Windows of the Heart

He turned his face up to her as
a prisoner who recovers light. . . .
Look Homeward, Angel

She was a voice that God seeks.
Look Homeward, Angel

WINDOWS OF THE HEART

The Correspondence of
Thomas Wolfe and Margaret Roberts

Edited by Ted Mitchell
Foreword by Matthew J. Bruccoli

The University of South Carolina Press

© 2007 University of South Carolina

Published by the University of South Carolina Press
Columbia, South Carolina 29208

www.sc.edu/uscpress

Manufactured in the United States of America

16 15 14 13 12 11 10 09 08 07   10 9 8 7 6 5 4 3 2 1

Library of Congress Cataloging-in-Publication Data

Wolfe, Thomas, 1900–1938.
    Windows of the heart : the correspondence of Thomas Wolfe and Margaret Roberts / edited
by Ted Mitchell ; foreword by Matthew J. Bruccoli.
        p. cm.
    Includes bibliographical references and index.
    ISBN-13: 978-1-57003-674-3 (alk. paper)
    ISBN-10: 1-57003-674-8 (alk. paper)
    1. Wolfe, Thomas, 1900–1938—Correspondence. 2. Roberts, Margaret, 1876–1947—
Correspondence. I. Roberts, Margaret, 1876–1947. II. Mitchell, Ted. III. Title.
    PS3545.O337Z48 2007
    813'.52—dc22
    [B]

                                                                    2006037509

The originals of letters 5, 12–28, 30–54, and 56–77 are in the William B. Wisdom Collection
of Thomas Wolfe at Harvard's Houghton Library. The library call number is cited in each letter's headnote. By permission of the Houghton Library, Harvard University

Frontispiece: Thomas Wolfe in 1916, the year he graduated from North State School, by per-
mission of the Thomas Wolfe Collection, Pack Memorial Public Library, Asheville, North
Carolina; Margaret Hines (Roberts) in 1901, at the age of twenty-five, courtesy of Jerry Israel,
Asheville, North Carolina

To Arlyn and Matthew J. Bruccoli, with my love and admiration
To Jerry Israel, with gratitude
To the memory of Margaret Rose Roberts and Martha Roberts Palmer

He opened one window of his heart to Margaret, together they entered the sacred grove of poetry. . . .

Look Homeward, Angel

⁂

I found your letter here when I came back. As usual, everything you say touches and moves me deeply. I wish my work deserved half of the good things you say about it: I hope that someday it will. The knowledge that you have always believed in me is one of the grandest possessions of my life. I hope it may be some slight return for your affection and faith to know that I have always believed in you, first, as a child, with an utterly implicit faith and hope, and later, as a man, with a no less steadfast trust. Life does not offer many friendships of which one can say this.

Thomas Wolfe (August 11, 1929)

⁂

Now, to the heart of the matter, which is you. . . . There is a sense in which I loved all of the boys, even the most trifling; because in each there was something worth loving, or something needing love. Then, again, there was a much smaller number that were loved with a really personal love. And one that I counted close – next to the dearest children of my heart. I shall leave you to guess Him. Old school teachers are always saying, "I knew this or that one when he was just a little fellow –." Well I Did, and my faith has never wavered.

Margaret Roberts (March 13, 1921)

⁂

Contents

Illustrations

Foreword

The Way It Was

Thomas Wolfe consistently—perhaps involuntarily—transferred readily recognizable, undisguised characters into his fiction. The claim in his note "To the Reader" for *Look Homeward, Angel* that "he meditated no man's portrait here" is untrue. His reply to Margaret Roberts's pained response to his novel is not persuasive: "Do you really think, Mrs. Roberts, that any artist ever gave body and blood night after night to any creation, for the sole purpose of making a bitter transcript of life? Do you think that if the reality in my book was only the same reality that walks the streets, I would take the trouble of writing at all?" Wolfe defended his technique only generally to Mrs. Roberts because he was denying the truth: that his greatest characters are supremely convincing because they were real. W. O. Gant or Eliza or Ben could not have been invented. If they were, they wouldn't be believable. Wolfe did not write straight transcripts from life; yet he worked much closer to life than other fiction writers. Certainly Wolfe cut and focused and improved his sources in order to strengthen the characterizations.

Wolfe had a compulsion to get it right, to tell it the way it was. He knew that his portrait of the Leonards would hurt Margaret Roberts, whom he had cherished. Yet the only thing that mattered to him was true-to-life fiction. Wolfe could have said that getting the Leonards right was worth any number of broken-hearted teachers, including the "mother of my spirit." Or he could have said, "That's the way they were. I gave them perpetual life."

Opaque critics have claimed that Wolfe was deficient in the power of invention because he worked "too close to life." All convincing characters are copied from life. That's the point of enduring fiction. The difference between Wolfe and other fiction writers who utilized this method is that he didn't try to disguise or obscure his sources, perhaps because to do so would have falsified his characters and diminished their truth for him. It didn't matter to readers in 1929, and it doesn't matter now whether John Dorsey Leonard is "too close"—whatever that is supposed to mean—to John Munsey Roberts or whether this characterization is an act of cruelty. What matters is that Leonard is one of the enduring characters in a novel populated by memorable characters. Psychiatrists—amateur and professional—blame the treatment of Leonard on Wolfe's sexual jealousy and resentment of the man who was married to the schoolboy's beloved teacher. Not necessarily. Wolfe treated all of his character sources the same way—except possibly Margaret Roberts.

Great fiction always requires believable characters. They are remembered after the plot is forgotten. One of the ways that fiction succeeds is through the reader's recognition that this is the way it was or this is how he or she must have been, based on the reader's experience and observation. The effects of a novel depend on what readers bring to it. Good readers are good noticers and good retainers. W. O. Gant is the richest and truest comic figure in American literature for readers who have known men who validate him. W. O. is almost as effective for the readers who have been deprived of Gantian figures; Wolfe tells the truth about him, and therefore the reader believes in W. O.

Recognizable characters are recognized only by the very few readers who have known the originals. Most readers are unaware of Wolfe's—or of any author's—sources or models. The test of the effectiveness of a character is the reader's belief in that character: whether the character behaves in ways that accord with the reader's experience and observation. The art of fiction is the art of getting it right. It enriches the pleasure of the readers if they possess the inside dope that enables them to judge what the writer did with his material. But writers don't write for the initiated. They write for an anticipated vast readership or they write for themselves. More than most writers, Thomas Wolfe wrote for himself: to preserve the life of his people. There are those of us who believe that there are no great fictional characters who are wholly invented.

Collation of the uncut *O Lost* against *Look Homeward, Angel* reveals that Wolfe removed material from the earlier text that provided an heroic impression of Leonard:

> John Dorsey Leonard met his wife Margaret for the first time when they were students at Vanderbilt University in Nashville. She was from Kentucky people, and very poor. She had taught school in a village in central Tennessee for several years in order to get money for college. At this time, Margaret was twenty-six years old and Leonard was almost thirty. They were both years older than most of the students about them; both had taught in country schools for several years before coming to the university.
>
> Leonard came from Tennessee farming people, strong, righteous, and comparatively enlightened folks. His father begat eleven sons and daughters, fed, clothed, and housed them with considerable difficulty by tilling 600 acres of land, and talked to them of the advantage of education. The elder Leonard was a large red well-developed Calvinist who led the good life, dragged his black sheep into the barn, and whipped

them with a cowhide in the name of Lord Jesus and the authority that devolves upon a Christian father. He was the master of his bed and board, and in his hale decline grew a long white beard, read only the best that had been thought and spoken by the men before him, and made sermons every Sunday at the Methodist church. Also, he gave to each of them as much schooling as he could afford, and offered a part of what he had for their course at a university. He expected them to get the rest for themselves.

John Dorsey Leonard worked on his father's farm until he was twenty-two. Seven years later, when Margaret first met him at Vanderbilt, he was a large solid countryman on whom the awful dignity of the schoolmaster and the judicial power of dealing punishment with a rod had put its starched and chalky stamp. He went arrayed in a boiled shirt and decent garments of pepper-and-salt; he discussed with keen interest questions of the day, attended meetings of the literary society every Friday night, took an active part in the debate, and once represented his university in the annual intercollegiate against Sewanee. He also taught a class in the Methodist Sunday School, which younger men interested in the application of religion to modern life attended.

When he went back home now the neighbors and members of his family called him "'Fessor." He liked the name even more than they did. He had a genuine desire to teach, but even more, perhaps, he liked the titles accruing to the office, the respect it exacted particularly in communities where life was lived upon the land and where, to respectable farmerfolk of the better sort it represented, with the law and the ministry, an advancement into gentility. Finally he thirsted for the great authority it put into his hands, the office of kingship, of stern but benevolent tyranny over the lives of others. He fantasied of the day when he would have his own school—a school for boys, modestly begun, which should become in time famous for the rigor of its discipline, the excellence of its instruction, the upright and Christian liberality of its policy.

. . . . .

He remained at the university a year after his graduation, doing graduate work. But really he stayed to be near her. In the spring she was desperately tired, confined for a month with influenza, and had a nasty cough. She had to give up her work. She went home to Kentucky, and wrote him after three weeks asking if he knew where she could find work teaching. Her people had no place for her.

The year was over; he had just returned to the farm. He took the first train to Kentucky and fetched her back with him. He told her she must rest; at the farm the big broad Leonards fetched and carried for her, much to her discomfort, insisted knowingly that she must get some meat on her bones, and stood over her sternly while she drank glass after glass of creamy milk. And they talked to her with violent energy of the "things of the mind"—reasoning, debating, roaring out the necessity of "cult-sher" in their strong sweaty unsubtle fashion.

. . . . .

One day she lay on a couch talking to him. He had come in from the fields. She felt a great deal better, she said. From time to time she coughed gently, with care, into her wadded handkerchief, and suddenly, his mind fixing sharply on the detail for the first time, he saw that each time she brought the cloth from her lips she had printed on it a small red blot.

John Dorsey Leonard was now past thirty and a Liberal Thinker. He argued persuasively from time to time with more dogmatic folk on the harmonious adjustment of Christianity to evolution. He believed in a cultural background, the things of the mind, and the higher life. He stood for enlightened suffrage, intelligent citizenship. He kept up with current events and read *The Nation*. Once he had debated the subject of Philippine Independence. He granted certain concessions in the law of monogamy to people like Byron, Keats, and Shelley that he denied to the common run. But he was willing to reason, to "get to the bottom of things," to thrash things out. In fact, he was the very model of provincial liberalism—an Advanced Thinker among the Methodists, a herald of light at noon, a bearer of the torch after daylight. He was reasonably convinced that the theory of evolution had been established fifty years after it had been conceded.

So—having come thus far after more than thirty years of toilsome growth, John Dorsey Leonard, observing that Margaret was about to die, married her at four o'clock that afternoon, and departed with her the next morning at eleven o'clock for Colorado.

They lived in the West for four years. Leonard found employment in a public school; at the end of two years Margaret had so far recovered that she was able to begin teaching again. When they finally returned to Tennessee her consumption had been checked, but all her combative and restoring energies were so depleted that she had little power for resistance and none for recuperation. She hung desperately to the tree of life like a withered leaf. Leonard found employment once more in a Tennessee school for boys, but, at the end of two years, when her health did not improve, and when she seemed in danger of losing the advantage she had gained, he brought her to Altamont. (*O Lost,* 240–43)

Wolfe added to *Look Homeward, Angel* a passage recognizing Margaret Leonard's uncritical devotion to her husband, commenting: "And the boy had trembled, with fear and nausea, to see her so."

Leonard himself was not a bad man—he was a man of considerable character, kindliness, and honest determination. He loved his family, he stood up with some courage against the bigotry in the Methodist church, where he was a deacon, and at length had to withdraw because of his remarks on Darwin's theory. He was, thus, an example of that sad liberalism of the village—an advanced thinker among the Methodists, a bearer of the torch at noon, an apologist for the toleration of ideas that have been established for fifty years. He tried faithfully to do his duties as a teacher. But he was of the earth—even his heavy-handed violence was of the earth, and had in it the unconscious brutality of nature. Although he asserted his interest in "the things of the mind," his interest in the soil was much greater, and he had added little to his stock of information since leaving college. He was slow-witted and quite lacking in the sensitive intuitions of Margaret, who loved the man with such passionate fidelity, however, that she seconded all his acts before the world. Eugene had even heard her cry out in a shrill, trembling voice against a student who had answered her husband insolently: "Why, I'd slap his head off! That's what I'd do!" And the boy had trembled, with fear and nausea, to see her so. But thus, he knew, could love change one. Leonard thought his actions wise and good: he had grown up in a tradition that demanded strict obedience to the master, and that would not brook opposition to his rulings. He had learned from his father, a Tennessee patriarch who ran a farm, preached on Sundays, and put down rebellion in his family with horse-whip and pious prayers, the advantages of being God! He thought little boys who resisted him should be beaten. (*Look Homeward, Angel,* 232–33)

Thomas Wolfe knew what he was doing with John Dorsey Leonard, and he knew that it would hurt Margaret Roberts. It is unlikely that he understood how much it would pain the woman to whom he acknowledged his prodigious debts in the novel. Or it could be that Wolfe was compelled to break with patrons when his indebtedness to them grew too great: Margaret Roberts,

Aline Bernstein, Maxwell Perkins. Wolfe made no gesture or effort at reconciliation with Margaret Roberts for eight years after publication of *Look Homeward, Angel.* That she—the aggrieved one—made the first move indicates how his friends responded to him. He was inconsiderate, touchy, bad-tempered, suspicious, demanding, unreliable. But having known him, they couldn't forego him. The force of his mind and the stimulation of his company made life without him incomplete.

Matthew J. Bruccoli

Acknowledgments

The letters of Thomas Wolfe and Margaret Roberts are published with the permission of the William B. Wisdom Collection, Houghton Library, Harvard University; the North Carolina Collection, University of North Carolina at Chapel Hill; Mr. Eugene H. Winick, Administrator, C. T. A. of the Estate of Thomas Wolfe; Martha Roberts Palmer, the Estate of Margaret Roberts.

For guiding this volume through publication I am especially grateful to Barry Blose, Karen Beidel, and Pat Callahan at the University of South Carolina Press, and to Charles Brower, who did a fine job of copyediting this manuscript. Matthew J. Bruccoli's helping hand improved all drafts of this book.

This book was facilitated by the library staffs at Houghton Library at Harvard University (Leslie A. Morris, Peter Accardo, Tom Ford, Susan Halpert); University of North Carolina at Chapel Hill Library (Robert Anthony Jr., Nicholas Graham, Keith Langiotti, Harry McKown); Pack Memorial Public Library, Asheville, North Carolina (Philip Banks, Laura Gaskin, Ken Miller, Zoe Rhine, Ann Wright).

I also wish to thank Beverly and Frank Amendola, J. Todd Bailey, Tim Barnwell, Deborah A. Borland, James W. Clark, Alice R. Cotten, Andrew A. Craig, Jackie Wharey Craig, Robert Ensign, Leslie Fox, Deborah Harry, Jonathan Haupt, Jan G. Hensley, John L. Idol, Jerry Israel, Joanne Marshall Mauldin, Russell J. Miller, the late Edna and Ilias J. Mitchell, Wilma Dykeman Stokely, David Strange, Dr. R. Dietz Wolfe, John Young, and Anne Zahlan.

Arlyn Bruccoli and Amber L. Coker greatly aided in transcribing the otherwise indecipherable words in the holographs. The Thomas Wolfe Society's William P. Wisdom Grant in 1998 enabled me to complete collecting materials for this volume.

The late John S. Phillipson and the late Margaret Rose Roberts generously served as advisers to this project since its inception in 1994. Without their help this book would not have been possible. Steve Hill and Chris Morton at the Thomas Wolfe Memorial sustained me with their faith and concern for my career even when my own hope was dim.

Aldo P. Magi generously provided his wise counsel throughout the twelve years of work on this project. I value his prudent and cogent advice as much as his unflinching integrity. Aldo P. Magi is truly the "father of my spirit."

Introduction

On March 30, 1914, thirteen-year-old Thomas Wolfe wrote his earliest surviving letter to Margaret Roberts, thus launching an exchange correspondence, of which seventy-five pieces are known to be extant. Mrs. Roberts, who taught Wolfe English and history at North State School,[1] became his first mentor, the surrogate mother he adopted as his aesthetic authority, just as Maxwell Perkins would later be the father that Wolfe was seeking. Moreover, Mrs. Roberts fed Wolfe's undernourished ego by recognizing his extraordinary literary gifts. As Perkins recalled in 1938:

> I have always had the greatest admiration for Mrs. Roberts. It is most remarkable, it seems to me, that she so quickly realized Tom's genius.[2]

Margaret Roberts's letters instantly disclose the intense original behind the so-called fictional portrait Wolfe renamed Margaret Leonard in *Look Homeward, Angel* (1929).[3] Her letters are openhearted, forthright, replete with the encouragement and advice she meted out to her former student. In 1921 she wrote:

> If you look back to your days in English composition, you will recall that I never corrected much except your mechanical mistakes. I was wise enough, though not naturally wise, to see that by nature you had the touch of the pen, and that you would soon be far beyond your teacher. Lord bless your bones, I feel a choking in my throat when I think of what you have done in eight years and of the god-like vista of the years to come.[4]

Wolfe's letters to Mrs. Roberts are candid and clearly admiring but, on occasion, his loyalty gives way to reveal a duplicity bordering on betrayal. Wolfe's most grievous sins, though, are sins of omission. His unwillingness to share with Mrs. Roberts the offensive autobiographical nature of *Look Homeward, Angel* before its publication estranged the devoted friends for seven years. In addition to revealing the intimate details of a complex relationship, Wolfe's letters document what his writing meant to him throughout the altering stages of his life. In 1925, longing for fame, the aspiring novelist wrote his former teacher:

The reason for all this is simply that I am tired of writing for the four winds: I realize the desperate lack and hypocrisy of pure expression. We are children – we must have an audience; and if my audience may be the people of a little North Carolina town, well and good. That is my whole desire for the present – perhaps there is a tiny feeling that if any of it is at all good it may reach the ears of the gods.[5]

Thirteen years later, having achieved the fame he long dreamed of, and having completed the bulk of his life's work, Wolfe wearily confided to Mrs. Roberts:

It is curious how many hard and thorny things we find out about life, and how strangely palatable they become to us. It is all so different from what we imagined it was going to be when we were children, and curiously in so many ways it is so much better. I suppose like so many other boys I pictured a future life of brilliant works crowned by success and fame and ease, and surcease from labor; but it does not work out that way at all. Work gets harder all the time because as one digs deeper one goes into the rock. And there is no rest – those periods of delightful relaxation as a kind of reward for work accomplished that I used to look forward to with such eagerness simply do not exist.[6]

Wolfe's later letters also explain in unaffected detail the intensifying social consciousness that shaped his final literary output (most notably, *You Can't Go Home Again*). Furthermore, the letters contain his most clear-cut statements of his creative objectives, as well as startling revelations of his inward life:

It just boils down to the fact that there is no rest, once the worm gets in and begins to feed upon the heart – there can never after that be rest, forgetfulness or quiet sleep again: somewhere long ago – God knows when, or at what fated moment in my childhood – the worm got in and has been feeding ever since and will be feeding till I die: after this happens, a man becomes a prisoner, there are times when he almost breaks free, but there is one link in the chain that always holds; there are times when he almost forgets, when he is with his friends, when he is reading a great book or a great poem, when he is at the theatre, or on a ship, or with a girl – but there is one tiny cell that still keeps working, working; even when he is asleep, one lamp that will not go out, that is forever lit.[7]

The *Atlantic Monthly* (Edward Augustus Weeks Jr., editor) became the first to publish a selection of Wolfe's letters to Margaret Roberts. "Writing Is My Life," twenty heavily edited letters, were published in installments (December

Margaret Rose Roberts,
New York City, 1937.
Collection of Ted Mitchell

1946–February 1947). Elizabeth Nowell's *The Letters of Thomas Wolfe* (1956) includes twenty-two letters, also edited for length and content, with Wolfe's punctuation and paragraphing emended. My own "Windows of the Heart: The Letters of Margaret Roberts to Thomas Wolfe," appeared in the *Thomas Wolfe Review* (Fall 1996, Spring 1997). Until now the correspondence has never been published in its entirety. In 1994 Mrs. Roberts's daughter, Margaret Rose, suggested to me that a volume of her mother's correspondence with Wolfe ought to be compiled. Miss Roberts proved to be a canny collaborator on this project. Intensely devoted to preserving the fascinating saga of her mother's friendship with Thomas Wolfe, she helped decipher Wolfe's illegible words and annotated first drafts of transcriptions with facts culled from eighty years of memories. Without her participation, much of the information about Wolfe, her parents, and students at the North State School would have been lost.

All of the known letters by Thomas Wolfe and Margaret Roberts have been collected in this volume. The letters are housed in the Thomas Wolfe collections at Harvard University and the University of North Carolina at Chapel Hill. Fortunately, a greater part of the correspondence survives, although some letters exist only in drafts and fragments. This volume publishes the letters complete and without omissions.

Mrs. Roberts's letters were among Wolfe's papers when he died in 1938. They were purchased from his estate by an ardent collector of Wolfe manuscripts, William B. Wisdom, who was buying Wolfe's papers with the intention of bequeathing them to a research institution. He eventually donated them to Harvard University. In 1946 Wisdom traveled to Asheville to retrieve what remained of Wolfe's manuscripts still in the possession of his family. While there, Wisdom also wanted to purchase Wolfe's letters that Mrs. Roberts owned. The moving description of Wisdom's visit, with Maxwell Perkins, to the Robertses is well worth quoting at length. Note, however, that Mrs. Roberts was not suffering from "the last stages of tuberculosis"; she died the following year of cancer.

On Saturday, May 11, or on Sunday morning, Max Perkins and I wanted very much to call upon Mr. and Mrs. Roberts for several reasons. First, Mrs. Roberts was Margaret Leonard, Tom's inspirational teacher in the North State Fitting School which Tom attended in Asheville. It was a very small school. Mr. Roberts was Mr. Leonard, the Headmaster about whom Tom wrote in uncomplimentary terms. In Tom's inscription on the flyleaf of *Look Homeward, Angel* which he gave to Mrs. Roberts, he referred to her as "Mother of my Spirit." The second overpowering reason for wanting to see Mr. and Mrs. Roberts, aside from the part she played in the molding of Tom's youthful years and education, was to attempt to purchase all of the letters and postcards that Tom had written to her.

Mr. Perkins and I found Mrs. Roberts in bed, in the last stages of tuberculosis. She invited us into her room. She had an extremely sensitive face, thin, greyish brown hair, keen, lively eyes, and an extremely alert mind. Tall and erect, Mr. Roberts had silvery white hair, pink healthy skin, and was a very stately gentleman. He read aloud that portion of "Portrait" from *The Face of A Nation.* Apparently, all rancor and hurt over Tom's treatment of Professor Leonard had disappeared with the years and the death of Tom. When Max and I broached the subject that I would like to purchase Tom's letters to Mrs. Roberts, she said that she had given them all to her daughter, Margaret Rose, she would have to get her permission and very possibly Margaret would not want to part with them. I also wanted to buy the first edition of *Look Homeward, Angel* with its wonderful inscription. She said she was sure that Margaret Rose would not want to sell this.

One must understand that this conversation had to be maintained on a very delicate plane, without any crass considerations and keeping the negotiation of price as unobtrusive as possible. I was willing to pay anything within reason, and we finally settled on $1,200 with the proviso that the letters should ultimately go to Harvard University and that I have four complete and separate photostatic copies of all the letters made for Mrs. Roberts, Mr. Roberts, her son, and her daughter. These negotiations were not concluded as rapidly as they sound here. They were initiated on this visit but were consummated later by correspondence. Mr. Perkins, a great ally, convinced Mr. and Mrs. Roberts that the letters were of great value to Tom's reputation and to the Robertses' memory and that they should be preserved carefully in an institution such as Harvard.

I was not able to obtain the first edition of *Look Homeward, Angel* and have not been able to do so to this day.

Our visit with the Robertses was heartwarming and sad. I felt that I had been in the presence of two remarkable people, and that I was elevated by their touching sentiment and love for each other, which they both knew was soon to be broken by her death.[8]

Wisdom finally acquired Wolfe's letters from J. M. Roberts in 1949 and the inscribed copy of *Look Homeward, Angel* in 1951. Its inscription reads:

To Margaret Roberts,
Who was the mother of my spirit,
I present this copy of my first book,
with hope and with devotion
Thomas Wolfe
Oct 15, 1929

Ↄ

The saga begins twenty-four years before Thomas Wolfe's birth. The sensitive and courageous woman who nurtured Thomas Wolfe's literary ambitions and first proclaimed him a genius was born Margaret Elizabeth Hines in Chillicothe, Ohio, on September 8, 1876. The daughter of Elizabeth (née Williams)

Margaret Hines at
two years old, ca. 1878.
Courtesy of Jerry Israel,
Asheville, North
Carolina

and Joseph Henry Hines, Margaret's father died when she was six months old. Her mother remarried, and she died when Margaret was fifteen.

Educated at East End College in Tennessee, Valparaiso University in Indiana, and Vanderbilt University in Nashville, Margaret Hines exhibited a remarkable aptitude for English composition but chose instead to become an educator. (Her 1947 death certificate gives her occupation as "teacher and writer.") Although she had no training in teaching the blind and knew no Braille, she won such distinction during two years of teaching at the Colorado State School for the Blind that she was invited to teach at the London School for the Blind. She had long dreamed of going to England, but she chose to marry instead.

While attending small, private East End College, Margaret became engaged to John Munsey Roberts (1874–1954), a Greek and Latin scholar, who had

Three undated photos of Margaret during the years she was calling herself Mattie Allbright. Courtesy of Jerry Israel, Asheville, North Carolina

LEFT: Margaret Hines, Nashville, Tennessee, 1898. Collection of Ted Mitchell

The North State Fitting School at 157 Church Street, Asheville. By permission of the Thomas Wolfe Collection, Pack Memorial Public Library, Asheville, North Carolina

been a teacher at the school. They married in Columbia, Tennessee, on August 26, 1904. Roberts, known as J. M., was teaching at the Vanderbilt Training School in Elkton, Kentucky, when the couple's first child, John Munsey Jr. (1906–1963), was born. Later, at the McFerrin School in Martin, Tennessee, a daughter, Margaret Rose Roberts (1910–1998), was born.

While at the McFerrin School, the Robertses began to plan opening a private school for boys. A mild case of tuberculosis Mrs. Roberts acquired before her marriage had been stabilized, and the couple chose to locate in Asheville, North Carolina, because of its elevation and climate. Arriving in the mountains in 1911, Roberts became principal of Orange Street School while deciding on a location for their private school. It was at Orange Street School that he first met eleven-year-old Thomas Wolfe.

Thomas Clayton Wolfe was born on October 3, 1900, at 92 Woodfin Street in Asheville, the last of W. O. and Julia Wolfe's eight children. When Wolfe's mother purchased the rambling boardinghouse Old Kentucky Home in 1906, the only child she took with her was five-year-old Tom, and a bewildering new era began in the boy's life. Shuffled from room to room to make space for his mother's boarders, when the house filled to capacity he was sent back to Woodfin Street, where his brothers and sisters lived with their father.

While composing *Look Homeward, Angel,* Wolfe wrote Mrs. Roberts:

I was without a home – a vagabond since I was seven – with two roofs and no home; I moved inward on that house of death and tumult from room to little room, as the boarders came with their dollar a day, and their constant rocking on the porch; my overloaded heart was bursting with its packed weight of loneliness and terror; I was strangling, without speech, without articulation, in my own secretions – groping like a blind sea-thing with no eyes and a thousand feelers toward light, toward life, toward beauty and order, out of that hell of chaos, greed, and cheap ugliness – and then I found you, when else I should have died, you mother of my spirit who fed me with light. Do you think that I have forgotten? Do you think I ever will? You are entombed in my flesh, you are in the pulses of my blood, the thought of you makes a great music in me – and before I come to death, I shall use the last thrust of my talent – whatever it is – to put your beauty into words.[9]

At Orange Street School, Principal Roberts held a writing competition to compare progress of students from grade to grade, as well as to find recruits for his new school.[10] Since his wife knew none of the students, Roberts took the papers home and asked her to help select the best one. After reading sixty

John Munsey Roberts in 1908.
Courtesy of Jerry Israel, Asheville,
North Carolina

or more, she came upon Wolfe's. Looking up, she declared, "This boy, Tom Wolfe, is a genius! And I want him for our school next year."[11] This marked the first time anyone recognized Thomas Wolfe as a genius. After more than a little persuading by Mr. Roberts, Wolfe's father agreed to pay the tuition of one hundred dollars a year, and Wolfe became the first student enrolled in the North State Fitting School. Wolfe described the years 1912–1916 at the Robertses' school as "the happiest and most valuable years of my life."[12] In *Look Homeward, Angel,* the Leonards' school becomes for Eugene Gant "the centre of his heart and life—Margaret Leonard his spiritual mother."[13]

The depths of Wolfe's complex feeling for Mrs. Roberts can never be fully fathomed. The correspondence affirms a deep and genuine love on both sides despite Wolfe's literary betrayal that led to their inevitable estrangement. At the age of twenty-four, Wolfe passionately proclaimed his devotion to the woman who had become a vital force in his life:

> She is one of the few great people I have ever known; she is one of the few women I have ever loved, greatly and permanently and magnificently. I have called for wine many times in twenty-four crowded and terrified years, and I have been mocked with vinegar; but from her I have never had less than my usurious demands exacted – and this is a

North State Fitting School students with the Robertses, ca. 1912–1914. Thomas Wolfe is to the right of center with arms folded; on right: Margaret Roberts with Margaret Rose Roberts, Emma Roberts, J. M. Roberts. By permission of the Thomas Wolfe Collection, Pack Memorial Public Library, Asheville, North Carolina

J. M. and Margaret
Roberts and their two
children, J. M. Jr. (Buddie) and
Margaret Rose, ca. 1912–1914.
By permission of the Thomas
Wolfe Collection, Pack Memo-
rial Public Library, Asheville,
North Carolina

Thomas Wolfe with students of North State School, 1915. From the left: Henry
Harris, Wolfe, Joe Taylor, Julius Martin, Junius Horner, Reid Russell, and Fred
Thomas. By permission of the Thomas Wolfe Collection, Pack Memorial Public
Library, Asheville, North Carolina

miraculous thing. Ah, believe me, I have never need of faith because I had evidence beyond all faith of the world's goodness in one person; and for me, who have the heart of a fool, that means eternal victory, for a million evil trickeries are forgotten or denied before a single glory.[14]

The biographer Andrew Turnbull described Margaret Roberts as "the fairy godmother of Tom's youth."[15] A major influence, she helped Wolfe cultivate his talent and awakened a love for fine literature. Before meeting Mrs. Roberts he had read indiscriminately. He later stated, "It was through her that I first developed a taste for good literature which opened up a shining El Dorado for me."[16] Because of her affection and compassion for young, awkward Tom Wolfe, she became the invincible mentor he told:

> Mrs Roberts, there's no estimating the influence you've had on me and the whole course of my life; what's done is done, each day causes me to see more plainly how tremendous an influence that was and I know I shall be even more emphatic on this score the last day of my life than I am now[.][17]

Wolfe did not extend such glowing praise to J. M. Roberts, whom he pronounced "a hoax"[18] in the autobiographical outline he drew up for "O Lost" (the original title of *Look Homeward, Angel*).[19] Wolfe's schoolboy crush on Mrs. Roberts may well have contributed to the ruthless portrait of John Dorsey Leonard,[20] the violent and obtuse pedant in Wolfe's autobiographical first novel.

At North State School, Wolfe read omnivorously and, despite his tendency to stammer, excelled in debate. During his four years at the school he received instruction in Latin, Greek, English, history, mathematics, and German. However, it was his study of English and American literature with Mrs. Roberts that he loved best. She guided him through Coleridge, Lanier, Longfellow, Milton, Sir Walter Scott, Shakespeare, and Twain, as well as the Old Testament.

On May 13, 1916, North State School participated in a Shakespearean pageant commemorating the tercentenary of Shakespeare's death. It was presented on the grounds of the Manor, a turn-of-the-century Tudoresque inn. "I Prince Hal," Wolfe recorded in his autobiographical outline, "The tights from Philadelphia—four inches too short."[21] Mr. Roberts's sister-in-law, Emma Roberts, substituted the remnants of a clown costume for the inadequate tights, and the audience roared with laughter at the sight of Wolfe's preposterous appearance. (Hoping to cheer Wolfe during his final illness in 1938, Mrs. Roberts recalled the amusing but humiliating incident in her last letter to him.)

Thomas Wolfe at fifteen, shortly before entering the University of North Carolina in 1916. By permission of the North Carolina Collection, University of North Carolina Library at Chapel Hill, and Eugene H. Winick, Administrator C.T.A., Estate of Thomas Wolfe

A month before the end of Wolfe's final year at the Robertses' school, Wolfe's essay "Shakespeare: The Man" won the bronze medal in the citywide essay contest sponsored by the *Independent Magazine* to celebrate the tercentenary. Mrs. Roberts persuaded Wolfe to recast the essay in oratorical form for the students' declamation contest, which he also won.

On July 1, 1916, Wolfe graduated from North State School with several awards but not magna cum laude or summa cum laude. Mrs. Roberts recorded in a memoir: "As far as regular class-room work was concerned, certain other boys with fine minds and regular habits of study, far surpassed him in other than literary subjects. We knew that this was not because he could not learn those subjects. They simply did not fire him."[22]

Despite the fact that Wolfe was only fifteen when he graduated from North State School, W. O. Wolfe announced that it was time for his son to go to college. Although Mrs. Roberts protested that Wolfe was far too young, she eventually relented and recommended the University of Virginia. However, W. O. Wolfe insisted on the state university at Chapel Hill; Wolfe was enrolled there on September 12, 1916.

↛

Their friendship did not fall short of mythological overtones. "Pegasus must be controlled, even tho by one of a lower order who has no wings,"[23] Mrs. Roberts chastised fourteen-year-old Thomas Wolfe in one of his composition books. In recognizing the boy as the symbol of poetic inspiration, the winged horse, she was astonishingly perceptive in defining the roles of the relationship that would endure another twenty-two years. Similarly Wolfe opened one letter thus:

> Dear Mrs Roberts: – If I saluted you as I dared, perhaps in another more gracious age, I should say instead "Best and Wisest of Mortals."[24]

More than merely a teacher to Wolfe, Mrs. Roberts illuminated his heart and mind, and she is portrayed as nothing less than a saint in *Look Homeward, Angel*—complete with a transfiguring light and mystical healing powers:

> Eugene went to see the Leonards several times. Margaret looked thin and ill, but the great light in her seemed on this account to burn more brightly. Never before had he been so aware of her enormous tranquil patience, the great health of her spirit. All of his sin, all of his pain, all the vexed weariness of his soul were washed away in that deep radiance: the tumult and evil of life dropped from him its foul and ragged cloak. He seemed to be clothed anew in garments of seamless light.

And on the same page:

> O! My lovely Saint! he thought. How close you have been to me, if any
> one. How I have cut my brain open for you to see, and would my heart,
> if I had dared, and how alone I am, and always have been.[25]

(Further confirming Wolfe's conception of Margaret Roberts as a saint, he once
wrote her that his friend Olin Dows was "almost as great a saint as you are."[26])

But not even Saint Roberts escapes the multitude of ugly details in *Look
Homeward, Angel*. When Eugene Gant first sees Margaret Leonard, her "wasted
figure" appears to him like a "draped stick."[27] Although Margaret possesses
"the most tranquil and the most passionate face he had ever seen," her skin is
"sallow with a dead ashen tinge; beneath, the delicate bone-carving of face and
skull traced itself clearly: the cadaverous tightness of those who are about to
die had been checked."[28] Grotesque descriptions notwithstanding, twelve pages
later, Eugene's bond with Margaret is fixed:

North State School at its new and final location at 57 Austin Avenue.
By permission of the Thomas Wolfe Collection, Pack Memorial Public Library,
Asheville, North Carolina

He opened one window of his heart to Margaret, together they entered the sacred grove of poetry.[29]

The idyllic walk through such groves, however, was abruptly interrupted by the publication of *Look Homeward, Angel* on October 18, 1929. Judging by the letters she received from Wolfe prior to the novel's publication, Mrs. Roberts could not have guessed the uproar that the novel would create in Asheville, nor that it would be condemned from street corner to pulpit and banned from the public library. Despite Wolfe's surviving ten letters written to Mrs. Roberts after the gestation of *Look Homeward, Angel* in 1926, she received little warning that she would appear in a leading fictional role. On May 30, 1927, Wolfe confessed:

> My book is full of ugliness and terrible pain – and I think moments of a great and soaring beauty. In it (will you forgive me?) I have told the story of one of the most beautiful people I have ever known as it touched on my own life. I am calling that person Margaret Leonard.[30]

However, in no letter did he inform Mrs. Roberts that her entire family—husband, children, in-laws, even the household cow—would join the extraordinary cast of characters of a highly provocative novel.

Mrs. Roberts reacted to the publication of *Look Homeward, Angel* with a mixture of bewilderment, pain, and humiliation. "Numb with misery,"[31] she read the pages about Wolfe's years at the North State School. She was deeply wounded by the portrayal of Mr. Roberts as John Dorsey Leonard, the "heavy-handed master" who puts down rebellion with "good cornfield violence." Nor is Leonard's cow spared violence: to milk her, Leonard laughs his "vacant silly laugh" and gives her "a good smacking kick in the belly to make her come round into position."[32] And in the next chapter, Mrs. Roberts found herself implicated in her husband's alleged brutality:

> [Leonard] was slow-witted and quite lacking in the sensitive intuitions of Margaret, who loved the man with such passionate fidelity, however, that she seconded all his acts before the world. Eugene had even heard her cry out in a shrill, trembly voice against a student who had answered her husband insolently: "Why, I'd slap his head off! That's what I'd do!"[33]

Mrs. Roberts's beloved relatives at the school fare only slightly better. Her sister-in-law Emma Roberts, portrayed as Amy, is "185 pounds," with "straight and oily" hair and "thick forearms," her dresses stained "below the arm-pits

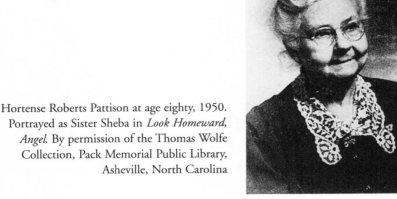

Hortense Roberts Pattison at age eighty, 1950.
Portrayed as Sister Sheba in *Look Homeward,
Angel.* By permission of the Thomas Wolfe
Collection, Pack Memorial Public Library,
Asheville, North Carolina

with big spreading blots of sweat," and while she sits naked before the fire after her bath, "her big body" is observed "steaming cleanly like a beast."[34]

Another cherished in-law, Hortense Roberts Pattison, is the "violent and garrulous"[35] teacher Sister Sheba. Even Mrs. Roberts's venerated father-in-law, William Orton Roberts, is rendered as "a Tennessee patriarch who ran a farm, preached on Sundays, and put down rebellion in his family with a horse-whip and pious prayers, the advantages of being God!"[36] Mrs. Roberts's humiliation must have been complete when she, a self-described "Victorian,"[37] encountered Eugene Gant's contemplation of Mr. and Mrs. Leonard's marital relations:

> Margaret Leonard was of middling height, five feet six inches perhaps. As the giddiness of his embarrassment wore off, he saw that she could not weigh more than eighty or ninety pounds. He had heard of the children. Now he remembered them, and Leonard's white muscular bulk, with a sense of horror. His swift vision leaped at once to the sexual relation, and something in him twisted aside, incredulous and afraid.[38]

After reading *Look Homeward, Angel,* Mrs. Roberts fired off an angry letter to Wolfe, declaring, "You have crucified your family and devastated mine."[39] This letter, among others that harshly criticized Wolfe (like another letter she wrote disapproving of his love affair with Aline Bernstein), is missing, perhaps destroyed by Wolfe—although he showed it to Maxwell Perkins before it disappeared. (Missing letters to or by Wolfe are conspicuous in their absence; he usually hoarded every scrap of paper with writing on it. Among the threatening letters denouncing *Look Homeward, Angel* that Wolfe claimed to have received, none survive.)

Although Mrs. Roberts's "You have crucified your family" letter is lost, in her next letter to Wolfe—*seven years later*—she disclosed her reasons for her outrage:

> It was just <u>hurtness</u> – hurt because the boy I loved so dearly had done this thing to the man I have always worshipped, and to others of a family that have been not merely "in-laws" to me, but rather sisters, close sisters, and a father. From the time when I was left absolutely penniless at 16, and hungry to learn, they were the ones who helped me to be able to shove forward in my head and heart and pocket book. Without them I could have never occupied even the small mental patch of ground that I have. You see, when you hurt not only Mr. Roberts, but Emma, and Mrs. Pattison, and even Grandpa R–, I felt wounded in the house of a friend.[40]

Wolfe continued to answer attacks on *Look Homeward, Angel* for the remainder of his career. In letters, in prefaces, and in his short book *The Story of a Novel* (1936), he attempted to clarify the distinction between a creative fusion of facts and literal transcription from life. Like every author, Wolfe may never have quite told the whole truth. We will never know how his subconscious transformed his life into fiction or to what extent he was simply settling old scores. In his preface to *Look Homeward, Angel*, "To the Reader," he insists that "this book is a fiction, and that he meditated no man's portrait here. . . . Fiction is not fact, but fiction is fact selected and understood, fiction is fact arranged and charged with purpose."[41] Wolfe further elaborates in his February 2, 1930, letter to Mrs. Roberts—a convincing defense that cannot be overlooked:

> all creation is to me fabulous, that the world of my creation is a fabulous world, that experience comes into me from all points, is digested and absorbed into me until it becomes a part of me, and that the world I create is <u>always</u> <u>inside</u> me, and never <u>outside</u> me; and that what reality I can give to what I create comes only from <u>within.</u> Its relation to actual experience I have never denied, but every thinking person knows that such a relation is inevitable, and could not be avoided unless men lived in a vacuum.[42]

Notwithstanding, upon completing the manuscript of "O Lost" in 1928, Wolfe admitted that certain passages had "done their work of catharsis, and may now be excised."[43] But other than an innocuous description of Mr.

Leonard's background, few negative characterizations of the schoolmaster were actually removed; one nasty jab, "Leonard lived for him at times in a brown murk of evil, a monster capable of Gomorrhean obscenity, reptilian deception,"[44] was excised. Evidently, Wolfe had second thoughts and took action to offset the treatment of his former teacher. While *Look Homeward, Angel* was in galley proofs, Wolfe wrote editor John Hall Wheelock at Scribner's, directing him to insert one paragraph beginning "Leonard himself was not a bad man" into the text. He wrote Wheelock on July 17, 1929:

> Will you look over Galley <u>62</u>? I have written in a paragraph to soften the harsh impression one gets of Leonard (where he beats the little boys), and I include Margaret, his wife, who seconds him out of love and loyalty – I did this on the idea that "misery loves company."[45]

And on July 19, 1929, he wrote Wheelock:

> I am sorry the printer was upset by my one long insertion – I do not think it will happen again: I did it here to round out one detail in Leonard's life – much that showed the man in a favorable light had previously been cut, and I thought it proper to add a little here.[46]

Although "Leonard himself was not a bad man—he was a man of considerable character, kindliness, and honest determination"[47] is a good start to soften the schoolmaster's harsh portrait, Wolfe then elaborates on Leonard's brutality toward schoolboys and adds Margaret's support of it. In addition, he includes a caustic description of Leonard's violent father armed with a horsewhip. Yet Wolfe ends the insertion to show Leonard in a more favorable light with "He thought little boys who resisted him should be beaten."[48]

Whatever the author's motives, the late insertion accomplished little to assuage Mrs. Roberts's distress. Creative process or not, she was never won over by any of Wolfe's entreaties. Seven years after the publication of *Look Homeward, Angel,* she complained:

> I have not changed in thinking that the wounding was needless. . . . I am not so dumb as not to believe that an artist has a right to get his material where he pleases and twist it as he pleases, but I maintain that he has no right to twist or invent, in making a pen-picture and then write under it the name of a living person.[49]

(Wolfe had used the Robertses' actual first names in *Look Homeward, Angel;* the identity of Eugene Gant's schoolteachers to anyone who knew the Robertses was no secret.)

ॐ

Whatever the past uproar in Asheville or the hairsplitting defense of literary methods, the bond between young Pegasus and his "Best and Wisest of Mortals" could never be annulled. Wolfe writes in *Look Homeward, Angel:*

> He turned his face up to her as a prisoner who recovers light, as a man long pent in darkness who bathes himself in the great pool of dawn, as a blind man who feels upon his eyes the white core and essence of immutable brightness. His body drank in her great light as a famished castaway the rain: he closed his eyes and let the great light bathe him, and when he opened them again, he saw that her own were luminous and wet.[50]

And:

> He was still prison-pent. But he turned always to Margaret Leonard as toward the light: she saw the unholy fires that cast their sword-dance on his face, she saw the hunger and pain, and she fed him—majestic crime! on poetry.[51]

The Robertses allowed Wolfe the final word. The quotation from *Look Homeward, Angel* carved upon Mrs. Roberts's gravestone proclaims the benevolent gift bestowed upon her former student:

> She remained, who first had touched his blinded eyes with light.[52]

Notes

1. Called North State Fitting School when founded in 1912; renamed North State School in 1915. Fictionalized as the Altamont Fitting School in *Look Homeward, Angel;* and as both the Leonard Fitting School and the Altamont Fitting School in *O Lost*. See Thomas Wolfe, *O Lost: A Story of the Buried Life,* ed. Arlyn and Matthew J. Bruccoli (Columbia: University of South Carolina Press, 2000), 241 and 243.

2. Maxwell Perkins to George McCoy, October 15, 1938, *Harvard*.

3. Wolfe's veneration of Margaret Roberts is unmistakable in his letters and in his portrayal of Margaret Leonard in *Look Homeward, Angel:* "For her, teaching was its own exceeding great reward—her lyric music, her life, the world in which plastically she built to beauty what was good, the lord of her soul that gave her spirit life while he broke her body" (*Look Homeward, Angel* [New York: Charles Scribner's Sons, 1929], 216). According to North Carolina novelist Wilma Dykeman, Wolfe's depiction of Mrs. Roberts was true to life: "I knew both of the Robertses. Tom's portrayal of them was right on target. She was so direct, so straightforward. He was different;

he took his time to get at or around a point" (Wilma Dykeman to Ted Mitchell, interview, August 16, 1994).

4. Margaret Roberts to Thomas Wolfe, March 13, 1921; letter 6 in this text. The following is one of Wolfe's compositions that Mrs. Roberts likely found striking: "To become a master of English one must not expect to grow fluent at once. Little by little, a word here and a word there and all the time you are growing richer. In other words the sun is struggling to break through the clouds. Then in the full halo of your glory you find yourself rewarded" (*Thomas Wolfe's Composition Books: The North State Fitting School, 1912–1915,* ed. Alice R. Cotten [Chapel Hill: North Caroliniana Society and the Thomas Wolfe Society, 1990], 20).

5. Thomas Wolfe to Margaret Roberts, March 21, 1925; letter 24.

6. Thomas Wolfe to Margaret Roberts, April 6, 1938; letter 72.

7. Ibid.

8. William B. Wisdom, *My Impressions of the Wolfe Family and of Maxwell Perkins,* ed. Aldo P. Magi and David J. Wyatt (N.p.: Thomas Wolfe Society, 1993), 41–42. The "Portrait" Mr. Roberts reads aloud is a physical description of Margaret Leonard excerpted from *Look Homeward, Angel* (213–14) in *The Face of a Nation: Poetical Passages from the Writings of Thomas Wolfe,* ed. John Hall Wheelock (New York: Charles Scribner's Sons, 1939), 99–100.

9. Thomas Wolfe to Margaret Roberts, May 30, 1927; letter 36.

10. "They were to write a paper on the meaning of a French picture called The Song of the Lark. It represented a French peasant girl, barefooted, with a sickle in one hand, and with face upturned in the morning-light of the fields as she listened to the bird-song. They were asked to describe what they saw in the expression of the girl's face. They were asked to tell what the picture meant to them. It had been reproduced in one of their readers. A larger print was now hung up on the platform for their inspection. Sheets of yellow paper were given them. They stared, thoughtfully masticating their pencils. Finally, the room was silent save for a minute scratching on paper" (Wolfe, *Look Homeward, Angel,* 207–8). In a memoir written ca. 1940, Mrs. Roberts claimed that she could no longer remember the subject of the composition. Wolfe may have drawn on his prodigious memory, or "The Song of the Lark" could have been a more interesting re-creation.

11. Margaret Rose Roberts to Ted Mitchell, interview, April 16, 1995. In Mrs. Roberts's memoir of Thomas Wolfe, she simply tells her husband, "You must be sure to get the little Wolfe boy" (Untitled memoir, Estate of Margaret Roberts, 2 [hereafter cited as Roberts memoir]). For another account of Mrs. Roberts's discovery of Wolfe's genius, see J. M. Roberts to John Skally Terry, June 23, 1947: "When I placed before Mrs. Roberts a batch of papers – compositions to be read – (among these it chanced that Tom had a paper) she read his and suddenly exclaimed: 'This boy is a genius.' I said, 'I'm not astonished to hear this; I have seen all along that he is outstanding.' She had never seen him, never knew him. . . . Perhaps this was the first time this had ever been said of him. I had heard him commended but none had said 'genius'" (ALS, 2 pp., *UNC*).

12. Thomas Wolfe to John Bryan, December 18, 1933, *Harvard.*

13. Wolfe, *Look Homeward, Angel,* 231.

14. Thomas Wolfe to Hortense Roberts Pattison, ca. 1924/1925, *Harvard.* Elizabeth Nowell transcription.

15. Andrew Turnbull, *Thomas Wolfe* (New York: Charles Scribner's Sons, 1967), 13.

16. *The Letters of Thomas Wolfe to His Mother,* ed. C. Hugh Holman and Sue Fields Ross (Chapel Hill: University of North Carolina Press, 1968), 23.

17. Thomas Wolfe to Margaret Roberts, September 2, 1921; letter 8.

18. Thomas Wolfe, *The Autobiographical Outline for "Look Homeward, Angel,"* ed. Lucy Conniff and Richard S. Kennedy (N.p.: Thomas Wolfe Society, 1991), 20.

19. On January 9, 1929, Wolfe signed a contract with Charles Scribner's Sons to publish the 1,114-page manuscript he titled "O Lost." The editing process reduced the 294,000 words manuscript by 66,000 words, a total of 147 cuts. The heavily edited novel was retitled *Look Homeward, Angel* in April 1929. Wolfe's complete manuscript was published by the University of South Carolina Press in 2000.

20. "The name 'Leonard' for Mother and Dad came from that of Leonard Roberts, my first cousin" (Margaret Rose Roberts to Ted Mitchell, March 2, 1995). Leonard Roberts appears as the nefarious Tyson Leonard in *Look Homeward, Angel* (320 and 325). The reasons for Wolfe's unflattering portrait of J. M. Roberts are unknown. Margaret Rose Roberts was convinced that the portrait of her father was fictionalized to contrast the divergent characterization of her mother and father: "I don't think people who read *Look Homeward, Angel* would realize that actually Thomas Wolfe was very fond of my father. Even as a little boy Tom was very fond of him. My father was a very fine Latin and Greek scholar, but he was not the inspired teacher that my mother was. And I think Tom—in order to make a good story—wanted to play up this difference between the two of them. Well, of course it hurt my mother very much when she read it, and she didn't get over it for a long time" (Ted Mitchell, "An Interview with Margaret Rose Roberts," *Thomas Wolfe Review* 15 [Spring 1991]: 94).

21. Wolfe, *Autobiographical Outline,* 27.

22. Roberts memoir, p. 8, Aldo P. Magi Series, Wilson Library, University of North Carolina.

23. Wolfe, *Thomas Wolfe's Composition Books,* 76.

24. Thomas Wolfe to Margaret Roberts, September 16, 1924; letter 20.

25. Wolfe, *Look Homeward, Angel,* 477.

26. Thomas Wolfe to Margaret Roberts, May 30, 1927; letter 36.

27. Wolfe, *Look Homeward, Angel,* 212.

28. Ibid., 213.

29. Ibid., 225.

30. Thomas Wolfe to Margaret Roberts, May 30, 1927; letter 36. Perhaps the portrait of Margaret Leonard would not have taken Mrs. Roberts quite so unaware if she had remembered this letter. According to her daughter: "Tom wrote her a beautiful letter which my mother said she forgot about when she received her copy of *Look Homeward, Angel* for the first time and was so shocked to find herself and my father in it,

but Tom had written to her when he began outlining *Look Homeward, Angel* in England. He said he was calling her Margaret Leonard. . . . But it's strange when she received the book she had forgotten all about that letter" (Mitchell, "Interview with Margaret Rose Roberts," 95).

31. Roberts memoir, 34.

32. Wolfe, *Look Homeward, Angel,* 207.

33. Ibid., 233.

34. Ibid., 222.

35. Ibid., 225. On the previous page Eugene Gant calls Sheba "Old Lady Latimer." For a "Who's Who" in *Look Homeward, Angel,* see Joanne Marshall Mauldin, *The People and Places of Thomas Wolfe's "Look Homeward, Angel": From the 1929 Scribners Edition* (Weaverville, N.C.: Privately printed, 2002).

36. Wolfe, *Look Homeward, Angel,* 233.

37. "I am a Victorian" (Margaret Roberts to Thomas Wolfe, July 31 / August 3, 1924; letter 19).

38. Wolfe, *Look Homeward, Angel,* 212.

39. Roberts memoir, 34.

40. Margaret Roberts to Thomas Wolfe, May 11, 1936; letter 60.

41. Wolfe, *Look Homeward, Angel,* preface, "To the Reader." Although Wolfe claimed that he "meditated no man's portrait," in truth, the resemblance between living persons and fictional characters was rarely accidental. In fact, his characterizations in *Look Homeward, Angel* are largely prose portraits of actual people.

42. Thomas Wolfe to Margaret Roberts, February 2, 1930; letter 58.

43. *To Loot My Life Clean: The Thomas Wolfe–Maxwell Perkins Correspondence,* ed. Matthew J. Bruccoli and Park Bucker (Columbia: University of South Carolina Press, 2000), 1.

44. Wolfe, *O Lost,* 252.

45. Wolfe and Perkins, *To Loot My Life Clean,* 12.

46. Ibid., 16. Wolfe's insertion totaled 319 words.

47. Wolfe, *Look Homeward, Angel,* 232.

48. Ibid., 233.

49. Margaret Roberts to Thomas Wolfe, May 11, 1936; letter 60.

50. Wolfe, *Look Homeward, Angel,* 214. For a perceptive interpretation of this passage, see Robert Taylor Ensign, *Lean Down Your Ear upon the Earth, and Listen: Thomas Wolfe's Greener Modernism* (Columbia: University of South Carolina Press, 2003), 91.

51. Ibid., 308.

52. Ibid., 216.

A Note on the Text

This volume assembles forty-eight letters from Thomas Wolfe to Margaret Roberts, twenty-seven from Roberts to Wolfe, and one letter from Wolfe to Frank Wells. The letters are published in their entirety and transcribed from the extant originals. No editorial emendations have been made in the texts of the letters, except for silent corrections of obvious typographical errors—strikeovers, transpositions, or misspacings. Missing punctuation has not been provided.

The identifications for these documents are ALS (autograph letter signed), AL (autograph letter without signature), and TLS (typed letter signed).

Transcribing Wolfe's and Mrs. Roberts's holograph documents requires decisions: commas and periods are often indistinguishable, as are colons and semicolons.

Bracketed words represent the editor's best guess; [*illegible*] indicates indecipherable words.

Dashes have been regularized to en-dashes unless a long dash seems deliberate.

Each letter has four items of data in its headnote:

To/From [if required]   *Description and location of document*
Assigned Date [if required]   *Address* [if required]

Dates that are on the originals are transcribed as part of the letters.

The following location abbreviations are used: *Harvard* (William B. Wisdom Collection, Houghton Library, Harvard University); and *UNC* (North Carolina Collection, University of North Carolina Library at Chapel Hill).

Chronology

August 15, 1874 Birth of John Munsey Roberts.

September 8, 1876 Birth of Margaret Elizabeth Hines; has one brother, Joseph Fennimore Hines.

1877 Margaret's father, Joseph Henry Hines, shot and killed by a berserk employee.

1879 Margaret's widowed mother, Elizabeth, marries Thomas Allbright; Margaret now has two stepbrothers, Thomas Jr. and Zack. Margaret calls herself Mattie Allbright until the age of fifteen, then goes back to Margaret Hines.

1891 Margaret attends East End College in Tennessee; meets John Munsey Roberts, a pupil at the school and later a teacher. The couple soon becomes engaged.

1899–1900 Margaret attends Vanderbilt University but does not graduate with a degree. Begins teaching at the Tennessee School for the Blind in Nashville.

1900 Margaret ill with a mild attack of tuberculosis, cared for in a Boulder, Colorado, sanatorium. After tuberculosis declared inactive, teaches at the Colorado State School for the Blind in Colorado Springs.

October 3 Thomas Clayton Wolfe is born at 92 Woodfin Street, Asheville, North Carolina, the last of William Oliver Wolfe and Julia Westall Wolfe's eight children.

August 26, 1904 Margaret Hines and John Munsey Roberts marry.

1906 John Munsey Roberts Jr. born while his father is principal of Vanderbilt Training School in Elkton, Kentucky.

August 30 Julia Wolfe buys the Old Kentucky Home at 48 Spruce Street to operate as a boardinghouse.

September Wolfe enters Orange Street School.

November 5, 1910	Margaret Rose Roberts born while her father is principal of McFerrin School in Martin, Tennessee.
1911	Roberts family moves to Asheville for its healthy climate. Plan to establish private school for boys. Mr. Roberts is principal of the Orange Street School, where Thomas Wolfe is in the sixth grade.
September 1912	The Robertses' North State Fitting School is founded at 157 Church Street on Buxton Hill. Thomas Wolfe is the first student enrolled.
1915	North State Fitting School renamed North State School and moved to 57 Austin Avenue.
May 13, 1916	Wolfe appears as Prince Hal in *Henry IV* in the North State School's pageant commemorating the tercentenary of William Shakespeare's death.
May	Wolfe's essay, "Shakespeare: The Man," wins the bronze medal in a citywide contest sponsored by the *Independent Magazine*.
June 1	Wolfe graduates from North State School.
September 12	Wolfe enters the University of North Carolina at Chapel Hill.
September 1918	Wolfe enrolls in Professor Frederick H. Koch's course in playwriting, the newly organized Carolina Playmakers.
October 19	Wolfe's brother Benjamin Harrison Wolfe dies; Mrs. Roberts sends a letter of consolation.
March 14–15, 1919	Wolfe's first play, *The Return of Buck Gavin,* is performed by the Carolina Playmakers with Wolfe in the title role.
Spring	Wolfe wins the Worth Prize in Philosophy for his essay *The Crisis in Industry.* It is published as a pamphlet by the University of North Carolina.
Fall	Wolfe is named editor in chief of the *Tar Heel,* the University of North Carolina student newspaper.
1920	North State School closes.
June 16	Wolfe receives bachelor of arts degree from the University of North Carolina.

September 13 Wolfe is accepted in the Graduate School of Arts and Sciences, Harvard University, to pursue a master of arts degree in English. Wolfe writes his mother that while traveling by train to Boston, he experiences "a rattling, tearing, sort of cough, full of phlegm" (Wolfe, *Letters of Thomas Wolfe to His Mother,* 8), soreness in his right lung, and coughs blood into his handkerchief. These symptoms are possibly the first signs of tuberculosis, which ultimately leads to his death.

Fall Wolfe studies playwriting as a member of George Pierce Baker's 47 Workshop.

January 25, 1921 Wolfe's *The Mountains,* a one-act play, is given a trial performance in the 47 Workshop's rehearsal hall.

March Wolfe works on a play called "The Heirs," which in 1925 becomes *Mannerhouse.*

Fall Mrs. Roberts begins teaching at Grace High School in Asheville, where Mr. Roberts is the principal.

October 21–22 Wolfe's revised *The Mountains, A Drama in One Act,* is staged by the 47 Workshop at the Agassiz Theatre, Radcliffe College.

June 19, 1922 Wolfe receives news his father is dying and returns to Asheville.

June 20 William Oliver Wolfe dies of prostate cancer. Wolfe receives his M.A. degree from Harvard University while he is still in Asheville.

September Wolfe returns to Harvard to study with Baker for another year and works on a full-length play that later becomes *Welcome to Our City.*

May 11–12, 1923 *Welcome to Our City* is staged by the 47 Workshop at the Agassiz Theatre.

August Wolfe revises *Welcome to Our City* and submits it to the Theatre Guild, an influential New York organization of stage producers, directors, and actors. (The Theatre Guild declines the play in December.)

February 6, 1924 Wolfe begins teaching English as an instructor in the Washington Square College of New York University, a position he holds for six years.

October 25   Wolfe leaves on his first trip to Europe, aboard the *Lancastria*. He begins writing a satiric treatment of his voyage, which he later titles "Passage to England."

December   Mrs. Roberts on verge of breakdown due to stress and overwork.

Wolfe in Paris, where the manuscript of his play *Mannerhouse* is stolen.

January 1925   Wolfe completely rewrites *Mannerhouse*.

March   Wolfe sends Mrs. Roberts the manuscript of the prologue of "Passage to England" and appoints her editor and censor.

June   Mrs. Roberts edits the prologue of "Passage to England" and turns it over to Wolfe's sister Mabel to locate a typist.

July 19   The *Asheville Citizen* publishes "London Tower," a short excerpt from "Passage to England."

August   Wolfe leaves for New York aboard the *Olympic*. On August 25, the day before the ship lands, he meets and begins an affair with Aline Bernstein, a set designer for New York theaters.

September   Wolfe resumes teaching at Washington Square College.

Fall–Winter   Wolfe's relationship with Bernstein deepens. He moves into a loft at 13 East Eighth Street that she rents as a studio.

June 23, 1926   Discouraged by the rejection of his plays, Wolfe leaves on his second trip to Europe, aboard the *Berengaria*. He travels in France and England with Aline Bernstein.

July   In Paris Wolfe begins an outline for an autobiographical novel.

August   Wolfe settles in London and begins working on the first version of his book.

December 22   Wolfe leaves for New York aboard the *Majestic,* arriving in the city on December 28. Settled back into the Eighth Street studio, he works for six months on his autobiographical novel.

July 12, 1927   Wolfe leaves on his third trip to Europe, aboard the *George Washington*. For two months he travels with Aline Bernstein in France, Germany, Austria, Czechoslovakia, and Switzerland.

September 18   Wolfe returns to New York aboard the *Belgenland*. He resumes teaching at Washington Square College and continues to work on his long manuscript.

March 1928   Wolfe moves into a more spacious apartment at 263 West Eleventh Street, where he completes the manuscript of "O Lost." He shares the apartment with Aline Bernstein.

May   Wolfe begins work on a new novel, "The River People."

May 20   Wolfe engages Madeleine Boyd as his literary agent for "O Lost" after it has been rejected by several publishers.

June 30   Wolfe leaves on his fourth trip to Europe, aboard the *Rotterdam.*

July 9   Wolfe lands at Boulogne and travels in France, Belgium, and Germany. He continues working on "The River People," which he soon abandons.

September   Madeleine Boyd submits "O Lost" to Maxwell E. Perkins of Charles Scribners' Sons.

September 30   Wolfe is injured in a brawl at the Oktoberfest in Munich and is hospitalized.

October 4   Wolfe is released from the hospital. He continues to travel, visiting Oberammergau in Germany to see its Passion Play. He also visits Vienna and Budapest.

November 16   Upon his return to Vienna, Wolfe finds a letter from Maxwell Perkins expressing interest in publishing "O Lost."

December   Wolfe travels in Italy and leaves for New York aboard the *Vulcania* on December 21. He arrives in New York on the last day of the year.

January 2, 1929   Wolfe has his first meeting with Perkins.

January 7   Perkins orally agrees to publish Wolfe's novel. Two days later, Charles Scribner's Sons formally accepts "O Lost." Over the next four months, Wolfe works closely with Perkins editing and cutting the manuscript.

February 5   Wolfe resumes teaching part-time at Washington Square College.

April   Wolfe changes the title of "O Lost" to *Look Homeward, Angel* at the request of Scribner's.

June   Manuscript of novel is sent to typesetter. Wolfe corrects proof of the novel while vacationing in Maine and Canada.

August	*Scribner's Magazine* publishes "An Angel on the Porch," a revised chapter from *Look Homeward, Angel.*
September 7	Wolfe makes a short visit to Asheville, his last trip to his hometown until 1937.
September 24	Wolfe resumes teaching full-time at Washington Square College.
October 18	*Look Homeward, Angel* is published. The novel causes a commotion in Asheville but generally receives favorable reviews.
October	Mrs. Roberts wounded and angered by the portrayal of her family in *Look Homeward, Angel.* She does not communicate with Wolfe for nearly seven years.
January 17, 1930	Wolfe resigns from Washington Square College, effective February 6. He never works as a teacher again.
February 2	Wolfe's last letter to Mrs. Roberts for over six years. Mrs. Roberts leaves it unanswered, and the friends are estranged until 1936.
March 8, 1935	*Of Time and the River* is published by Charles Scribner's Sons.
November 14	*From Death to Morning,* a short-story collection, is published by Charles Scribner's Sons.
April 21, 1936	*The Story of a Novel* published by Charles Scribner's Sons.
May–June	Mr. and Mrs. Roberts in New York to visit daughter Margaret Rose; Mrs. Roberts extends an invitation to Wolfe to call on her, but he avoids her while she is in New York.
early January 1937	In New Orleans Wolfe meets William B. Wisdom, who later purchases Wolfe's personal papers and manuscripts and donates them to Harvard University. Wolfe mails letters severing his relations with Scribner's.
May 3–15	Wolfe's first return to Asheville since the publication of *Look Homeward, Angel.* Returns to New York.
July 2	Wolfe returns to North Carolina and moves into a rented cabin at Oteen, near Asheville.
September 2	Unable to find undisturbed privacy to work on his manuscripts in Oteen, Wolfe returns to New York, eventually moving into the Hotel Chelsea.

Fall Wolfe's break with Scribner's becomes public knowledge. He searches for a new publisher and chooses Harper and Brothers; Edward C. Aswell will be his editor.

December 31 Wolfe signs a contract with Harper for a novel titled "The Life and Adventures of the Bondsman Doaks."

January 1938 Wolfe launches into intensive work on his new novel.

February Wolfe enlists Mrs. Roberts to collect research for a proposed book about Asheville's ruin and Central Bank scandal.

March Wolfe changes his mind about his new book and decides on an autobiographical chronicle, titled "The Web and the Rock," with George Webber as the protagonist.

May 17 Wolfe delivers first draft manuscript to Edward Aswell.

May 19 Wolfe gives a lecture, "Writing and Living," at Purdue University.

June 20–July 2 Wolfe takes a two-week tour of the western national parks.

July 5 On a ferry from Seattle to British Columbia, Wolfe contracts a respiratory infection that activates dormant tuberculosis in his right lung.

July Wolfe enters Firlawns, a private sanatorium, twelve miles from Seattle at Kenmore.

August Wolfe is hospitalized at Providence Hospital in Seattle.

September 10 Wolfe arrives in Baltimore and is admitted to Johns Hopkins Hospital.

September 12 Dr. Walter E. Dandy performs an operation called a cerebellar exploration on Wolfe.

September 15 Wolfe dies of tuberculosis meningitis at 5:30 A.M.

June 22, 1939 *The Web and the Rock,* a novel assembled from Wolfe's manuscripts by Edward Aswell, is published by Harper and Brothers.

September 18, 1940 *You Can't Go Home Again,* a continuation of *The Web and the Rock,* is published by Harper and Brothers.

October 15, 1941 *The Hills Beyond,* which includes a fragment of Wolfe's final novel as well as short stories and sketches assembled by Aswell, is published by Harper and Brothers.

1945   Mrs. Roberts ill with cancer; bedridden for nearly two years.

May 9, 1947   Mrs. Roberts dies; buried at Riverside Cemetery.

July 12, 1954   John Munsey Roberts dies of a stroke; buried next to Margaret.

February 8, 1963   John Munsey "Buddie" Roberts Jr. dies.

February 4, 1998   Margaret Rose Roberts dies.

THE LETTERS
ॐ Part I

You say in your letter that you never knew many things about my
life when I was a child and that many more you did not discover
until years later. I am afraid there are still other things that you are
yet to learn. . . .

Thomas Wolfe to Margaret Roberts
(ca. August 1929)

THE EARLIEST EXTANT WRITINGS between Margaret Roberts and Thomas Wolfe date from 1912, the year eleven-year-old Tom Wolfe enrolled in the Robertses' North State Fitting School. Three of Wolfe's English composition books from 1912 to 1915 survive; the following is a sample of Mrs. Roberts's comments preserved upon their pages:

1912/1913[1]

Not so long as I wanted but well written. Dot your i's. [2]

You are not doing as good work as you can. [5]

Your work since Christmas has not been satisfactory. I shall be forced to call your mother up to get her co-operation unless you begin to do your work more faithfully. You are a boy of great ability, but you must study too. You read a great deal, and that is good, but too much reading is not to be desired any more than two [sic] little. [6]

You must be neater in the arrangement of your pages. Your sentences are good indeed. [11]

1. red-headed, not red headed. You must avoid leaving so much space between words. [11]

Tom, you are capable of doing excellent work, so I can have no patience with such scrawling. [14]

Tom, this work is truly distressing to me. You are a boy capable of doing exceptional work in English, but you grow worse in your written work instead of better. Your ideas are good and well expressed but slovenly written beyond endurance. Understand now that from now on, I shall require you to rewrite every bit of such careless work. [17]

Tom, you are capable of doing English work of the very highest quality. Carelessness is your besetting sin. Please make up your mind this summer that you will overcome this. [22]

Such an improvement gives me much pleasure. Be continually careful not to leave wide spaces between words. [1] Too much space. [25]

You must be neat in your work. [26]

Remember not to leave such big gaps between words that all your thoughts leak out. [30]

You must be more careful as to neatness. [32]

Why do you leave such a street between your words? [34]

1914[2]

[Thomas Wolfe's English composition on p. 50]
I was born October 3rd, 1900 and there begins the story of my existence. In 1904 I went to the world's Fair and stayed there seven months. At the age of five I was sent to school and in in [*sic*] month or so learned the Rudiments of reading and writing. At eleven I started to school with a gentlemen [*sic*] by the name of Roberts and for the past two years have been going to the school of same. Here my brief existence and manuscript must close as I am not a futurist and therefore cannot continue.

[Mrs. Roberts comment on the above composition]
You might have been a "Pasterite," and told more of your early life. [50]

Tom, I feel quite as if the Albatross had fallen from my neck – To think that I have actually got so much written work from you at one time. Keep it up and tread the path to glory. [55]

Please number your exercises. Your worked [*sic*] much improved in neatness. You omit part of the lesson. [58]

Excellent in words, but pretty badly disfigured as to penmanship. [60]

Tom Wolfe, turn to Wooley,[3] 179–180, and study till it burns your eye balls. [64]

Fine story finely told by a fine boy. [65]

1915[4]

This is the best-looking work you have done, but you <u>have not done</u> what I called for. [72]

Very good work, but poorly arranged on the page. [74]

I have graded your last paper, unless you get paper and put it in properly, and follow my directions. Pegasus must be controlled, even tho by one of a lower order who has no wings. [76]

1. The cover of the earliest surviving composition book is dated 1912 and contains pages from 1912 to 1913. Wolfe's three composition books are part of the Thomas Wolfe Collection at the University of North Carolina at Chapel Hill. Quotations are from *Thomas Wolfe's Composition Books: The North State Fitting School,*

1912–1915, ed. Alice R. Cotten (Chapel Hill: North Caroliniana Society and the Thomas Wolfe Society, 1990). This instructive book reproduces both Wolfe's exercises and Mrs. Roberts's comments.

2. "1914" and "#3 English" are written on the cover of the second composition book; March 30, 1914, is the only date written inside.

3. According to Alice R. Cotten's introduction to *Thomas Wolfe's Composition Books,* Wooley "appears to be Edwin Campbell Woolley's *Handbook of Composition.* . . . There are many editions, but the Boston: D.C. Heath, 1907 edition seems to match the corrections noted" (viii).

4. The third composition book is dated 1915. Note on the inside back cover by Wolfe's sister, Mabel Wolfe Wheaton: "Written by Thos. Wolfe while at Roberts School known as North State School at Asheville N.C. Year 1915." Wolfe wrote "English IV" on some pages.

ॐ

WOLFE'S APPRAISAL of the North State Fitting School is recorded in his 1914 composition book:

I am a pupil of the North State Fitting School and shall explain the reasons why I prefer it to other schools I have gone to. I like the fairness and the justice meted out by the teachers and I have a personal regard for them. I like especially well the student ~~life~~ body as they are all fine boys. The manner of instruction is new and novel, the lessons often being suggested by the pupils. On Fridays the literary society meets and we spend an enjoyable afternoon. The school-house is set far back in a grove of oaks of several acres and is situated on a high hill. There is ample ground afforded for recreation and we spend an enjoyable time. There is not one thing around or about the school that I dislike and I therefore spend an enjoyable time (Wolfe, *Composition Books,* 52).

2

THOMAS WOLFE's first surviving letter to Margaret Roberts is written in two drafts in his 1914 North State Fitting School composition book.

ALS, 2 pp., UNC

Asheville, N. C.
March 30th, 1914.

Dear Mrs. Roberts, –
    English is very hard and I wish you to shorten my lessons. Co operate, if you are my friend and I am yours –
    Tom Wolfe.
(Apologies to Benj. Franklin)
    Asheville, N. C.
    March 30th, 1914.

Dear Mrs. Roberts –
Will you shorten my English lessons as they are hard.
    Sincerely
    Tom Wolfe.
    Desha asks would the teacher shorten the lesson.[1]

[Mrs. Roberts's comment on the above letter]
Not until you learn to use the interrogation mark.
The last pages are neat – but – those others.[2]

    1. Mrs. Roberts's nephew Desha W. Dodson, son of Novvie Roberts Dodson and D. W. Dodson.
    2. Wolfe, *Composition Books,* 62–64.

3

THE FOLLOWING POSTCARD was written as the United States entered World War I. Wolfe was too young to enlist and remained at the University of North Carolina.

Postmarked November 8, 1917

Postcard of South Building,
U.N.C. Chapel Hill. N.C.;
Harvard, bMS Am 1883.2

Wolfe's postcard to Margaret Roberts, November 8, 1917. By permission of the William B. Wisdom Collection, Houghton Library, Harvard University, and Eugene H. Winick, Administrator C.T.A., Estate of Thomas Wolfe

Mrs. Margaret Roberts,
The North State School
Austin Ave,
Asheville, N.C.

My school mates are leaving in numbers to enlist. Will lose both my room mates after Christmas. Again Carolina has answered the call. I'll try to stand it the rest of the year. We're all very proud and rather sad.

I wish you a very happy Thanksgiving – Thos Wolfe.

[Handwritten upon front of postcard]
Do you remember what I said about Carolina?
This scene is typical.

4

THE REFERENCES TO Wolfe's "heavy heart" and "the war question," combined with Mrs. Roberts's condolences, date the following letter as 1918, the year Wolfe's brother Ben died (October 19, 1918). Also, according to Central Methodist Church records, Dr. Charles Wesley Byrd, the minister referred to, died January 3, 1918, after four consecutive terms of service. Mrs. Roberts's daughter, Margaret Rose Roberts, was puzzled by the religious sentiments in this and other letters to Wolfe; Miss Roberts maintained that her mother was an atheist.[1]

Ca. October 1918   *ALS, 4 pp., UNC*

Sunday After noon.

My dear Tom,

Realizing with what a heavy heart you left home, and that going back to school on such a grey day as this, cannot lighten your heart very much. I am sending you this little note, hoping that it may break the lonliness just a little.

You have been constantly in my thoughts since you telephoned last night, and Mr. Roberts and I both want you to know how much our sympathy is with you.

My eyes have just fallen on the last words Dr. Byrd wrote (you knew of his sudden death). They found them on his table unfinished. Somehow, they seem to me the very words that you need just now. At any rate, I risk sending them. Perhaps they will help you to face what may prove (Pray God, it may prove not so) dark days ahead. "O God, we know Thou art the God of light, liberty, love and life and we ask Thee to illumine our hearts, and send us forth to the duties of this new day and new year with the joy of faith, the gladness of obedience welling up in our hearts, and with a vision of truth and duty, that will equip us for better service. Thou has given us the sublime and awful gift of the freedom of the will. Make us to know the responsibility that is involved in this endowment. And help us to realize that <u>our will is ours that we make it Thine,</u> and may enter into the highest liberty by becoming– – –."

Write when you can, and remember if I am slow about writing it is because "Ole Man Work" is riding my shoulders full gallop and not because I forget our Sophomore.[2]

Since I failed to send the stamps due the university when I returned the books, I am enclosing them here and will ask you to give them to the librarian.

Some day find out if I can get "Osbornes Origin and Evolution of Life," and "Under Fire."[3]

I have had a good many bitter sorrows to bear in my life. And I have always found that of all earthly helps, <u>hard work</u> is the best comforter. I know you will do this – Of course, not too hard.[4]

Always write how your pulse is on the war question, and on all other questions that stir you. We keenly regretted not having you and Thomas[5] together.

Your sincere friend,
Margaret Roberts

1. Margaret Rose Roberts to Ted Mitchell, interview, November 5, 1990: "I don't
think she had a religion. She really was an atheist, but she never told us that. She never
let on in any way or tried to influence us in any of our beliefs. She read the Bible to
us. She knew the Bible upside down and backwards, and she thought just as Tom did,
that there was no literature in the world as great as the Bible. And my mother had us
memorize verses of it, and at Christmas time she had us recite the Christmas story in
front of the Christmas tree. After I was grown and had come home [from college] I
didn't believe in religion myself. All of my friends were kind of shocked, and I said to
my mother, 'You know everybody's shocked with me when I tell them I'm an atheist.
Why did you have us recite all of those things when you didn't believe in them yourself?' She answered, 'Well, I wanted you to know the historical background of why
people celebrate Christmas, and I wanted you to know the literature of the Bible. I've
brought you up to do your own thinking. I never wanted to influence you.'" Wolfe's
own religious convictions are open to wide interpretation. In the 1930s he claimed to
be an atheist: "I do not think that I have believed in God for fifteen years. Sometimes
it seems that I never believed in him save when I was a little child, saying my prayers,
mechanically, at night" (Turnbull, *Thomas Wolfe,* 327).

2. Clearly an oversight; by the time this letter was written, Wolfe had become a
junior.

3. No book has been located with this title for this period. Mrs. Roberts may have
meant *The Undying Fire* by H. G. Wells. See letter 12, note 1.

4. When Wolfe caught his first glimpse of Mrs. Roberts, she was typically hard at
work. In the autobiographical outline for *Look Homeward, Angel,* he recorded: "The
first trip to the North State—She was sweeping the floor" (Wolfe, *Autobiographical
Outline,* 18). In *Look Homeward, Angel* Wolfe transforms this first impression into:
"The huge trees made sad autumn music as they entered the grounds. In the broad
hall of the squat rambling old house Eugene for the first time saw Margaret Leonard.
She held a broom in her hands, and was aproned. But his first impression was of her
shocking fragility" (Wolfe, *Look Homeward, Angel,* 212).

5. Thomas Wallis, a North State School student. Tom Davis in *Look Homeward,
Angel.*

5

FOLLOWING HIS GRADUATION with a B.A. degree from the University of North
Carolina on June 16, 1920, Wolfe set his sights on graduate study at Harvard
University. He was convinced that his dream of becoming a playwright would
be realized when he enrolled in George Pierce Baker's renowned playwriting
course, English 47, familiarly called the 47 Workshop.

The "great Baker"—
George Pierce Baker.
By permission of the Harvard Theatre Collection,
Houghton Library,
Harvard University

Postcard of Harvard College, Pierce Hall, Cambridge, Mass; Harvard, bMS Am 1883.2 (294)

Postmarked December 23, 1920

My Dear Friends, I have worked almost to exhaustion and I welcome the respite of the holidays which started today. I'm writing you a long letter to make up Coming here was the greatest thing I could do. I have written a one-act play for the great Baker[1] which will be put on, I think.[2] I have gone through my silent moment of self doubt in this lonely place but I know myself now God Bless You and a happy Christmas be yours.

My address 48 Buckingham St Cambridge

1. Professor George Pierce Baker (1866–1935). Wolfe wrote his mother, Julia E. Wolfe, in 1920: "[Baker] is the greatest authority on the drama in America and in the last six years he has developed in this class some of the best dramatists in the country, several of whom have plays on Broadway now. I was in the depths of despair at the time but his talk has lifted me up again" (Wolfe, *Letters of Thomas Wolfe to His Mother*, 13). Baker was portrayed as Professor James Graves Hatcher in *Of Time and the River*. "Eugene was now a member of Professor Hatcher's celebrated course for dramatists,

and although he had come into this work by chance, and would in the end discover that his heart and interest were not in it, it had now become for him the rock to which his life was anchored, the rudder of his destiny, the sole and all-sufficient reason for his being here" (*Of Time and the River* [New York: Charles Scribner's Sons, 1935], 130).

2. Wolfe's one-act play, *The Mountains,* was given a trial performance in the 47 Workshop's rehearsal hall on January 25, 1921.

6

It is not difficult to understand why Wolfe, after six years of suffocating existence in his mother's boardinghouse, chose Mrs. Roberts as the first of three parental substitutes that he idolized. (Aline Bernstein and Maxwell Perkins were the others.) Her response to the notice of Wolfe's one-act play *The Mountains* is typical of the declarations of praise and encouragement that drew him to his boyhood teacher.

ALS, 7 pp., UNC

Asheville, N.C. Box 1116
Sunday, March 13, 1921

My dear Boy,

I think you can hardly realize how much joy your letter brought us. Very few hours have passed over my head that you have not been in my thoughts, and nearly as often in our conversation. So why shouldn't you come for the lump of sugar and the pat on the head? Especially since you know perfectly well that you would get it. For you have been not merely a good doggie but a transcendent one. I have had a letter dribbling off the end of my pen ever since the notice in the paper about your play, but physical conditions with us have been of ponderous, prostrating power.

Before coming to the real things, I shall say, briefly, that we have sold the beloved 26½ acres of our farm and are now in town. It gave us a sore-wrench, but we have been having our "It's for the best" teeth extracted for so many years that we have tried to be manly enough not to scream over the extraction of this loved molar. We found we could sell it for almost as much as the whole 121 acres cost us. So, with the money market depressed and our needs great, we felt it no time for sentiment.

He (Mr. George Stephens) wanted possession almost at once, so we moved to Kenilworth[1] where we were miserably smoked for six weeks by a diabolical flu. After a most disagreeable altercation with the landlord, we came out here on Victoria Road to as lovely a location as heart could wish.

As far as the rest, our chronicle is brief. Mr. Roberts has continued to improve. I am stronger than in fifteen years. Munsey[2] is a young giant – larger than last fall – confiscates all his daddy's shirts and socks. Margaret Rose continues to be our joyous skylark. Thus endeth the tale of "We'uns." Roy[3] is teaching at State College. Saw Thomas,[4] an enthusiastic and progressive farmer.

Now, to the heart of the matter, which is you. I wonder how much more joy I shall get from Munsey as a young collegian. There is a sense in which I loved all of the boys, even the most trifling; because in each there was something worth loving, or something needing love.[5] Then, again, there was a much smaller number that were loved with a really personal love. And one that I counted close – next to the dearest children of my heart. I shall leave you to guess Him. Old school teachers are always saying, "I knew this or that one when he was just a little fellow" —. Well, I Did, and my faith has never wavered. Miss Roberts[6] used to worry about your Math. But I told her not to bother – that your road lay not over the plough-shares of x + y.

If you look back to your days in English composition, you will recall that I never corrected much except your mechanical mistakes. I was wise enough, though not naturally wise, to see that by nature you had the touch of the pen, and that you would soon be far beyond your teacher. Lord bless your bones, I feel a choking in my throat when I think of what you have done in eight years and of the god-like vista of the years to come. Just let old ugly Prudence saw her saw. You can't burn the candle at both ends. Keats did. Shelly did. Coleridge, De Quincy! What might they not have done if they had conserved their powers.

Another thing, you <u>must lay aside foolish pride.</u> Let your <u>people help</u> you until you are <u>through school.</u> It is their simple duty. If they were living in want or even painful economy it would be different. I don't give names, but I know of one family where the lives of a whole family of younger children have been made gloomy for ever by the overweening greed of an older brother. He didn't take the education that was his for the asking, and in all these years he has squeezed and squeezed until the family for years has almost bloodless, damaged educationally, financially, and spiritually. Such wounds do not heal overnight.[7]

Now, don't let yourself be crowded into the same wrong corner. And above all, don't lose faith. A man must suffer before he can write. I believe that. But I don't believe any man who has lost faith in God and man (whether his be an orthodox conception or not lies with him) ever wrote a line that was a farthing's worth to the world.

Mark Twain says that a man is a fool who is a pessimist before he is forty, or an optimist after that age. I am pretty close to the time when I can enjoy the misery of being a pessimist without at the same time being a fool. You are a long ways off. An intense nature like yours must above all guard against being too tense. The string snaps, or as you suggest,[8] the temptation comes to make it snap when the tension not is, but seems unbearable. But you don't need me to preach to you any more than you needed me to correct your themes thoughts.

I have been twisting that Harvard Prof's hand ever since your letter came. If only they could realize the comfort to the student of the personal touch. But, after all, he is often such a pack animal that he has no time or energy for much besides routine. Anyway, this particular one has found you out, and I rise up and call him blessed.

Another preachment, and I am done. Don't you shoulder too much of the sorrows of our beautiful world. The pens that profess to know how to write seem able to paint only feebly the awful world conditions, so it seems useless for me to try to tell you how my heart is wrung – just as yours is, and those of all other people who have any remnant of soul left. Sometimes I feel as if the greed for gold has about overwhelmed us all. To me, the spots of glory are the souls of a few like you, young and glowing with ideals. "The old men dream dreams, and the young men see visions"[9] The seers are our only salvation now, of which, thank God, you will be one. Most of the good, fine boys I know will grow to be honest gentlemen – but getting the "squiddy"[10] is their aim, and every hour I live I see more clearly that that aim will bring its own retribution.

But enough. I don't ask you to write. You should not. Only let us have just a postal about the welfare of the new play and the climb to Parnassus of the old one. Two lumps of sugar and numberless pats will be your reward. If you could only come over after them this afternoon, you would love North Carolina and forget that All's not right with the world.

I never fully realized how lovely Asheville is until we came out here. This house stands on what was a part of the Vanderbilt estate, and looks to the mountains on every side. They are lovelier today than usual. You know how the shadows lie some days, with the brilliant color shining through the haze.

The river winds just at the foot of our hill on one side and joins with the Swannanoa on the other, both gleaming in the sun. It's a golden world and makes me long to measure up to its high calling. If I were you and had the gift of the pen, I'd rather be able to interpret the beauty of the world; the beauty and tragedy and mystery in men's lives than to have all the gold that has ever been mined. I hope I have made you homesick for these mountains – so homesick that we may at last have a glimpse of you next summer. By – the – way, the Frazers[11] are now at 22 Pleasant Avenue, South Montclaire, New Jersey. Some chance might bring you near them.

Please understand that while I do the writing, Mr. Roberts speaks through me. He, too, is a firm, believer in your star.

By the way, William Cocke[12] and Munsey saw their first Shakespeare last week – in two of the plays which we had "acted." I never had such a good time watching anybody. I was surprised at their trenchant comments and their keen appreciation. Never before had I realized how much they had entered into the spirit of the plays. Do read "Thomas Bewick and His Tail Pieces" in the "Freeman," March 9, if you can find time. A charming sketch.

Love from us all,

Margaret Roberts

At last I have kept my promise and here enclose the letter. My earnest request is that you never show it to anybody. In those days I lived on the run, and this letter certainly shows it. For it is about as carelessly thrown together as any letter could well be.[13]

M.R.

1. "It was a little log house on Caledonia Road" (Margaret Rose Roberts to Ted Mitchell, interview, March 17, 1996).

2. John Munsey Roberts Jr., nicknamed Buddie by the family; also called Munsey.

3. Leroy "Roy" Dock, a former North State School student, portrayed as Guy Doak in *Look Homeward, Angel:* "Guy Doak was five years his senior. He was a native of Newark, New Jersey: his speech was touched with Yankee nasality, his manner with Yankee crispness. . . . He was foppishly neat in his dress. People called him a good-looking boy" (319–20).

4. Thomas Wallis.

5. Mrs. Roberts's compassion for her students is shared by her fictional counterpart, Margaret Leonard: "Boys were her heroes, her little gods. She believed that the world was to be saved, life redeemed, by one of them. She saw the flame that burns in each of them, and she guarded it. She tried somehow to reach the dark gropings toward light and articulation, of the blunt, the stolid, the shamefast. She spoke a calm low word to the trembling racehorse, and he was still" (Wolfe, *Look Homeward, Angel,* 307–8).

6. J. M. Roberts's sister, Emma Roberts, taught Wolfe math at the North State School.

7. The family Mrs. Roberts describes is her husband's: "Daddy's older brother Andrew Pitt wheedled out the deed for the farm at Roberts Bend outside of Columbia [Tennessee]. Emma, Daddy, and Horty paid to keep the farm and take care of

Grandpa Roberts and his family for years. Mother never got over it" (Margaret Rose Roberts to Ted Mitchell, interview, March 17, 1996).

8. Wolfe's suggestion is in a now missing letter.

9. Joel 2:28: "your old men shall dream dreams, your young men shall see visions."

10. Slang for money.

11. Mr. and Mrs. Spaulding Frazer were former neighbors of the Robertses. According to Margaret Rose Roberts, Mr. Frazer came to Asheville to be treated for tuberculosis. In 1920 Mrs. Roberts had consulted Frazer about the possibility of Wolfe teaching at the Bingham Military School in Asheville. Frazer recommended Harvard instead. He was dean of Newark Law School.

12. William J. Cocke, one of Wolfe's friends and a fellow student at North State School, nicknamed Wee Willie. Portrayed as Johnny Parks in *Of Time and the River.* "Once or twice a week Eugene went into town and had tea in the rooms of a boyhood friend whom he had known at school and who was now a Rhodes scholar at Merton College" (627).

13. The "carelessly thrown together" letter has not been preserved.

Note: In reference to Mrs. Roberts's March 13, 1921, letter to Wolfe, Wolfe wrote his mother on April 19, 1921: "I got a nice letter from Mrs Roberts a few weeks ago which stirred me considerably. They have had a hard time and have been forced to sell their last home in Chunn's Cove to which they were attached. Mr Roberts has been very sick with stomach trouble, you know, and the one strong thing about Mrs Roberts since I have known her has been her invincible spirit that is as brave and true as any I have known. They have been two dear wonderful friends to me and when I get a letter from her I flush at her praises for I know I am not big enough yet for them. It was through her that I first developed a taste for good literature which opened up a shining El Dorado for me. If you see her I wish you'd give her my kindest regards" (Wolfe, *Letters of Thomas Wolfe to His Mother,* 23).

7

In August 1921, Mrs. Roberts asked Wolfe to write on her behalf to Frank Wells, superintendent of Buncombe County Schools. She requested that Wolfe attest to her abilities as a teacher in the hope that it would enable her to obtain a higher rating (and thus a better salary) at Grace High School. Although she had attended the private East End College in Nashville as well as Vanderbilt University, she had not acquired a degree. For this reason, she needed to establish her teaching credentials.

ALS, 2 pp., UNC
North State School letterhead

August 21, 1921.

My dear Tom,

Your last letter brought good tidings.[1] I'm happy that your caterpillar spring came out such a gorgeous butterfly summer.[2] Only I'm afraid you have worked too hard. Let us have your plans for the fall and winter:

I'm sorry to say I haven't gotten the play yet.[3] For days I've had company steadily with no time to think about anything. Aunt Emma was here ten days sick all the time. She has ruined herself with hard work, but people without money have to do that these days. It seems useless to kick against the inevitable. I'm going to your house to-morrow.

Now, I have time for a note only, and that to ask a favor which you may be too honest to grant. I'm going to teach this winter at Grace H.S.

By the new scale of salaries, because I lacked (because of a break in health) all of the work for my degree at V.U.[4] Now in order to get the highest rating and thus get a decent salary, I've got to blow a big horn about my vast and valuable teaching experience to make up for that degree.

So I am told to get the best that those who know me will say about my work, especially that at the N.S. School. It has occurred to me that possibly, in the interest of a full dinner pot, you wouldn't mind doing a little judicious lying in my behalf. I have always maintained that if I wanted to get the truth about a teacher, I'd go to the pupil rather than a former employer. I shall be glad to have you do this at once if it won't embarrass you. Please allow me to request that you write something good and write so that it can be read, or else, if you have nothing good to say, write in your usual handwriting such as I have to walk on my hands and balance on my nose to read. In the latter case, he would think I have some great genius praising me, and because I am even known by such, will give me a $300 salary. All nonsense aside, I shall feel very grateful to you if you can have the will and the time to do this for me. Address Mr. Wells, Supt. Buncombe Co. Schools, Asheville. With much love,

Margaret Roberts

1. Wolfe's letter has not been located.
2. Referring to Wolfe's arduous study at Harvard in summer school. "I put in five weeks of hard study in the Summer school which closed August 13, and although I have heard nothing yet as to my grade I am reasonably certain it is high—a B plus at any rate" (Thomas Wolfe to W. O. Wolfe, August 1921, Wolfe, *Letters*, 15).
3. Perhaps the three-act version of *The Mountains*.
4. Vanderbilt University, Nashville, Tennessee.

8

ALS, 12 pp., UNC

Sept 2 1921
Camb. Mass.

Dear Mrs Roberts: Your letter finally came a day or two ago and I am getting a glowing testimonial under way to Mr Wells. <u>Glowing</u> I say, and the term is mild: if I didn't restrain my leaping pen it would be a red hot paean. And I find the difficulty in writing such a letter is the tempering it down to a point where the man won't think you hired me. I know you were joking when you asked me if I would do this as a <u>favor</u> but I wonder if you really have any idea what a joy and a privilege and an honor I esteem it. I only fear I may hurt your own cause by my own fervor. Under any condition I fear the letter will have an over-eulogistic flavor to one who doesn't know me – or you. I am therefore making the letter informal, as I know Mr Wells slightly, for I feel I will better create the impression of utter earnestness I am so desirous of creating.

But I shall certainly tell him that I have had only three great teachers[1] in my short but eventful life and that you are one of these.

Harvard, fine as it is, has as yet been unable to submit any candidates to my own Hall of Fame tho I hope within another year to nominate and elect a fourth.

This 'point system' of selecting teachers is a relic of barbarism, when I compare you not only in actual culture but in the more vital quality of stimulating and inspiring the love of fine and beautiful literature in the heart and mind and soul of that boy lucky enough to claim you for a teacher (my sentence is becoming attenuated; I'll have to get a fresh breath) – when I compare you in these respects to the average college grad, comparisons, as Mrs Malaprop[2] says, become odorous.

Mrs Roberts, there's no estimating the influence you've had on me and the whole course of my life; what's done is done, each day causes me to see more plainly how tremendous an influence that was and I know I shall be even more emphatic on this score the last day of my life than I am now

Your friendship, and that of Mr Roberts, and your faith and hope in me, one of the most cherished possessions of my life, causes me ghastly suffering at times when I doubt myself and wonder if you are fooled in me. Yes, I have actually writhed in my sheets in the dead dark night thinking of this and this alone. It has been my yoke and will continue to be my burden to bear the flagellations of a passionate, at times, almost uncontrollable temperment, but, somehow or other, this summer, in my loneliness and despair I have got my hand on the throat of Mr Hyde, and I believe, with the grace and help of God, I'll ride the waves in safety now.

You are always reading. Well so am I. Curiously enough when you wrote me you had been reading Francis Thompson's[3] essay on Shelley I had been doing the next best thing, that is, reading Shelley.

I reread Alaster[4] and Adonais[5] a few days ago and was inexpressibly thrilled by that mighty poetry. I don't think anyone has ever said such vast and powerful things in so vast and powerful a way as Shelley.

When I read the following (from Adonais) my feelings were between a wild extant shriek and downright weeping, so deeply did it stir me up:

"The One remains, the many change and pass;

Heaven's light forever shines, Earth's shadows fly:

Life, like a dose of many-colored glass

Stains the white radiance of Eternity," – Forgive me for quoting these well-known lines but when a man can talk like that the world is literally nothing but his footstool.

It goads me to fury to hear the cant and the clap-trap daily bandied about which would divorce a man like Shelley from Life and Reality and call him a cloud gatherer and laud a writer of debauched plays such as Wycherley[6] or Congreve[7] for his _infinite_ knowledge of life. What rot! Those who spend their lives searching around pigsties, bask in the favor of the unthinking while those who take a broadcast view of things or, as Shelley did, identify themselves with the wind – "tameless and swift and proud"[8] – are hooted at because they won't stay to be shod!

Francis Thompson was a unique figure and had a good deal of the Coleridge mysticism about him. I have read his "Hound of Heaven" and some of his other poems.

He too was a drug addict and a street waif, the people who finally unearthed him and supported him finding him almost barefoot. I suppose he could have satisfied the utmost desires of the worldly with "knowledge of life" if he'd cared to exhibit that "knowledge" but fortunately the glory and significance of things struck him as more important.

Well, I mustn't rave any more or I'll be at it all night. I am desperately tired and weary of limb. We are having another hot spell, – it was almost 100 today. I want to go home. I've _got_ to go somewhere, but I'm afraid they won't want me to come back next year and I've _got_ to do that also.[9] Give my kindest regards to Mr Roberts

Tom

1. The others were Horace Williams, head of the Department of Philosophy, and Edwin Greenlaw, head of the Department of English, both at the University of North Carolina.

2. Mrs. Malaprop, character in Richard Sheridan's comedy *The Rivals* (1775) noted for her misuse of words. "As headstrong as an allegory on the banks of the Nile" is one of her gross misapplications.

3. Francis Thompson (1859–1907), English poet.

4. "Alastor, or the Spirit of Solitude" (1816), a poem by Percy Bysshe Shelley (1792–1822).

5. "Adonais" (1821) by Shelley. When Keats died in 1821, Shelley was moved to compose this elegy for his friend. Considered one of the greatest elegies in the English language.

6. William Wycherley (1640–1716), English dramatist, noted for the savagery of his satire and his cyncial, mordant wit.

7. William Congreve (1670–1729), English dramatist, usually considered the great master of the Restoration comedy of manners.

8. "Ode to the West Wind" (1820) by Shelley.

9. Wolfe's parents had not yet consented that he be allowed to re-enroll for 1921–1922.

9

To: Frank Wells   *ALS, 8 pp., UNC*

Sept 5 1921
Cambridge Mass.

Dear Mr Wells: My friend and former teacher, Mrs J. M. Roberts, has lately written me, explaining that some testimonial is desired as to her quality as a teacher, and asking me if I would care to record any opinion I have on that subject. I esteem it an honor and a privilege to do this altho I find myself in constant difficulties when I try to keep my pen from leaping away with a red-hot panegyric.

But – with all the moderation and temperance and earnestness at my command I can no do less than consider Mrs Roberts as one of the three great teachers who have ever taught me, – this with all honor to Harvard who has not yet succeeded in adding a fourth name to my own Hall of Fame.

More than any one I have ever known Mrs Roberts succeeded in getting under my skull with an appreciation of what is fine and altogether worthwhile in literature. That, in my opinion, is the vital quality. That is the essential thing, – the mark of a real teacher

I didn't know until Mrs Roberts wrote me that she had no university degree but that is a matter of not the slightest consequence to me. So far does she surpass certain college graduates I know, who are teaching, in respect to actual knowledge, appreciation, and the ability to stimulate and inspire that any difficulty as to a degree would be negligible, I think.

I have spoken of Mrs Roberts merely as a teacher. This is perhaps the only testimonial you want. But I cannot stop before I speak of another matter that has been of the highest importance to me. During the years Mrs Roberts taught me she exercised an influence that is inestimable on almost every particular of my life and thought.

With the other boys of my age I know she did the same. We turned instinctively to this lady for her advice and direction and we trusted to it unfalteringly.

I think that kind of an elation is one of the profoundest experiences of anyone's life, – I put the relation of a fine teacher to a student just below the relation of a mother to her son and I don't think I could say more than this.

You can readily understand that the intimacy of such a relation is much more important in those formative years at grammar school or high school than afterwards at college.

At college you don't get it but you don't need it so much. The point is that I did get it at a time when it was supremely important that I get it. It is, therefore, impossible that I ever forget the influence of Mrs Roberts, she is one of my great people and happy are those who can claim her as their teacher!

I am

    Very Truly Yours

    Thomas Wolfe

10

Ca. November 1921   *ALS, 4 pp., UNC*

Sunday Nov.
135 Hillside St.
Asheville, N.C.

My Dear Tom,

I can hope for nothing but utter condemnation from you. I have waited from day to day and week to week, hoping that my over weighted body would somehow join forces with my weak mind and enable me to write at least a coherent letter. Now, I believe you have faith enough in me to believe me when I tell you that this is the first hour that I have felt that I could scrawl anything. I shan't bore you with details. Only believe that my long delay has not been caused by any lack of appreciation for your wonderful and much undeserved letter, or by any lack of love. I do not speak with any assumed modesty when I tell you how far beyond my deserts your letter went. The big tears rolled down my cheeks after I had read it. It is a very great joy to me that you should feel that my teaching meant any thing to you. I feel only too keenly my deficiencies as a teacher, both from inadequate preparation, and a body so tired for many years that I have been able to add only by piecemeal to that slender preparation. But perhaps I have made up for this in part by my love for the work, and for chaps.[1]

Anyway, I have no words with which to thank you, not simply for the letter which I hope will bring in the extra shekels but far more, do I thank you for the heart of your letter.

Again, you will feel sure that the above is all idle talk, that I care nothing for you and your development when I tell you that I have not yet been to your house for your play. But again I beg you to have faith. I knew it useless to get it until my body got rested enough to trot along beside my mind. I have seen the notice in the paper that your play is to be presented now. Please show a Christian spirit. Forgive my seeming lack of interest and let me have even a card to say how it is received.[2] We talk about you everyday and daily we delight in you and in your work. I can't see how anything short of ill-health can stop you. Oh, Boy, I wonder if you can realize how close we feel you are to us, and how eager we are about every phase of your development. I know that life is too full for you to do any writing but whenever the moment comes that you have time for a card, let us have that full moment. Every word you write is seized upon by this family with avidity and will be all the more so now, because my little sister-in-law[3] whom you met when here, is with us for the winter. She has always been a great admirer of you, and always eagerly inquires about you.

I am glad to know that you were able to see your father. He can't have many more days or years with you and each meeting you can have with him will be very sweet for you to remember[4]

As for this family, after weary weeks of searching for an empty house we are established in our new quarters. Mr. Roberts says he can't stretch his legs freely in any direction but if you will come to see us we will knock out a wall and give you room for expansion.

We love the teaching work at Grace.[5] I have never enjoyed work more, but with the home work in addition I am simply an animated jumping-jack. Mr. Roberts is holding out pretty well, tho always there is the fear at my heart that there might come another break.[6]

Margaret Rose is, as ever, our joyous skylark, very pretty, to me at least.

Buddie is at Davidson, very enthusiastic, and working hard. He was not so well prepared as he should have been and hence has to study pretty hard. But he likes his work. He seems to do especially well in English. Of course that is because he has always loved to read. His teacher told him last week that his short story was so good that Professor told him he wanted him to work it over and give it to the college magazine. When Marg heard this she said, "Well, Mother, he may be a Tom Wolfe yet."

As for me, I am in a state of coma so far as reading or thinking is concerned. A mere head-liner. Of course my every thought and heart-beat is with the Washington conference. If one only could hope that they would cease to be politicians and diplomats and be human beings! But can one hope, remembering what they have done for the world, and failed to do in the past four years. But it is not in me to see things all black. Write what you think about everything. When will you come home again? No hopes, I suppose, for Christmas? That would be too good. James Gillespie still in bed. Wee Willie Cocke leading his class at the University. I hear old George McCoy[7] doing fine work. Both the Cheeseborough boys[8] there. Wee & George will carry on the torch. Munsey said he himself got so interested in French Revolution (Carlyle) that he sat up all night to read it. Not bad for fifteen, is it? With much love from all of us.

Margaret Roberts

[On left margin]
Stately State Board has not yet ambled around to my case, so I am not yet able to draw but a fraction of a cook's wages. So much for the red tape.[9]

1. In *Look Homeward, Angel,* Wolfe captured Mrs. Roberts's misgivings about her teaching qualifications but defended her high degree of excellence. Describing Margaret Leonard's lessons in literature, he wrote that "she was afraid that what she had to offer was not enough. What she had to offer was simply a feeling that was so profoundly right, so unerring, that she could no more utter great verse meanly than mean verse well. She was a voice that God seeks. She was the reed of demonic ecstasy. She was possessed, she knew not how, but she knew the moment of her possession. The singing tongues of all the world were wakened into life again under the incantation of her voice. She was inhabited. She was spent. She passed through their barred and bolted boy-life with the direct stride of a spirit. She opened their hearts as if they had been lockets. They said: 'Mrs. Leonard is sure a nice lady'" (314).

2. On October 21 and 22, 1921, the 47 Workshop staged *The Mountains* at the Agassiz Theatre at Radcliffe College. The production was received unfavorably, and Wolfe was both disappointed and angered by the criticisms. The most frequent

criticism was that the audience found it depressing, to which Wolfe responded to Professor Baker, "If the audience is depressed over my play, I am depressed over my audience" (Wolfe, *Letters,* 20).

3. Mary Linn Roberts; called Aunt Dolly by the Robertses.

4. W. O. Wolfe died the following year, on June 20, 1922.

5. J. M. Roberts was the principal at Grace High School, where Mrs. Roberts was now teaching.

6. A reference to Mr. Roberts's recurring ulcer complications.

7. George W. McCoy, a friend of Wolfe's and student at the North State School. McCoy later became the managing editor of the *Asheville Citizen.*

8. Jack and Tom Cheeseborough, Mrs. Roberts's former students at the North State School, called the Cheesebrough boys in Wolfe's *O Lost* (357). The Cheesebrough brothers were excised from the manuscript before the publication of *Look Homeward, Angel.*

9. Mrs. Roberts did not receive the higher scale of salary that she hoped for from Grace High School.

II

Ca. December 1921   *AL fragment, 2 pp., UNC*

[First part of letter missing]
were a chap (what more are you now in years?) I felt you were so young to read such sophisticated plays. But I didn't realize that you were not to be held back – that there was already at work in you that spirit which had made Shaw[1] what he is. Incidentally, have you read this "Methusalah?" He has surpassed himself in that?

If you should by any chance strike New York, try to see the Frazers, 22 Pleasant Ave. Montclaire, N.J. I think they would enjoy seeing you, because they have the spirit of youth, and appreciation.

Let us know your plans for next year. I wonder if you will plunge straight into Literature and starve to death or try to feed your long frame by selling ice as last summer. As for us, life goes as usual: If you have ever seen a western jack-rabbit splitting the wind with its ears laid back – that's – me. But I love my work as much as any I have ever done, and Mr. Roberts seems to be as well as any could hope, considering his little demon hidden away in his stomach.

The chaps are fine and sweet, so what more could one call for in the way of homely joys?

We all of us send warm love. And best wishes for a true Christmas

"I heard an angel singing

When the day was springing,
  'Mercy, Pity, Peace
    Is the world's release.'"
And release can come only through "Souls' of vision" like yours. Surely, we must wake up and let Mercy, Pity, Peace, do their healing work for the world, broken as it has never been before.

[End of fragment]

1. George Bernard Shaw (1856–1950), British (Irish-born) author. Shaw was Wolfe's favorite playwright in his senior year at the University of North Carolina.

12

Ca. February 1922   *ALS, 12 pp., Harvard, bMS Am 1883.2 (294)*

Sunday Night

Dear Mrs Roberts: I am still paving the infernal road with my good intentions. Yet, failure to answer promptly letters from one who never fails to send hope and to invigorate me with new strength is not merely bad manners but bad judgment. If the press of work and examinations but recently ended can not come to my aid by way of excuse nothing else can.

Yesterday the secretary of the graduate school sent me a note saying he was "happy to inform" me I would get my M.A. with distinction upon removing the French requirement. I am sure his happiness can not equal mine. I have heard from only one course – but that is the one course I need. By their generosity my grade was A – altho I would hardly have dared to mark myself so well. So far I have made but one B and that was B+ last year in the Workshop. The rest have been As. When the year is over I will not only have completed the four courses required for the degree but will have received credit for two more as well. Six in all. This does not include the French.

My second year in the workshop did not count for the degree since not more than <u>one</u> composition course may be counted and, of course, 47 last year went down for that.

I am reading heavily. I will give you some idea of my labors for I take a grim delight in counting the victims of my insatiable bookishness, tho I despair at ever really knowing anything. Today is Sunday. This morning I finished Well's Undying Fire,[1] which I began last night. This is one of the few moderns I have had time for but rarely have I been more stimulated. He's not a profound man, but he's a very sound man. Not, i.e. what Emerson would call a "primary man" but one who is a living proof of the benefits of a broad and intensive education applied to the training of a first-class mind. But to go on with the tally: this afternoon I took a walk and read half through Swift's Tale of a Tub. Tonight I have read two essays of Emerson's and will finish Leslie Stephen's excellent life of Pope before I retire.

I suppose I make a mistake in trying to eat all the plums at once for instead of peace it has awakened a good-sized volcano in me. I wander through the stacks of that great library[2] there like some damned soul; never at rest, – ever leaping ahead from the pages I read to thoughts of those I want to read. I tell you this in all its monotonous detail because it is illustrative of the war that is being waged within me now—between what forces? For it brings me acute discomfort even in my writing. Still, as ever, I am seized with these desires to scribble but this thing wiggles at me like some demon and says, "Not yet, not yet. In two, three, or five years! Then, you'll be ready." But this is folly! If it continues the weight of my ignorance will fall on me like a stone, to crush me.

There is something in that potential serenity of Emerson that gives me courage. I reread for the second time today his essay on Books. He is

[A portion of this letter is missing.]

with death" The reference, of course, is plain, namely, that the drama can not deal successfully with the supreme moment. But is not this a little unfair? I know of no other art form which can treat the subject with more truth. The interesting thing about Liliom[3] is that this play gets off to a new start in interest after the hero kills himself. The next scene is the suicide court in heaven (as he thought it would be) But I will tell you no more. There is humor, even farce comedy, while he dies, there is comedy almost of a slap-stick variety in the heaven scene but all the time one says "why not?" For if we look at life intelligently we realize what a curiously woven fabric it is. The calloused police officers in Liliom drag the body of the dying man out to an open place and while he lies there groaning his life away, talk about the heat, curse the mosquitoes, the new wage scale, etc.

Let me add a gruesome touch of my own: When my brother died a few years ago I went around to the undertakers with Fred[4] to see him. The particular undertaker who met us, a pious, mealy-mouthed man, took us back, asked us to wait a moment, as an artist would ask his friends to wait until he got the light adjusted on his picture. Then he called us back and showed us Ben's body. As we stood there watching, filled with emotions and recollections of indescribable pain, the man began to talk. He was proud of this job. It was one of the best he had ever done. No other undertaker could do a better one. Then, with true artistic pride, he began to point out the little excellencies in

Benjamin Harrison Wolfe. According to his death certificate, Wolfe died at four o'clock in the morning, October 19, 1918, of "Pneumonia following Influenza." By permission of the North Carolina Collection, University of North Carolina Library at Chapel Hill, and Eugene H. Winick, Administrator C.T.A., Estate of Thomas Wolfe

his finished work that showed the hand of the master. It was too much for me. I went into howls of uncontrollable laughter. It was no doubt a reflex of my condition at the time but to this day I think of the incident with a smile[5]

That is one reason I defend Sir J.M. Barrie whenever he is criticized. I think Barrie is the most significant dramatist in the English speaking world today because he really is carrying on the great tradition of our drama. This is an arch-heresy here where some of my young critical friends consider him 'sentimental.' Is it not strange how the academic, critical point of view shrinks nervously away from the sympathetic. I have never read a play of Barrie's that didn't give me this curious 'mixed' feeling. He is not trying to 'prove' anything (thank heaven) but like Shakespeare and other old fogies is more interested in the stories of human beings than in the labor problem. That's why I believe his plays will outlast those of his contemporaries because people at all times can understand and appreciate the emotion of other people. Sceptics are referred to The Trojan Woman.[6] This is the universal, eternal element in drama.

After all, the conditions of which John Galsworthy wrote in Strife are becoming changed already; in twenty years we will still have a labor problem no doubt, but it will be one altogether different from the one Strife sets forth.[7]

During the most inventive and mature years of his genius G.B.S. expended his great powers of satire on the one thing he thought worthy of drama – the thesis. Then a war comes along that kills twenty million people and destroys nations and suddenly we can't convince ourselves that Mrs Warren's Profession or Widower's Houses deal with the biggest things in the world after all. If I were Shaw now I think I should feel as if I had been equipped with a mighty bludgeon but had spent my life braving gnats.

I agree with you about Eugene O'Neill[8] He's the beacon light in our own drama today; he's kept his ideals and now seems in a fair way to prosper by them. Two new plays of his are shortly to come to New York; Anna Christie is there now enjoying a popular success. I saw 'Beyond The Horizon' not long ago. It is a fine play. O'Neill is still a young man, c. 35, I think. I don't believe he has reached his greatest development yet. When it comes! There's one thing that worries me: In a forecast of his new play, The Hairy Ape, which is to be produced soon, I see the subject is to be a stoker on an ocean liner. During the successive stages we will see him go back steadily to the primitive man. I hope O'Neill won't let this tendency run away with him. You see, he was 'looking backward' in the Emperor Jones and, to a degree, we find this in other plays. Tragedy if continued in this vein, will become sordid and brutal. Surely this does not represent his outlook on life, great tragedy, I think, must look ahead.

[A portion of this letter is missing.]

and I have come to like her immensely because she pretends to be such a dunce. I don't believe she is at all; that's where our Southern girls are clever. It goads me beyond endurance when one of these Maidchen impossibles disgorges, as if it were her own, the content of her reading for the past month. But I refuse to be dazzled by high sounding talk.

J. S. Mill,[9] whose autobiography I was reading the other night, said the greatest lesson the Greeks taught him was to dissect an argument, as did Socrates, and find its weak spot. If men ever needed to use that method now is the time. There is so much claptrap, so much nonsense veiled behind intricacies that we need all our sanity and common sense to tear the arguments of these buffoons to pieces. Oh, for a Swift to flay the free versists!

Well, I really must be going. I hope Mr Roberts is feeling well. Give him my kindest regards and send my best wishes to Munsey when you write to him at Durham.

With Much love

Tom

67 Hammond St

Cambridge, Mass

Your criticism of the last scene in my play was unerringly accurate. I've not cut Mag's speech. I've written the first two acts of the play as a three act, (also a prolog).[10]

1. Wolfe admired H. G. Wells's modernized Job saga, *The Undying Fire* (1919), and based "The Old School," one of his early plays written at Harvard, on it. (The manuscript survives only in fragments.)

2. The Widener Library. "I read prodigiously. The Widener Library has crumpled under my savage attack. Ten, twelve, fifteen books a day are nothing" (Wolfe, *Letters,* 44–45). Letter probably to Merlin Mcf. Taylor.

3. *Liliom* (1909), by Ferenc Molnár.

4. Wolfe's brother, Frederick William Wolfe (1894–1980). Portrayed as Luke in *Look Homeward, Angel.*

5. For Wolfe's employment of this incident with undertaker Claude B. Holder (called Horse Hines in *Look Homeward, Angel*), see Wolfe, *Look Homeward, Angel,* 567–72.

6. *The Trojan Woman,* by Euripides (ca. 484–450 B.C.E.).

7. John Galsworthy's (1867–1933) plays reflected his interest in social documentation. His play *Strife* (1909) led to prison reform.

8. Mrs. Roberts's assessment of O'Neill may have appeared in the missing material of letter 11, ca. December 1921. Mrs. Roberts also praises O'Neill in letter 14.

9. John Stuart Mill (1806–1873), English philosopher and economist; his *Autobiography* was published in 1873.

10. *The Mountains.* Mrs. Roberts's criticism of the last scene has not been located.

13

Ca. September 1922   *Fragment, 6 pp., Harvard, bMS Am 1883.2 (294)*

coming home this last time I have gathered enough additional material to write a new play,[1] – the second fusillade of the battle. This thing that I had thought naive and simple is as old and as evil as hell; there is a spirit of world-old evil that broods about us, with all the subtle sophistication of Satan. Greed, greed, greed — deliberate, crafty, motivated – masking under the guise of civic associations for municipal betterment. The disgusting spectacle of thousands of industrious and accomplished liars, engaged in the mutual and systematic pursuit of their profession, salting their editorials and sermons and advertisements with the religious and philosophic platitudes of Dr Frank Crane,[2] Edgar A. Guest,[3] and The American Magazine[4] The standards of national greatness are Henry Ford, who made automobiles cheap enough for us all, and money, money, money!! And Thos. A. Edison who gave us body-ease and comfort. The knave, the toady, and the hog-rich flourish. There are three ways, and only three, to gain distinction: (1) money, (2) more money, (3) A great deal of money. And the matter of getting it is immaterial. Among the young people here there is one, who spends two-thirds of his time in the drug store, and who announces boldly, and as a kind of boast, that he is going to "marry money." This boy's father is an engineer on the rail-road – an honest, industrious, straightforward sort of man who walks to his work every morning with a tin dinner-pail swinging from his hand. Meanwhile the boy rides through the streets of the town, in pursuit of his ambition, in a spick-and-span speedster which he has inveigled from these hard-working people, or, perhaps from the very foolish woman, his aunt. Another boy, of good but common stock, who had all his advances repelled, to within a few months back, with contempt or indifference, has unlimited money, and with a part of it has purchased an expensive roadster, like a foolish fellow. Now they cluster about him like flies, and feed upon his bounty. These are but mean and petty things, which I could multiply indefinitely. But what of the darker, fouler things? What of old lust, and aged decay, which mantles itself in respectability, and creeps cat-footed by the stained portals of its own sin? What of the things we know, and that all know, and that we wink at, making the morality we prate of consist in discretion? I assure you I am not barren in illustrations of this sort. The emotion I experience is disgust, not indignation. Moral turpitude on the physical basis does not offend me deeply – perhaps I should be sorry to confess it – but my attitude toward life has become, somehow or other, one of alertness, – one which sustains and never loses interest, but which is very rarely shocked or surprised by what people do. Human nature is capable of an infinite variety of things. Let us recognize this early and save ourselves trouble and childish stupefaction later. I desire too much to be the artist to start "playing at" life now, and seeing it through a rosy or vinous haze. Really, I am unmoral enough not to care greatly how the animal behaves, so long as it checks its behavior within its meadow. The great men of the Renaissance, both in Italy and England, seem to me an amazing mixture of God and Beast. But "there were giants in the world in those days,"[5] – and they are soon forgiven. What do their vices matter now? They have left us Mona Lisa. But what of this dull dross that leaves us only bitterness and mediocrity? Let pigs

[A portion of this letter is missing.]

I suppose the alarmist means that the time will come when the strength of our national life will wither and decay, just as all preceding national lives have served their times, and have withered and decayed, and passed on. But what is there in this either to surprise or alarm us? Surely a nation has no greater reason to expect imperishability than has an individual. And, it is by no means certain that a long life, whether for man or nation, is the best one.[6] Perhaps our claim to glory, when our page is written in the world's history, will rest on some such achievement as this: "The Americans were powerful organizers and had a great talent for practical scientific achievement. They made tremendous advances in the field of public health, and increased the average scope of human life twelve years. Their cities, altho extremely ugly, were models of sanitation, their nation at length was submerged and destroyed beneath the pernicious and sentimental political theory of human equality."

I do not say that this is utterly base or, mean, or worthless. It will be a very great achievement, but it has left no room for the poets. And when the poets die, the death of the nation is assured.

———— Well, – I have returned to all this at midnight. The fires of the hearth have burned to warm-grey, cones of powder. There is a roaring in the wind to-night, the streets are driven bare, and my "autumn leaves" are falling already upon the roof, in a dry, uncertain rain. The annual taint of death is in the air, – these

[The remainder of this letter has been lost.]

1. Wolfe is describing "Niggertown," which later became *Welcome to Our City.* There is no evidence to indicate whether this letter was written in Asheville or upon his return to Cambridge.
2. Dr. Frank Crane (1861–1920), Methodist clergyman whose pious, platitudinous essays were syndicated in newspapers in the 1920s.
3. Edgar A. Guest (1881–1959), English-born American writer of sentimental verse. His folksy, moralistic doggerel was widely syndicated and extremely popular throughout the United States.
4. *American Magazine,* Crowell Publishing Company, Springfield, Ohio.
5. Genesis 6:4: "There were giants on the earth in those days."
6. Written on the left margin next to this in Mrs. Roberts's hand: "That's an American Life."

14

AL, 2 pp., Harvard, bMS Am 1883.1 (545)

135 Hillside Street.
Asheville, N.C.
December 24, 1922

My dear Boy,

Christmas brings you one affliction – a letter from me – so brace up and take the dose. But we can wait no longer to hear from you, our erstwhile ugly duckling, now no doubt a swan. I know you are working at a white heat all the time, but it matters not. Now, we <u>must</u> have news of your progress, spiritual, mental and physical.

Write plainly enough so that we can read at least two. thirds of it without
an expert.

The days roll with us as usual, its joy, its trouble and its work. Of course
this is one of our happier times – the old boys coming to see us. It's so fine to
watch them grow. Old George, Wee Willie, Lud[1] etc. not to mention our own
Big Boy.[2] He is at Carolina[3] this year, and enjoying it so much. Story too long
to tell as to why he left Davidson.[4] He has Greek and Latin under "Bully
Bernard"[5] and full of enthusiasm. He heads the list now for next man on "the
Tarheel."[6] So we think that fine for a new boy.

Mr. Roberts not so well as last year.

Aunt Emma teaching with us this year. As for me, I work and try to steal
a little time to read, but I have to run like a turkey to get the time. Robinson's
"Mind in the Making" on hand just now. Can you write a play as good as
"The Hairy Ape."? O'Neil is coming – and coming fast, don't you think?
Do write what you are doing. Not only in play-writing but in other work.
How are you and Prof. Baker making it. Do tell everything. It is the most
beautiful thing in this world to be a master of words – and I believe you are
on the way.

> "God wove a web of lonliness
> Of clouds and stars and birds,
> But made not any thing at all
> So beautiful as words.
>
> They shine around our simple earth
> With golden shadowings,
> And every common thing they touch
> Is exquisite with wings.
>
> There's nothing poor and nothing small
> But is made fair with them.
> They are the hands of living faith
> That touch the garment's hem.
>
> They are as fair as bloom or air,
> They shine like any star.
> And I am rich who learned from her {The child's mother.
> How beautiful they are.

This is what you are going to make words do. I feel it in my bones. Make them
shine, Tom. You are a star, and you must make your words shine like stars. All

of us send love, and more love. Let Tiny Tim speak for us, "God bless us every one." Christmas joy and peace to you.

[Unsigned]

[Written on margin, p. 1]
Jim Gillespie[7] very ill. – had to insert a tube in his throat to keep his breath going. Munsey just now told me he had read a letter you wrote to George.

1. Ludwig Lauerhass, a former North State student.
2. John Munsey Roberts Jr.
3. The University of North Carolina at Chapel Hill.
4. John Munsey Roberts Jr. was involved in a vandalism incident (defacing a dormitory) at Davidson College and was suspended. He chose not to return and enrolled at the University of North Carolina.
5. William Stanly "Bully" Bernard, who was also Wolfe's colorful teacher of Greek studies at the University of North Carolina. Portrayed as Edward Pettigrew "Buck" Benson in *Look Homeward, Angel*. The study of ancient Greek under Bernard greatly influenced Wolfe's first two novels, in which he made extensive use of Greek philosophy and myth.
6. *The Tar Heel.* The student newspaper at the University of North Carolina. Wolfe became managing editor in his junior year (1918–1919) and editor in chief in his senior year (1919–1920).
7. Jim Gillespie, a mutual friend of Wolfe and Mrs. Roberts; died soon after this letter was written.

15

Through the Harvard appointment office, Wolfe learned of an opening at a branch of New York University, Washington Square College. He began teaching on February 6, 1924, and continued intermittently until February 6, 1930. Wolfe accomplished little creative work during his first two years as a teacher, finding it impossible to both teach and write. For the most part he spent his time, like Mrs. Roberts, correcting papers.[1]

ALS, 22 pp., Harvard, bMS Am 1883.2 (294)

Room 2220
Hotel Albert
Eleventh Street & University Place
New York
Sunday, Feb 10, 1924

Dear Mrs Roberts: I am writing at length to answer your last heartening letter, which was written after I left home, and which has grown old, but more
precious.

I have seen a great many people, witnessed a number of events, and, like
Satan, have grown, for the moment, weary of my goings to and fro, and up
and down the earth.[2] It seems now that I will be fastened for several months
in this great madhouse of a city; – for good or ill, who can say? – but I think
I have chosen wisely.

Briefly – since I saw you I have been in New York for six weeks, when I was
busy with the Graham Memorial Fund[3] at the University; later I went to
Boston and Cambridge for the holidays and remained a little more than a
month. The Guild held my play[4] for three or four months, as you perhaps
know; held it until I was on the verge of madness and collapse, and finally
returned it, after wining me, dining me, telling me I was "a coming figure,"
and so on, and trying to extract a promise that all my future work would be
submitted to the Guild for consideration before any other producer got hold
to it. Of course, I made no such promise.

Before I left the city, however, one of the Guild directors, – a Jew by the
name of Langner,[5] and, I believe, a very wealthy, patent lawyer, had me in to
his apartment. He wanted me to cut the play thirty minutes, – a reduction I
concede it needs. He wanted me, also, to cut the list of characters, – this means
cheaper production, – and to revise, – he insisted it needed no re-writing, –
with a view to "tightening": – that is, to develop a central plot which will run
through each scene, and which would revolve around a small group of central
figures, – Rutledge, the negro, the girl, etc. Of course this would mean a more
conventional type of play. I told him I had deliberately tried to avoid writing
such a play; that I had written a play with a plot which centered about the life
and destiny of an entire civilization, – not about a few people. If I consented
to this revision, Langner promised his support and added that he was fairly
certain he could place the play. He observed, cheerfully, that he had really
asked for very little: that I could make all necessary changes in a week. This
was a bit of optimism in which I did not share. However, I promised to make
the effort, and departed for Cambridge. Professor Baker was properly horri-
fied when I communicated the evil tidings. Not only, he said, would the proposed revision greatly cheapen the play, but it was also impossible since my
play had been hailed and praised as a new departure in American drama; its
fate was on the rails. Thereupon, he read to me from a book on the American
Theatre just published, by Oliver Saylor, in which my play is described at
some length as "the most radical and successful experiment ever made in the

American theatre."[6] The Workshop comes in for its share of praise for doing my play.

This is, of course, sweet music to my ears, but my heart is assuming a flinty cast, and the sound of the shekel is not unpleasing. I told Professor Baker as much, as gently as I could, and he accused me of having allowed New York to "commercialize" me in my six weeks' stay. This opened the flood-gates; I had heard enough of such talk. All the old and cruel sentimentality of the world, in its relation to the artistic, struck me with a bitter blow. It was not a question of desiring cake and wine, I told him; it was a question of naked need: – Bread! Bread! Bread! Was this commercialism? Then, indeed, was Christ a materialist when he multiplied the loaves. Christ, by the way, unlike many of his present followers, was base enough to recognize that men and women must be fed.

I broached the question of my future again. What must I do? The answer came, as always: Write! Write! Do nothing else. Yes, but how? I had been told this for three years; it was all, no doubt, very true, but not very helpful. I suggested teaching. At the suggestion, he looked as if he were being rent limb from limb. Of all possible suggestions, this was the worst, – and he seemed to think that all of mine were incredibly bad. Finally, – supremest irony of all! – he confided that, after mature consideration, it seemed to him that a year abroad was the very thing I needed most. The full humor of this is apparent when I tell you that no later than August he had descended on me in his wrath when I suggested this very thing, and he had told me this would be colossal stupidity at the time. Now, plainly, he has forgotten he ever made such a statement; the wind, for unknown reasons, has veered from another corner, and he has tacked.

At any rate I began to understand – a bitter draught it was – that Professor Baker was an excellent friend, a true critic, but a bad counsellor. I knew that, from this time on, the disposition of my life was mainly in my own hands; that one profits, no matter how good the intention, not by the experience of others, but only by such experience as touches him. At that time I heard that New York University needed several new instructors for the February term, and I directed the Harvard appointment bureau to forward my letters, grades, and papers. I applied; I had friends in New York speak for me. In two days I had their answer. An instructorship was mine if I wanted it. I came to New York on a flying trip. I liked the men. The offer was more than reasonable: $1800 for seven months over an eight-hour-a-week teaching schedule; my work was to be concerned entirely with English composition. The men here at the University assure me that I should easily complete my work, in and out of class, with three hours a day. If this is true, I should have time to write. There is one other advantage, – a decided one. The college – this branch of it – is but eight years old, and has no traditions. I am given great liberty; personal idiosyncrasy is recognized and allowed. The students, moreover, mainly Jewish and Italian, have come up from the East side; many are making sacrifices of a very considerable nature in order to get an education. They are, accordingly, not at all the conventional type of college student. I expect to establish contacts here, to get material in my seven months' stay that may prove invaluable. I am here until September; I must teach through the summer.

I am here where the theatre is, – the theatre I love, – and if I can't write plays, at least I can see 'em. What Professor Baker will say, or has said I don't know. I never told him my decision

But I have taught for two days now, and I am living; and nothing about me, so far as I know, has "suffered a sea-change"

And this is all that I have to tell you for the time, – over that which you know already: that you wax immensely in my affections and that, as ever, I am

Faithfully yours,
Tom Wolfe.

P.S. And – glory of glories – I'm free. The world is mine, and I, at present, own a very small but satisfying portion of it: – Room 2220, at the Hotel Albert, where I hope presently to have the joy of reading one of your letters.

The new play[7] comes; I read it to a friend[8] in New Hampshire, who also writes 'em. He said I would sell it in spite of "hell and high water." The words are mine. And, by the way, I was in New Hampshire for four days and fished through the ice of the lake. This is the history.

1. On April 4, 1924, Wolfe described his hectic existence to his mother: "Just a few lines are all my time allows. I must go back to the interminable work of correcting papers:—like a brook, *that* goes on forever. On three days a week—or four—I can sleep late, and generally do, because, on my teaching days, I am so worn by nightfall that I sleep as though drugged. I don't know how to conserve nervous energy; I burn it extravagantly. However, I am not unhappy. I believe I am learning much although I am doing no writing. What time I have is usually spent at the theatre, or at the library, or in the open. When I am through grading papers, and writing my comments on the back, I don't feel in the mood for composition of my own. You can't serve two masters; I have selected to serve one, and I must see it through" (Wolfe, *Letters of Thomas Wolfe to His Mother*, 61).

2. Job 1:7: "From going to and fro on the earth, and from walking back and forth on it." The Old Testament book of Job was a favorite of Wolfe's.

3. In November 1923 Wolfe held a temporary job soliciting contributions from University of North Carolina alumni for the completion of Graham Memorial building

at Chapel Hill. Edward Kidder Graham had been the much beloved, idealistic president of the university when Wolfe was a student there. Graham died in 1918, during the height of the Spanish influenza epidemic.

4. *Welcome to Our City.* Later written on the margin by Mrs. Roberts to her daughter: "Marg he read us this play in Chunn's Cove."

5. Lawrence Langner.

6. Oliver M. Sayler, *Our American Theater* (New York: Brentano's, 1923). The actual quote is "Then, last year, there was produced in course, 'Welcome to Our City,' by Thomas Clayton Wolfe, a play as radical in form and treatment as the contemporary stage has yet acquired" (128).

7. Called variously "The Heirs" and "The House" in some manuscripts; titled *Mannerhouse* in 1925.

8. Probably Henry Fisk Carlton, according to Elizabeth Nowell (Wolfe, *Letters*, 60). Carlton was a member of the 47 Workshop in 1920–1922 and an instructor of English at New York University from 1925 until 1928.

16

Undated; ca. 1924   *Postcard, Harvard, bMS Am 1883.1 (545)*

Asheville, N.C. R. R. 2.[1]

My dear Boy, I am not writing a letter because I know you are too busy to even read it. Of course we are gleaners after news about you – every smidgeon of it. Couldn't you just write a postal-card about your play. I feel so impatient to get some first hand information about you and your brain-children. What are your plans for next year and are you coming home this summer. <u>Must hear</u> about your play. Mr. R. sends love.

With much love,
Margaret Roberts

1. The Robertses' Chunn's Cove home.

17

Ca. spring 1924   *AL, 6 pp., Harvard, bMS Am 1883.1 (545)*

Sunday.

My dear Boy,

It's a shame that any of God's creatures, especially you, should be shut up in a hole like New York, when there is a Chunn's Cove[1] to do your breathing and gazing in. It's so beautiful; it hurts.

"Granpa Roberts," William Orton Roberts.
"He was the master of his bed and board, and
in his hale decline grew a long white beard"
(*O Lost,* 240). Courtesy of Jerry Israel,
Asheville, North Carolina

You haven't been far from the paling-fence of my mind since you left here, and you may know from that how I've devoured your letter – your wonderful letter.

I had hoped to hear that you were in Europe – but, after all, Tom, don't you find all the phases of life that you can mentally digest, right there in your college. I don't mean to imply by my questions that your powers of mental digestion are weak – but that rather, Life, in all its variety, can be found almost anywhere. If there is material there, I know you will find it. I wonder if you realize how I exult in your mental and spiritual growth.

I have loved all my life beauty, both in books, life and nature, but only in an appreciative way. So I suppose I rejoice all the more when I see those I love, develop the interpretive powers. And you are going to do this, as sure as the sun is beautiful enough to be worshipped to do. I don't use "are going" in the sense that you have not yet, but rather, that your powers will grow, and the world will stop to hear.

Don't let yourself get "out" with the world – this "Tom-fool of an old world," as Grandpa Roberts used to call it – (He was your Man – a Master Man in mind and spirit, if you could put him on paper, your future would be secure.[2] But it would be a Russian play, not an American one.). The world often butts its brains out because of running blindly against stone walls that refuse to move.

Genius has often suffered cruelly because of this blindness – but there are a good many stone walls still standing. By-the-way, why wouldn't "Stone Walls" be a good subject for a play? It seems to me you have enough acrid acid stored up now to make a true thing of it.

We are curious and anxious to know how you like teaching, – about the men with whom you come in contact; about your plans for next year, and above all, about the old play and the new one. Can't you write again, right away? I have been so long in answering simply because I put in sixteen hours every day, seven days in the week. It has been a tremendous year, from the standpoint of work, – but there are always compensations, – the fun of watching some one pupil grow, just as I used to rejoice in you. I have one now, a poor, cramped boy of eighteen, an orphan's home product. He is rare in soul; has natural ability with his pen, and has a smile that would illuminate hell. However, it comes only by rare flashes, because of a melancholy (He's in a period of revolt) engendered by his hard life. Tom, don't swear too much by the aristocracy of the intellect – or at least, remember that it is found in any chance hovel. And it must have its little spoonful of public school education – so that somebody may have the opportunity to discover where there is enough vitality to justify further feeding.

This boy must go to college – or have somehow the opportunity to find himself. Here's your tragedy of wastage – milking cows for his board when he could be doing constructive work with his head. There are plenty of milkers in the world.

This makes me think of George McCoy. He couldn't graduate at Carolina without Latin or French – so he went to Chicago this year. He has made a splendid record; Phi Beta kappa grades, tho he can not get a key because of having only one year's residence.

He is as fine material as I know of in every way. He has specialized in Hist, Economics and kindred subjects, and wants to teach next year. If you can tell me of anything, won't you write. He's another good piece of granite that came near being made into crushed rocks for road-making. We have to have good roads but it kills me to see splendid material that can be made into beautiful statues, or at least into sturdy obelisks, being crushed for high-powered autos to whirl over.

While I am on "Boys," I'll ask you too, if you have any political influence now at Carolina, and have no reason against, and have time to spare, to cast a word for Wee Willie Cocke as Pres. of Student Body. He's a splendid fellow, and I don't believe they will get a better. From the standpoint of ambition, it puts him in line for a Rhodes Scholarship. They are hard-up, and the scholarship would mean worlds to him. He means to specialize in International law.

But please don't let my meddling have weight if it should not.

Now, for a slice from life in our own family that may not be uninteresting to a playwright.

Munsey, as you may remember, will not be eighteen until July. Last fall, (he was a Junior) he was getting along well in his work, when he fell madly in love with a girl five years his senior.[3] He simply went all to pieces in his work; couldn't study; eat, nor sleep unless he could see her – she lived at Durham.

He had not told her but allowed her to think that he was twenty-three. So he came home Christmas utterly miserable – down in his work and afraid to tell her the truth about his age. Our entire Christmas was spent trying to re-adjust him. Finally we three all agreed that if he couldn't study there was no need to go back to the University now, so if he could get some newspaper work he was to do it. He made quite a name for himself on the Tarheel and The Magazine last year. It so happened that the editor of "The Durham Herald" had noticed his work and was trying to get in touch with him at that very time. He offered Munsey a place with him at $25 a week, and he has been there since January 10. He is making a good name for himself, and is very happy to feel that he is tangibly at something.

Now, I have inflicted all of this upon you for a purpose. We want your advice. Of course we want him to go back to College. He has the attitude that so many of the courses are "bunk" (and professors, too) – that only now and then does one strike a vital course and a vital man etc – all the usual indictment of the American College. Of course we know all of this, but nevertheless there is much to be gained there, and he must go on. He knows a great deal for a chap, and he is learning a great deal in his new work, but you know what must be our reasons for wanting him to go on.

If he goes back to Carolina, he will be in danger of repeating his mistake of being absorbed in the girl; if he stays in Durham he certainly will not get a chance to fall out of love – (The girl seems to be fine, but you know 5 years is too much difference especially with him a kid in years). He will be eighteen in July, and has I think, credit for Sophomore and Freshmen, perhaps all but one course.

What would be your advice about his going to Harvard next year? Consider him from every standpoint, keeping in mind the story. Is he too young to stand the strain of life there? There is no question about his mental ability; physically, I think there is no doubt but that he is clean; He assures me that he has never done one thing that he would be ashamed for us to know and I have reason to believe that it is true. He will study on subjects he likes, such as "Bully's" Greek, but slights others; kills time playing cards when he should be at work etc.

He is intemperate in that if he walks, he walks too far; if he gets interested in a book, he will read all night. (He has read much good stuff): if he eats, he eats irregularly and too fast; if, if, if.

It will be hard for us to get up the cash for him to go to Harvard. How cheaply can a boy actually make it and have good food etc?

Tom, if you can possibly spare the time, write to us <u>now</u> what your advice is, and also to him, 822 Cleveland Street, Durham N.C. I think I have told you enough so that you will know how to make the approach. Of course if you don't think it wise for him to go to Harvard, no need for you to write to him unless you are in a philanthropic mood. I am sorry to take up your time this way, but that boy is a brilliant boy and I hate bitterly to see it all come to naught. He is dearer to us than life and light, and I think he feels the same way toward us. 'Nuff said. Any help you can give us in this, to our difficult and delicate situation, will be precious to us.

By-the-way, the Fraziers are living at 22 Pleasant Avenue, Montclaire, N.J. I know you would find them company well worth while. They are a very unusual pair, delightfully so, big-hearted, big brained. If you can spare the time, and would write them a note that you would like to call on them; or I would do it, if you care for me to do so.

Now, Tom, to come back to you. I am worried about you. You think too much "Such men are dangerous."[4] At least, your present state of mind is dangerous to your physical welfare – and without physical welfare your brain children can't grow. You are in a highly nervous state all of the time.

You must grab your thinker and choke it into submission.

You have genius; that is sure. That you should succeed with your first play would be indeed a miracle. What man has! I was reading in "The Citizen" a sketch of Kreymborg's[5] struggles. They all have to die before this world will bat an eye. It is so easy to be wise after the event. I met K—and had a talk with him about you. Don't forget that your every movement is of interest to us. Don't worry about Dr. Baker's change of position; that is just one of the many things that pester one's feet in the forward march.

Must get breakfast. Have no time to read. Just now trying to steal a line in Brandeis's "Creative Spirits in 19 Century"

[Unsigned]

[Written on left margin, p. 1]
I carried a Christmas card – 3 weeks – trying to get your address. Nobody seemed to know where you were. Can't you write now.

[Written on left margin, p. 5]
Wee Willie won by good majority – largest ever – Pres. Student Body also Pres. of IBK.

[Written on left margin of last page]
Wish you could be here this morning.

    1. Chunn's Cove, east of downtown Asheville. Depicted as the paradisiacal Lunn's Cove, where Eugene Gant and Laura James picnic: "a rich little Eden of farm and pasture" (Wolfe, *Look Homeward, Angel,* 452).
    2. J. M. Roberts's father, William Orton Roberts (1840–1923). Although Wolfe accepted his former teacher's suggestion and eventually incorporated W. O. Roberts into his literary work, the result greatly offended Mrs. Roberts. For her reaction, see letter 60.
    3. Verna Britt.
    4. Caesar's words about Cassius in Shakespeare's *Julius Caesar* 1.2.191.
    5. Alfred Kreymborg, New York City poet and playwright.

18

IN 1924 WOLFE DECIDED to travel to Europe after his summer term at New York University was over. His initial plan was to take a leave of absence from teaching and to write undisturbed while traveling through Europe for two months. He resolved to write 1,500 words a day while abroad. He maintained his resolve but did not return to teach until the fall of the following year.

ALS, 26 pp., Harvard, bMS Am 1883.2 (294)

Hotel Albert
New York
May 5, 1924

Dear Mrs Roberts: This, briefly, to thank you for your fine letter, and to render my poor judgement on the subject nearest your heart – Munsey's future. I think I understand his position. Did you know I fell in love when I was sixteen with a girl who was twenty one? Yes, honestly – desperately in love. And I've never quite got over it. The girl married, you know; she died of influenza a year or two later. I've forgotten what she looked like, except that her hair was corn-colored.[1]

A woman five years older can make putty of a boy of eighteen. In one way, she is as old as she will ever be, and a great deal depends upon her own quality. I think that you have handled the affair with fine understanding The encouraging thing, of course, is that he will love not once, but a dozen times, before he marries. And, if he is like me, – a thousand. You are everlastingly right, I believe, in allowing him to quit school for a year: even in allowing him to find work in Durham near the girl, there's a good chance that in a few months his passion may waste itself, and he will begin to look around for new worlds to conquer. It seems that at this period man comes to grips with something elemental beyond him. I'm beginning to question the wisdom of mixing education with adolescence; Greek with Seventeen, – literature with love. Perhaps the academics should come later when we have leavened our madness with a grain of method. I'm not sure. And, I suppose, there's not time enough.

But, back to our bacon; – Perhaps, in a few months he may have adjusted himself sufficiently to be willing to return to Carolina. If not, the question, I suppose, is "What other university can we send him to?"

You speak of Harvard. That's most difficult. I don't know what to say. But I'm sure of this: —

If I had gone to Cambridge instead of to Chapel Hill – when I was sixteen – the result would have been catastrophic. Of course, Munsey is a big, fine, strapping fellow, well-grown, mature in appearance, with associations with wealthy boys which may have given him a kind of balance. But this, I think, is now true of Harvard. No boy should go there now until he is ready to mine his own ore. If he is still in need of dependence on someone or something – a very real and honest need, by the way – Harvard is not the place, I think.

A sensitive young Southerner – fond of companionship and warmth, will find the sledding rough, I'm afraid. Of course, with a student of one of the great academies – Andover or Exeter – the situation is different, I believe He is graduated with his class and accompanies them to Cambridge. This occurs as naturally as the transition, say, from Asheville High to Chapel Hill.

But I have seen hundreds of boys submerged in the student life of Harvard – Unknown they enter – are swiftly apalled by the vastness of the system, and its impersonality – and unknown they leave, at the end of four years, with a feeling of disenchantment and futility.

The quality of Harvard instruction is very high – the highest, I believe – but, again, many succeed in evading all attempts at education on the part of the University faculty. It is not difficult to slide through; and, in addition, you must be prepared to calculate the probable effects of a metropolitan community of over one million people upon a fascinated young stranger thrust suddenly in from the provinces.

A change of climate and geography might be intensely valuable to him now. Remember, there are a number of first-rate small colleges in New England, beautifully located, with admirable scholastic standards.

There is Amherst, for example, which still demands Greek, I'm told. And Williams, a lovely place, walled in by mountains not unlike our own. And Bowdoin – and, of course, Dartmouth, – one of the best. In all these places a young fellow might assert himself, and grow.

Whatever you do – don't tell Munsey you wrote me about him, or that I returned to make any comment. At eighteen we resent this as interference – properly – I'm not sure that twenty-three has any right to pass judgment on eighteen.

As for me – I work and am fairly happy. Really, I'm having a wonderful experience This place – particularly the University – swarms with life, Jewish, Italian, Polish. My little devils like me – I tell them every week that I'm no teacher. I suppose they can see that for themselves; and perhaps that is why they like me. The head of the department[2] has asked me to come back next year, but I have given him no answer. The desire to write – to create – has, for the first time, become almost a crude animal appetite. And this is because of the obstacles thrown in the path of creation. During the few hours left to me I write like a fiend on one of the finest plays[3] you ever saw. My first term is almost over – two weeks more, in fact. Gone like a flash!

And did you know that I'm going to Heaven in September. That is, to England.

From September 1, six months pay will be due me – Sep – Feb (inc) This is $900. With economy I can stay over five or six months. I'm going down to Cornwall first – it's very beautiful, I'm told — and bury myself in a country village for two months. There I shall write my heart out. Then over the country, into London for a few days, Scotland, and France.

This is all for the present. I've snatched Time to write this. But, during the examination period, you shall have greater detail. The Provincetown Theatre has had my play five months.[4] I can hear nothing.

One of the editors of D Appleton left a note at the hotel this morning. He wants my play – the Theatre Guild suggested it – to read for publication. I shall let him read it; I doubt that I shall let him publish – even if he wants to. Certainly, not as long as someone may produce it.

The new play is an epic. I believe in it with all my heart. Dear God! If I but had the time to write. Professor Koch[5] of Chapel Hill bounded into town a week or so ago, and looked me up. He wants to put one of my juvenile one acts – the <u>Buck Gavin</u> thing – in his new book[6] which Holt is bringing out soon. He is insistent, and has just sent me a copy of the thing.

I'm not ashamed of the play, but I wrote it on a rainy night when I was seventeen, in three hours. Something tells me I should hate to see my name attached now. Of course I couldn't tell Koch that.

Besides, he had his chance two or three years ago, when he brought his first book out. Please don't <u>publish</u> – but I'll give you my honest opinion: I believe his eagerness to publish the little play now comes from a suspicion that I'm going to get famous in a hurry now – God knows why! – and he wants to <u>ticket</u> me, so to speak. This is a rotten thing to say, but its my honest opinion

I sent Koch an act or so of my new play – you heard the prolog[7] – and he did everything but break down and weep. It was the greatest thing ever; I was the American Bernard Shaw, etc.

Everyone, you see, is enthusiastic, but I notice that <u>I</u> earn my own living. The Theatre Guild is cordial. When am I going to bring my new play in? Their officials want to know me. Will I have lunch? Their play reader, Lemon,[8] trumpets my name abroad. He told me recently he had spoken of me at the banquet of some dramatic association. I am grateful, but how I wish someone would <u>produce</u> one of my plays. The Guild, by the way, recommended my play to Appleton.

But – I learn. I am acquiring patience. And I'm quite willing to wait a year or two for the unveiling exercises. Do you know, all that really matters right now is the knowledge that I am twenty three, and a golden May is here. The feeling of immortality in youth is upon me. I am young, and I can never die. Don't tell me that I can. Wait until I'm thirty. Then I'll believe you.

I never hear from you but my respect for your intelligence waxes. You are a lovely, a beautiful woman. Other women I have known – young and old – who wanted to mother me, to ruffle my hair when it's curly, or to feed me. But you mother the minds and spirits of young men until they grow incandescent. That is a nobler, finer thing.

So, it seems, you are a great woman.

To you all, as ever, my deepest love –

Tom.

1. In the summer of 1917 Wolfe fell hopelessly in love with one of his mother's boarders, Clara Paul, from Washington, North Carolina. Portrayed as Laura James in *Look Homeward, Angel,* Clara was five years older than Wolfe, and his desperate love for her was one-sided. She was already engaged to a young soldier, Wallace M. Martin.

2. Homer Andrew Watt, chairman of the Department of English of Washington Square College. See *The Correspondence of Thomas Wolfe and Homer Andrew Watt,* ed. Oscar Cargill and Thomas Clark Pollock (New York: New York University Press, 1954).

3. "The House"—later became *Mannerhouse.*

4. *Welcome to Our City.*

5. Frederick H. Koch, founder of the Carolina Playmakers at the University of North Carolina.

6. *Carolina Folk Plays, Second Series,* ed. Frederick H. Koch (New York: Henry Holt and Company, 1924). Wolfe's first play, *The Return of Buck Gavin,* was one of the first plays to be presented by the Carolina Playmakers. It was produced on March 14 and 15, 1919, and because no actor could be found to convincingly portray Buck Gavin, the tall mountain outlaw, Wolfe himself was enlisted to play the title role.

7. The play that later became *Mannerhouse.* Wolfe had read the prologue to Mrs. Roberts when he was in Asheville in October 1923.

8. Courtenay Lemon.

19

July 31 and August 3, 1924

ALS, 10 pp., Harvard, bMS Am 1883.1 (545)
Grace High School Letterhead

July 31, 1924.

My dear Tom Wolfe,

How strange it is that I should deprive myself, just for the sake of sweeping and dusting, of the joy we have in hearing from you. Perhaps if I had answered more promptly, I should now know full details of your wonderful European plans,[1] and all the other things about you that are as meat and drink to me. We certainly buy bubbles with "a whole soul's tasking," and yet somehow the daily round of sweeping, mending and trying to keep the paunches of this family filled must be done.

I just wonder if you can get it in your dull pate how happy I am that you are really going to Europe. You are taking Europe with you, so there can be no doubt of what you will find.

Before coming to your work, I must tell you how much we appreciated your prompt and full letter about Munsey and his future. It's no wonder you can write plays. Your attitude toward him and our problem and young love in general shows a pretty old head on very young shoulders. You are altogether right, I think, in saying that it all depends upon the girl. In this case, she is quite as much in love as Munsey, and so far shows no sign of letting go. She is coming home with him next week for his vacation. I must take your time enough to tell you that he has really made a remarkable record for a chap with his newspaper work. His editor told him he was big city paper material, and complimented him from several different angles. He says that if they knew he is barely eighteen that they would kick him out. But why should they? Its the grey matter and not years that count, as has been so ably demonstrated in the person of my young friend, Thomas Wolfe, erstwhile of Asheville, now a citizen of the world.

I had quite a chat with Dr. Koch Tuesday. He is very enthusiastic about you, and to me he seemed whole heartedly so very much so. He says you are going ahead of Eugene O'Neal – and that your new play is a remarkable piece of work. Said for me to remember him to you – spoke about seeing you in April and that Buck Gavin would be in his new volume of plays. Of course "I kep on say in' nuffin" about what you had written to me about that. I may have told you that I also had met Kreymborg and he told me about seeing you. Have you seen the Citizen and have you noticed about the Chronicle House movement? If so, do you think it is a truly vital movement. Such a colony would mean much here if it had the stuff in which real life and art are made.

I suppose it is utterly selfish in me to ask or to expect that you can spare us any time as you fare forth into that brave new-old world of Europe. But if there comes a time, a moment even, when you feel that you can spare a blessed moment, write what you can of how much it has gone to your head. It has been the dream of my life. Since I was fourteen at any rate. Every real poem, play, story and bit of history that I have ever read has almost literally carried me across the Atlantic The richest years of my meager intellectual life were thru at a boarding school in Nashville a sharp roof – flat roof on main building. [drawing of roof with comment: my room] There were few days that the flat roof was not warm because it had a tin roof and a protecting parapet. So, stocking-footed to keep from slipping on the cone-shaped intervening roof, all day Saturday and Sunday, I spent on that roof. The library, belonging to Mr. Roberts's brother-in-law,[2] had been picked up in the various countries of Europe. Much of it was beyond me but I gnawed on it. – and much of it I reveled in. Shelley, Keats, Coleridge, histories, all of Dickens, Scott, George Eliot, etc. etc. All the things that this swift generation considers so hopelessly old-fashioned – Whatever there is in me to-day that flat roof, unknown practically to all the boarding girls, did for me. I began making my own living at seventeen – with the break for going to Vanderbilt – and since all my golden moments have been stolen. It is literally true that I have read nothing since I was twenty that has not been read with me sitting on the edge of a chair, my conscience prodding me because I was not doing "the duty that lay nearest me" as a dear old maid room-mate once wrote in my autograph album. Tom, don't ever do your duty. It's a tyrant tyranical beyond words. I don't know how in the world I switched off on this – and expected you to be interested. But perhaps in the back of my head the idea lurked that, because of those golden days, I can in some degree at least, appreciate what you with your mind so clear and cultivated, and your spirit as taut as a bowstring, will get out of your – I won't say "trip," because I want you to stay so long that "trip" will not be the applicable word.

If you are not going right off, tell me about the new play, its prospects, and also of the old one. Now, for Heaven's sake, don't work yourself into a nervous fever if it doesn't hit the stage at 9 P.M. the day after your ink is dry on it. Make your spirit content to let your plays "lie on the laps of the gods" for as long as need be. Your art will be growing finer and more mature all the while. Recognition must come to you sooner or later, and you are so young that you can afford to let the gods act as nursery governesses for a lengthy period. What if your growing pains do seem unbearable! When you were a chap, did you have the "leg–ache" as we chaps used to call it? If you did, I am sure your mother put bags of hot salt on them, just as my mother did. The remedy was almost as severe as the disease. But just let the gods alone for a while. They will rub hot salt on your spiritual growing pains – and it will eventually do the work. If you are as wise as I think you are, you will not worry one iota about the plays you leave behind you, accepted or unaccepted. You will plunge head-long into the new life, drain the cup <u>to</u> the dregs, – but no more. As I write this, I have in mind certain ideas you put in your next to last letter.

I am Victorian, I suppose, but I think you are wrong in that. Many of the great geniuses of the world in all the different fields of art, did drink the cup of experience not only <u>to</u> the dregs, but they inserted their tongues in the not always silver goblet and drained every dreg. I have studied and studied about that phase of their lives. Were they made the greater artists thereby? Or did the bitterness they found in the cup so embitter their lives that it often short-ened their lives, and tarnished their genius. They were supremely great in spite of drinking the wine of life to the lees, rather than because of it. I do manage to keep up enough with the trend of the new time and the new literature to know that what I am saying sounds, not 1840, but antediluvian and you cry out, "prating old fool." So be it.

I suppose you see the Citizen and know that Asheville is still more or less a good target for your bitter satire. I know of no news that can interest you except that Henry Harris[3] finishes at the University of Virginia this summer, and that Thomas Wallis is the proud possessor of a marvellous son. Can you get that into your cranium?

As for us, we creep on our petty pace from day to day. It surely, in its regular commonplace duties, must appear to others that our life is indeed a petty pace. But I can say with truth that no day seems petty to me. I get more and more joy out of my efforts to teach, and of course Mr. R. and I are keenly alive to the momentary changes in Marg and Munsey, so to us it's a great old world in spite of the often – Sunday – Aug. 3. here I had to break off so you are spared whatever platitude it was I meant to write.

I suppose you noticed an account of Van Brown's death[4] – fell from a bridge in Panama where he was doing engineering work. He and Marcus Irwin Junior were buried that same afternoon. Marcus killed in the explosion of the Mississippi at San Diego.

Are you "inpolita's" and what have you been reading? An answer to that last question would, I have no doubt, be an avalanche for my complete entombment. How you have managed to digest it all is a complete mystery to me. Your spirit glows, your mind glows, but I always fear that you will burn up your bodily vitality by being always in a nervous tension. I wish, when you allow yourself to get so taut, that you would make your mind come back to your great need of keeping physically fit. You are going to do great things for us, and you will need every bit of stamina that you can muster. Listen to the old lady's warning – and the old "you can't burn the candle at both ends." This brings me to the part of your last letter in which you spoke of me far beyond my deserving. It would be a direct lie to say it did not warm the cockles of my heart, even tho I know that in your generosity of spirit you appraised me far above my worth. If I have been of any help to you or any other boy or girl with whom I have come in contact it has been through no conscious purpose of "uplift work" on my part, but because I could not help it – by that I mean, if I can find a way to say it – that there has always been within me a something that made me love with an abiding love the brightness of spirit in a boy or girl – that quality, whatever you call it, that makes them the glory of the world.

It breaks my heart to see their lights put under a bushell; and if they are only ordinary chaps – the dough instead of the yeast of the bread of life – I love them too, because I am so sorry for them that they miss the glow of life that comes to such as you. So, bright and glorious like you, medium like myself, and the really slow and stodgy – I love all of them. I'm always hoping that there may be a spark of the divine fire in every child who touches my life. To me, to-day the supreme tragedy of the world is the way we butcher little children in our schools, in our industrial life, and sometimes even more in our homes. They are so surely butchered as if we led them to Swift and Company, and had them turned into hams, leaf lard, and sausage. However, I don't really believe that we make many hams, or fine leaf lard; it's all sausage. So, if I deserve your praise in any small degree, it is because the older I grow the more determined I am to be as little of a butcher as possible. But the trouble is that I am so poorly equipped myself for the solemn task, or whatever words describe it, that I must needs fail at a million points. If this civilization is to be saved those of you who have the creative genius must use it with so high and solemn a reverence for the needs of the ungifted that your yeast will leaven our dough until the whole great mass will be permeated with the same idealism that will smash to smithereens the crassness that is devouring us, soul and body.

That sounds as if I mean that your art should be made utilitarian – a sort of machine for "uplifting the masses" instead of allowing it be as free as the winds to blow where it listeth. Well, – Tom, I'm just an old fool and should not consume the time of a distinguished "Professor" in the college of the city of N.Y. Do take time to tell us snatches, anyway, of your work, your hopes. Did you chance to meet at the college a professor named John Turner. He is a V.U. man.

Hope you can get in touch with the Frazers. If you care to, I can arrange it. They are unusual people, interested in all phases of life.

Mr. Roberts and I often talk of you, – from your kidhood on up.

I say "Bon Voyage" but I mean that "bon" in its three little letters to include every joy which you have anticipated that this trip to Europe will bring you.

Lord bless you, boy. We love you dearly and rejoice in all that rejoices you.

Your sincere friend,

Margaret Roberts

1. Wolfe eventually made seven tours of Europe—a total of fourteen ocean voyages. In 1927 he recorded in one of his pocket notebooks: "Dream: A ship—didn't get off in time—Make 7 trips over instead of one—see Mrs. Roberts and J. M. in dining saloon—she is looking around for me" (Wolfe, *The Notebooks of Thomas Wolfe*, ed. Richard S. Kennedy and Paschal Reeves, 2 vols. [Chapel Hill: University of North Carolina Press, 1970], 1:110).

2. D. W. Dodson.

3. Henry Harris, a former North State student. George Graves in *Look Homeward, Angel;* plays the Moor of Venice on p. 327.

4. Vance Brown, a former North State School student; Van Yeats in *Look Homeward, Angel.*

20

ALS, 6 pp., Harvard, bMS Am 1883.2 (294)
Hotel Albert Letterhead

Tuesday, Sep 16, 1924

Dear Mrs Roberts: – If I saluted you as I dared, perhaps in another more gracious age, I should say instead "Best and Wisest of Mortals."

This can be only a page or two. Glory to God I'm through – my last grades went in yesterday. Now I must make frantic preparations for departure My family keeps me ready to jump both ways. Mabel[1] has "been about to be" ready to come to New York three times – now it looks as if she will not. Fred has been on the way twice or oftener. Mama writes this morning, asking me to come home for a short visit instead, if Mabel doesn't come; and she believes she won't, although you never can tell, etc. The whole thing is a mass of conditions.

I may see you, therefore, in a few days. If not, I'll write. I'm terribly tired <u>above</u> the shoulders, but fairly well below.

You know, I really don't want to come home – except to see you and my people. I no longer grow husky when the name of my home town is mentioned.[2]

I bought a copy of the esteemed <u>Citizen</u> the other day – my first touch with local affairs since leaving. It is simply revolting I tell you honestly and earnestly that nowhere in the world have I even seen a point in geography where love of money and of cheap notoriety is more blatantly exhibited. This is treason, I know; but loyalty to the things for which the townsfolk live would be dishonorable pretenses on my part.

And I tell you, if I should face them, and become a celebrity, I should hate them for their applause.

You are quite right. I am discovering the world in October. Nothing can destroy the thrill with which I go.

But perhaps I shall see you first.

Tom

1. Wolfe's sister, Mabel Wolfe Wheaton (1890–1958), portrayed as Helen Gant in *Look Homeward, Angel.*

2. However, despite his reluctance to return home before going abroad, Wolfe returned to Asheville and stayed several weeks, during which time his finances were closely scrutinized by his mother. Despite Julia Wolfe's parsimonious nature, she generously helped pay for Wolfe's trip to Europe and assured him that she would provide future financial assistance as well: "When I left home, you may remember, the understanding

was that I should go as far as I could on my own, and that I should ask you for help when that was gone" (Wolfe, *Letters of Thomas Wolfe to His Mother,* 87).

21

ALS, 2 pp., Harvard, bMS Am 1883.1 (545)
October 16, 1924   *Grace High School letterhead*

[On top margin]
The boy, between his hard work and mental strain looks like a wreck.

October 16.

My dear Boy Tom,

Your letter has come into a broken house. It hurts me that I cannot send you a word of cheer for your voyage, but our house is as broken to-night as if death had come into it. Munsey was <u>married</u> last night at 7.30, P.M.[1] Last Saturday I went to Durham; came back 1 a.m. train Monday. I used every argument, that could be even imagined. The boy is literally rent in twain by his desire not to hurt us, and his love for the girl. I could get no definite promise from him. Mr. R. was so distressed that I had left him to fight the battle alone that he insisted that I go back. I got there just an hour <u>after</u> the marriage. He had finally accepted the Citizen's offer and the girl was not willing to let him come with out marriage – feared our influence. They had gone to Raleigh but her mother phoned him that I was there and he came back from R – in 28 min. My exactness may seem inconsistent with pain – but it shows you his state of mind. The meeting tore us both to shreds. They went on back to Raleigh. I had reached there on 9 P.m. train and came back at 1 a.m. My mind seems so stunned or so stone-like that I can think of nothing but trivialities. We may have done wrong not to forbid it, or to take steps to have it annulled but we have striven so hard to be decent to him; to respect his individuality. We would have sold our souls into bondage to have saved him.[2] There is no need for me to express our gratitude to you that you entered so perfectly into our troubled thoughts. If possible, you are knit more closely to us than ever before.

As for your mother, her face has haunted me since that day, and I had already made up my mind to go see her when this trouble came to a head. I shall go as soon as I can get myself in hand.

I'm happy that your students expressed themselves to you – it does warm the cockles of the heart. Of course their needs must say it. Moreover it is a blessed assurance to you that when or if stored-up cash and potboilers fail, the profession of teaching may suck you into its capacious maw.

Margaret Rose
Roberts, her first
cousins Patricia
Pattison and Penelope
Pattison, and her
brother, John Munsey
"Buddie" Roberts Jr.,
September 1925.
Courtesy of Jerry
Israel, Asheville,
North Carolina

Europe calls you. I'm sore-hearted that I should cloud your glorious adventure with my griefs – our griefs. You were good beyond words to agree to let the cub follow at your bearish heels. Well, the cub is grown and will not follow you this time. You are to have a riot of delight in this journeying. With you – "the mind is its own place."[3] The poetry in you "defeats the curse which binds you to be subjugated to the accident of surrounding impressions." Count yourself a free spirit. I should say a disembodied one if I could forget that 6 ft. 4 hulk of yours with its two enormous appendages.[4] It will take much poetry and exaltation of spirit to disembody you. Now may God have mercy upon all those that go down to the sea in ships,[5] – and to us all is Tom Wolfe. You are very dear to us. Dad and Margaret join me in this. Drink deep. Good-bye. M.R.

1. Verna Britt and John Munsey Roberts Jr. were married October 15, 1924.

2. Mrs. Roberts was distraught because she feared her son's marriage would impair his future career as a writer. "Munsey told our parents that he was planning to be married at once. Mother, who had taught him in the North State School until he graduated, had recognized that he possessed a considerable talent for writing. When she learned the news of his intentions of taking a job and not returning to college, she was distressed and concerned about his future. She wrote him at once and begged him to postpone the wedding until he graduated from college, but it was to no avail" (Margaret Rose Roberts to Ted Mitchell, interview, April 28, 1996). Roberts's career suffered little due to his youthful marriage; he became a foreign affairs analyst and later foreign news editor at the Associated Press.

3. Satan in Milton's *Paradise Lost,* 1.253.

4. Thomas Wolfe had in fact reached his adult height of 6'6".

5. Psalm 107:23.

22

ON OCTOBER 25, 1924, Wolfe sailed aboard the *Lancastria* for his first of seven trips to Europe. He made good use of his ocean journey by recording his thoughts, observations, and memories. This manuscript grew over the next five months as he extended his stay in Europe. He titled it "Passage to England / Log of a Voyage Which Was Never Made." It became a blend of fact and fiction, containing unsavory details about his ocean voyage and satires of daily life in Asheville. The manuscript was not published in its entirety during Wolfe's lifetime, although a small excerpt, "London Tower," appeared in the *Asheville Citizen* on July 19, 1925, thanks to George McCoy's influence.

Ca. fall 1924	*Postcard of Queen Victoria's Memorial and Buckingham Palace, London; Harvard, bMS Am 1883.2 (294)*

Am. Express Co
London

Got clipping of Munsey's marriage. Cheer up. It will all come right. Am writing you. Everything is marvellous beyond my dreams. I have written up the voyage over as it has never been done before.[1]

1. The eleven installments Wolfe planned for "Passage to England," perhaps fifty thousand words altogether, were never completed in their entirety. The manuscript also contains miscellaneous travel notes and sketches (such as "John Dempsey Gant, Prizefighter" and a memoir of Wolfe's brother Ben). Manuscript copies and drafts for installments one through nine and eleven, as well as typescript copies and carbons of

the first, sixth, and ninth installments, have been preserved in the William B. Wisdom Collection, Houghton Library, Harvard University. The missing tenth installment was a part of four installments titled "The Passenger."

23

IN DECEMBER, WHEN MRS. ROBERTS WROTE WOLFE, she disclosed aspects of an impending breakdown—a part of her personality captured in *Look Homeward, Angel:*

> This face was the constant field of conflict, nearly always calm, but always reflecting the incessant struggle and victory of the enormous energy that inhabited her, over the thousand jangling devils of depletion and weariness that tried to pull her apart. There was always written upon her the epic poetry of beauty and repose out of struggle—he never ceased to feel that she had her hand around the reins of her heart, that gathered into her grasp were all the straining wires and sinews of disunion which would scatter and unjoint her members, once she let go. Literally, physically, he felt that, the great tide of valiance once flowed out of her, she would immediately go to pieces.[1]

However, Mrs. Roberts's stoicism prevailed, and she describes her life as a catalog of blessings and felicitous resignation.

AL, 4 pp., Harvard, bMS Am 1883.1 (545)

December 21, 1924   *Grace High School letterhead*

[Handwritten on upper-left margin]
I am sorry that I have not yet seen your mother, tho I mean to this week. I have really been almost on the verge of a real breakdown, and have had to save every bit of myself for the day's work.

[Handwritten on upper-right margin]
All send love and wishes that this may be the rarest Christmas you have ever known.

Sunday, December 21.

You blessed Boy,

It has been good to get your two cards – good to know that you, in the midst of your exuberance could still remember us. By coincidence we had just had a history lesson about Bath and had read a little play called "the Beau of Bath" so that your card did double service.[2]

Thomas Wolfe in Europe, 1924. By permission of the North Carolina Collection, University of North Carolina Library at Chapel Hill, and Eugene H. Winick, Administrator C.T.A., Estate of Thomas Wolfe

I could feel the delight in you perking out in each word and also a full exemplification of "No Europe unless you take it with you." I had fully meant to get you a letter there by Christmas day at the latest – but I have had not a minute in weeks to do anything more than to tread the daily wine press.

I hear that the whole Wolfe family congregated at the Citizen office to read your letter to George.[3] I mean to see it this week if I can get my eyes on him.

I am ashamed to say it, but from the purely personal standpoint, you and your wandering joys are the brightest spots in my Christmas horizon. Practically every person I love except Margaret and you, is in some valley of Despair, Doubt, Distress of some sort –. Margaret is always bright and fair – and you now, at least, plays accepted or unaccepted, are standing tip-toe on the mountain tops – not misty ones, but those flooded with golden light. You have in you everything to make Europe all that it can be to any human. Go to! – and I must be selfish and impudent enough to beg that you will some day, somehow steal an hour to let us know how your soul fares.

As for us, our little round needs no annals. That sounds disheartened – but it is not meant so. Some are made for broad fields with a wide view: Others must find their joys in a narrow circle – and I do get much from my well-stuffed days with my boys and girls. So here's to full hearts for all of us, whether at home or abroad, even if the stockings on Christmas Eve hang rather limply from lack of stuffing.

You ask me about Munsey. I enclose a letter I wrote you which was returned to me, because you had already sailed. It is the first chapter. As for what has followed, I am at a loss to know what to tell you. I told him that his marriage would leave me a grey-hearted old woman. It has done so, inwardly. I have not given way. My every effort and thought goes to doing all in my power to canceling from them my feelings and toward making the marriage a success. I can truly say for myself that from the outside I am a "good sport." Inside is desolation. This isn't because I am wrapped up in the so-called "Mother" point-of view, the point of view that I only could guide his steps. If only I could feel assured that she is made of the stuff that would fight by his side, regardless of all opposing devils, but I can't feel it, — at least she has not satisfied me yet. She's pretty, she's capable in her line, but I can't see that she has in her either any Aaron or any Moses. I don't believe she will either lead him into any promised land, nor do I see any signs that, even tho she lacks the leading quality, she will atone for that lack, by Aaron-like, holding up his tired hands when he is no longer able to lift them in aspiration. A woman must do one or the other if she would prove herself a real wife. Moreover, I am cut off from any real communication with them (all lovely on the surface), because she is bitter toward us because we tried to get them to postpone the marriage. I suppose it serves me right for my worship of the boy. He had, in his particular line, wings, but I fear they are clipped past all flying. He is already thirty years old in his manner, and the weight of making ends meet has left him absolutely with no buoyancy. However, he is tending strictly to business, and learning some ordinary principles of everyday life that he sorely needed to know.

I think, if she will develope a little vision, that they may pull through. Anyway, we are hoping or trying to hope for the best, and we are trying, by every deceit deed possible, to break down the silly barrier which her pride has erected. We feel that we are old enough to stick our pride in our pockets – and do so daily. They love each other. If it prove strong enough to stay them over a very difficult, right now they can make the landing.

So. –

You will never know how much your presence here just at that time meant to us.

George was to us the good scotch granite that only he can be, and you the flame. School teaching is a hard road, but it has brought to me, through contact with certain boys and girls, the supreme joys of life – and the contact with you, Tom, will be to me as long as I live, one of my brightest joys.

If Munsey fails (God forbid!) to go to the heights to which his natural wings can easily carry him, I will get a double joy from you – you in your own right, and a sort of vicarious joy for Munsey.

Asheville still stands; L. B. Jackson's gorgeous sign still points the primrose path to a gorgeously commercialized Heaven of all material comforts.[4]

A bad piece of news is that Emily Westall,[5] riding on the running board of another girl's car, was bumped off, knocked insensible, and remained so for several hours. At our last telephoning, she was much better.

Be sure to tell us all about the fate of "Welcome to our City" and "The House." What new ideas are teeming in your head? How about pot-boilers? We are eager to know every "writing" step you take. Incidentally, Margaret is vitally interested in things French, and is making a French scrap-book in which she already has some really worthwhile material. So, won't you some times direct a card to her – she is especially interested in Anatole France – reads all she sees about him. So a picture card pertaining to him would give her much pleasure. A word to the wise is sufficient.

Another request. I do hope, if in your wandering you should come to Solesmes, Sarthe, France, won't you stop long enough to say one word to Mme. Coulergue and her little son and daughter, Raymond and Madeleine.[6] I know it would give them much pleasure. Besides, they tell me that nothing is more difficult than to get real access to even the humblest French home. I think our name would give you "open Sesame," and it might be a personal contact that would be worth while to you, he writes me letters that show a fine simple soul.

[Unsigned]

1. Wolfe, *Look Homeward, Angel,* 213
2. Wolfe's postcard from Bath has not been located.
3. George W. McCoy. Wolfe's letter of November 8, 1924, to McCoy was written in a vain attempt to sell "A Passage to England" to the *Asheville Citizen.* See Wolfe, *Letters,* 71–73.
4. Real estate magnate L. B. Jackson plastered huge "SEE L. B." billboards across western North Carolina. Ironically, the Jackson Building at 22 South Pack Square, opened in 1923 on land previously owned by W. O. and Julia Wolfe, was the site of W. O.'s monument shop. Asheville's veneration of real estate is the topic of Wolfe's play *Welcome to Our City* and his novel *You Can't Go Home Again.*
5. Emily Westall was Wolfe's first cousin once removed on his mother's side.
6. A family in France the Robertses adopted during World War I, sending packages to them.

24

ALS, 15 pp., Harvard, bMS Am 1883.2 (294)

Avignon   March 21, 1925

Dear Mrs Roberts: My only plea for my tardiness is that my own life has had a little private hell and heaven of its own[1] and I have been involved in my own wonder, my own emotion, my first bewilderment at a new civilization, and a new tongue, which is now beginning to unfold magically as I take hold.

I am wandering across France like a ghost, alone and glorious in loneliness, knowing not at all my next step – save vaguely; trusting to miraculous accident to find the enchanted harbor for me – and at times it does.

My play was finished long ago in Paris – in the little Latin Quarter hotel where Oscar Wilde died[2] – where I wandered one night, after having been robbed of an old suitcase containing the mss. of the old play. For a month I shut myself in, wrote madly, and <u>finished</u> the new play – a much better one, I believe.[3]

There followed a month in which I had an experience so filled with burlesque horror that I jerk a little in my sleep even now; I began to write again. I have an enormous mss. of my voyage – enormous notes.[4] I do not know where to peddle it – my one impulse is to write – and to send it to you. If you care to – you, mind, are my sole literary executor and censor, you may give it to George McCoy for the Citizen with this one condition which I make <u>absolute:</u> my name is not to be mentioned or published under anything I write. This is the one binding restriction, and I insist on it.

A few days ago, from Paris, the day I departed for Lyon I entrusted the prolog of the <u>Passage To England</u> to a lady, a friend, giving her your address and requesting that she send it at once.

In that prolog, about 10000 words, I judge, I said nothing of my actual voyage: I indulged, under a rather fantastic plot-work, certain speculations of mine on <u>voyages</u> – the true <u>voyages.</u> The idea came to me when, on going over the notes of the actual voyage, it occurred to me that the account I gave of events and people, if ever published, might get the author and the publisher into trouble. I had honestly made these notes while at sea, and while feeling none too gay; but I wanted even then to do what, to my knowledge, had never been done, – to isolate a transatlantic voyage, beginning and ending abruptly the moment the ship docks or sails, acting upon the belief that the sea and a ship disorganizes the whole social scheme for a few days, and that the social scheme reorganizes a new pattern before the voyage is over. I did this absolutely without malice; you may accept the whole when you get it as a melange of fact and fiction, with fiction emphasizing the truth of the business as I saw it.

That explains the sub-title: (Log of a Voyage That Was Never Made) This occurred to me at first purely as a device to escape libel: I changed the name of the ship and the characters. Then I remembered that I had not sailed on the day I had originally planned – that I had remained in Asheville a week longer, and that during that time I had had a queer feeling that I was or should be on the Atlantic. This led to the fantastic prolog, and my own growing conviction in the spiritual need of true voyages.

The whole, when you get it will amount I believe to 40000 or 50000 words, – a short novel It is queer journalism, I know, but since I give it, I feel that I am able to do and speak as I please You may tell George that I have amusing and interesting notes on England (I believe they are), and a story of Orleans, France – a true one – about the town and a genuine Countess who drinks horse's blood for anaemia, and an old villain of a Marquise, which, if I told it well, would make my future.[5]

I think, also, I may say things about people, about politics, about social differences, which may be superior to the banalities of the greater part of foreign correspondence, which, nevertheless, earns its authors good living.

The reason for all this is simply that I am tired of writing for the four winds: I realize the desperate lack and hypocrisy of pure expression. We are children – we must have an audience; and if my audience may be the people of a little North Carolina town, well and good. That is my whole desire for the present – perhaps there is a tiny feeling that if any of it is at all good it may reach the ears of the gods.

I shall send you lots of mss – I want to write, nothing else – and I have neither the patience nor the time nor the inclination to pull wires with literary agents, and so on And honestly, I know of no one who would publish my account now; because, as I said, I shall write this one as I please. Let him put it all in print, if he wants, but my name must be absent. Some of it may be fiction; most of it may be fact seen imaginatively[6] – it should have the same relation to reality as most autobiographical novels, as Childe Harold[7] – if you like.

I appoint you censor:[8] I have not been careful of myself in what I have said or am going to say – careful, that is, of what the townsfolk may think. That would be too petty, too dishonest. You must not be careful of that either in going over the mss. – it is not at all important. I think the sole thing – the principal thing – is the relation any of it may have to my family, to their position in the community. I shall never be too "advanced" to respect that.

It may be before I am done that I shall say something important – that in the mad rush to get it down, something of high worth may come out.

A letter has come – a very flattering and friendly letter – which asks me to return to N.Y.U. in September at $2000 – composition and Soph lit.

I shall accept, hoping that the heavens may rain manna before, or that a syndicate of county newspapers will appoint me representative at the councils of the League of Nations. For God's sake, say a word to my people, and get them to extend sustenance as long as my period of sufferance lasts.

I am reading French like mad – I came here alone, ignorant of the language and for two months wretchedly unhappy. Now I am jabbering villainously but adequately, and the world is brightening again.

I can not even make a gesture as to your own tragedy. What can I say? It was said before. In God's name let us pray for a time of loaves and fishes again. We must have miracles. Give Munsey my sincerest regards, my condolences in his illness. Poor boy – things have not gone too happily for him. What I am saying is so banal, so trivial – forgive me. I am emotionally <u>stretched</u> – a little too much – and I can say very little about these things.

The duty I impose on you is arduous and long – but I turn to you in trust and hope in this, as in all things. Do not hesitate to deny the responsibility if it's too heavy – I'll understand that. And if the paper doesn't care for the stuff, keep it for me. After all, I'm <u>embalming</u> the moments for future exhumation.

To you all my deepest love. Forgive me again if I send no cards, no letters. I'll give them to you on my return.

Meanwhile, read and accept my chroniclings as for your self.

It has been mad, bold, unhappy, lonely, glorious!

<u>Mail will be forewarded</u>

Tom.

Mailing address: American Express Co, Paris, 11 Rue Scribe

1. Referring probably to his passionate love for Helen Beal Harding ("Ann" in *Of Time and the River*), a wealthy Boston woman Wolfe had fallen for in Paris. "I'm hopelessly, madly, desperately in love with a woman who doesn't care a tinker's damn about me" (Wolfe, *Letters,* 78). For Wolfe's "hell and heaven" account of his adventures in France with Helen Harding, Marjorie Fairbanks, and Kenneth Raisbeck, see Wolfe, *Of Time and the River,* 687–794.

2. The Hôtel d'Alsace, 13 Rue de Beaux Arts, where Oscar Wilde died on November 30, 1900.

3. In Paris the manuscript of Wolfe's play "The House" was stolen in December 1924. By January 3, 1925, he had rewritten the play and retitled it *Mannerhouse*.

4. On March 16, 1925, Wolfe wrote his mother from Paris: "Meanwhile I am writing like a fiend. I have written, in addition to my play, what amounts to a short-sized

novel in length called *Passage to England*. It grew out of my notes on the voyage. I am
sending the first instalment off to Mrs Roberts to-day to give to George McCoy of the
Citizen. I don't know if they will take it—but if they will they may have it—I *must*
get published. . . . If the Citizen is afraid to publish my voyage (which may get them
in a libel suit) Mrs Roberts will give you mss. The thing now is for me to get it all on
paper. . . . I'm going to drown Mrs Roberts in mss. beginning right away. If you're at
home, warn her" (Wolfe, *Letters of Thomas Wolfe to His Mother*, 89–90). Although
"Passage to England" has not been published, in 1998 the Thomas Wolfe Society published a representative selection edited by John L. Idol Jr. and Suzanne Stutman.

    5. Countess Constance Hillyer de Caen is portrayed as La Comtesse de Caux in
Of Time and the River, 816: "by the doctor's orders I take horse's blood." La Marquise
de Marnaye appears on pp. 829–48.

    6. This succinct statement offers a valuable insight to Wolfe's fictionalization
process—especially the fact vs. fiction controversy over *Look Homeward, Angel*.

    7. *Childe Harold's Pilgrimage*, a long narrative poem by Lord Byron (1788–1824).
Wolfe undoubtedly related to Byron's romantically melancholy hero, Childe Harold,
who, disillusioned with life, embarks on a solitary pilgrimage through Europe.

    8. Wolfe's confidence in Mrs. Roberts's aesthetic propriety is resolute. Four months
earlier (without her knowledge), Wolfe had already appointed her his censor. On
November 8, 1924, he wrote George W. McCoy: "If it is suitable for publication in
the *Citizen*—I don't know that it is—take it to Mrs. Roberts at once, read it to her,
and ask her to censor it, if necessary. Much of it is so personal, written so rapidly, and
I am so *close* to it—not enough detachment—that I don't know whether I work myself
an injury (in the eyes of the burghers, you know) at times. Let her word go: if she gives
the word to print it as it is, and the paper wants it, print it" (Wolfe, *Letters*, 72). However, the manuscript at Harvard shows no evidence that Mrs. Roberts censored anything; she edited little except for correcting misspelled words and a few grammatical
errors. She emended the title of the first installment from "Log of a Voyage That Was
Never Made" to "The Log of a Voyage Which Was Never Made."

25

1925   *ALS, 1 p., Harvard, bMS Am 1883.2 (294)*[1]

Dear Mrs Roberts:

    Here is the next section of the grocer's daughter story, which I promise to
finish next time. I've been dragging in <u>dangerous</u> backgrounds – the thing has
grown so. Maybe some mad fool will print it.

                        Love
                        Tom

Please attend to punc. here also – as this story is being told by someone, watch
the "at the beginning, but not at the end of each ¶

1. Note accompanying sixth and ninth installments of "Passage to England." The sixth installment is untitled, but Mrs. Roberts has written "Tall Young Man" upon the first page of the manuscript; the ninth installment is titled "The Grocer's Daughter."

26

1925   *ALS, 1 p., Harvard, bMS Am 1883.2 (294)*[1]

<u>Ambleside, England Aug 4.</u>

Dear Mrs Roberts:

Attach this to the other. I shall send the rest on tomorrow; after that a story

<u>   Tom   </u>

1. Note accompanying seventh installment ("The Passenger") of "Passage to England."

27

1925   *ALS, 1 p., Harvard, bMS Am 1883.2 (294)*[1]

Dear Mrs Roberts: —

I will send the remainder of this silly thing to-morrow Then a really good story. The English lakes are unbelievably lovely.

Love to all

       Tom

1. Note accompanying a portion of seventh installment ("The Passenger") of "Passage to England."

28

1925   *ALS, 1 p., Harvard, bMS Am 1883.2 (294)*[1]

Dear Mrs Roberts:

Keep this even if it makes you shudder. I'll send the remainder tomorrow

       Tom

1. Note accompanying a portion of seventh installment ("The Passenger") of "Passage to England."

29

1925   *ALS, 1 p., Harvard, bMS Am 1883.2 (294)*[1]

Dear Mrs Roberts:

  Some more wretchedness just before my departure. Store it up
  Tom

  1. Undated note on torn sheet of paper that may have accompanied an installment of "Passage to England." The note is preserved in a folder of Wolfe's letters once owned by Mrs. Roberts. Verso reads "For Mrs Roberts."

30

                              ALS, 6 pp., Harvard, bMS Am 1883.1 (545)
June 7, 1925   *Grace High School letterhead*

                                        Sunday. June 7.

My dear Tom,

  Now to give you an account of my very unfaithful stewardship.[1] I feel as faithless in having postponed so long my duty that I feel that you must also have lost all faith in me. I can only say like the Western girl that I truly "have done my durndest," conditions being as they have been. Every one of my normal days is filled to the minute; then when we have as much sickness (and heart-aches, though they are not supposed to interfere with our "Carry On" system), as we have had this year, I get behind so, that even catching up seems a fox-fire pursuit indeed. Mr. Roberts's sickness in April (I can't remember whether I wrote you that the old ulcer on his duodenum burst again). Besides all this, my work at school has been heavier than ever in my life. I could find no minute when I felt that I could sit down and with any degree of intelligence, read your manuscript. I put this down so that you will understand that my long delay has been of the necessity of the flesh, and not because of lack of eagerness of spirit.

  It is all finished now – and goes to Mabel tomorrow. We all think it necessary that it be type-written. I could not stop after once started; you have done something both from standpoint of subject matter and style that I haven't seen done anywhere. That may not be saying much, because my life and time are so clipped off that I see almost nothing. But what I don't know and see, I can feel. I can see you in it, in every line of it; it was almost as good as having you here, with your torrential flow of speech. Boy, nothing can stop you. It's in you; it's the marrow of your bones, writing is, and your people must be made to realize it. I think they do, now, more than ever in their lives. But no need for me, in my feeble way, to try to say how it has all impressed me. You know me well enough to know what I think and feel. So that's enough.

Now, as to the practical side of getting it accepted, it won't be, not by the Asheville Citizen. At least, I fear not. Do you think Asheville, as represented by the Citizen, will be content to sit as a great Tar baby, and let you hit her with your hands, and your feet, and your big, thought-bulging head, and then let you lightly escape by flinging you into your native vastness of briar patch. No, sonny, rather than that, they will "tare out your har, and scratch out your eyeballs." I think George will favor it, and Buddie says they think George everything. Anyway, two or three more days will tell the tale. It hurts me that I have been so slow, but I believe you will understand and not be hurt. Don't let this end your confidence in me. I am not always such a snail. After it is type-written I will go over it again to be sure that it is as it should be. I don't see why you worry about your punctuation. It is about ideal; – just fits the thought in most cases, like a well-made glove.

The packages came through the mail in very poor condition. Several had been rewrapped in New York. Your wrappers are not substantial enough to hold so much dynamite. Once three were held up in Washington as fit subjects for customs restraint. I think the odor of the contents must have been unpleasant to the official's nose.[2]

What do you advise in case the Citizen refuses. What about the Nation? Don't wait too long to answer this question. If only you had left us one little smug-faced idol. But you smash every one dear to the Asheville heart. Gulliver picked his way carefully among the Lilliputans. As you say, with you it is all done in sadness of heart. That I know and understand, but it is done nevertheless, and your big foot, however much of sadness may be controlling your leg muscles, comes down with squashing force upon the godlets of our daily lives and Sabbath meditations.

Besides, the fantasticality of it will not appeal to those who are always wanting to look behind the fawn's ears.

On the other hand, The Citizen may see how unusual it is. Buddie will suck it in. He's a brilliant chap, if only —. I chuckled and chuckled when I came to your Meadow Lake Realty Deal.[3] The description was just to – a tee, what your mother had pictured only a day or so before could be done with our place. She, Mabel and Mr. And Mrs. Pettus were out.[4] Her keen black eyes took in at a glance the wonderful "possibilities" of the place, aside from its natural lovliness. In leaving she said in what was a hungrily pathetic tone, "Come to see me, Mrs. Roberts. I can talk about something else besides real estate."

Julia E. Wolfe in 1942 among her flowers in the front yard of her boarding-house, Old Kentucky Home. "As you grow older, try to come more and more into a sympathetic understanding with her, Tom." Photo by John S. Phillipson. By permission of the Thomas Wolfe Collection, Pack Memorial Public Library, Asheville, North Carolina

As you grow older, try to come more and more into a sympathetic under-standing with her, Tom. My heart-aches of this year have made me very sym-pathetic toward the mother term in these hard equations.

Coming back to Meadow Lake, you hit American "vision" hard – and no harder than it deserves. Yet there is another side to the shield. Take us. Ours is a Meadow Lake, – so beautiful naturally that I want to live here all of our lives and beautify it year by year. Yet we were forced to have American "vision" when we bought it – and it looks now as if we are about to reap an abundant harvest, (Knock on an Oak-tree.)

Go back a little. Can you blame us? See what the past has been – and what the money will mean to us. My father,[5] a prosperous man, was completely ruined when I was away my first year at boarding-school. From that year I have known nothing but unceasing toil with painfully scanty returns, both in money and education, tho I have worked hard for both. Mr. Roberts was even likewise. There were so many children that each of the older ones had to pay back into the family treasury the money spent on their education so that the younger ones might not be held up. That means all his young working days were spent in paying his early way; for fifteen years he and Emma have been the <u>sole</u> support of three invalids.[6] People in Asheville have wondered why we have always worn shabby clothes, lived in shabby houses, and deprived ourselves of all the usual pleasures. Some of them have been indelicate enough to put their wonder into words. We have toiled incessantly, not to accumulate money, but to make a bare living, and to try to educate our chaps. All the years that you have known us, it has been literally to scourge ourselves out of bed, so tired have we been, and then to be "good sports" and try to hide it from our pupils. This life has had much of fine joy in it, the joy that comes to all people who love their work, the joy that comes from knowing and having worked with such fellows as you, and George and Wee etc.[7]

But it's been hard. I've sometimes thought that I've been driven as full of nails as Mag Tulliver's doll.[8] Now, if things go as it now looks they will, American "vision" will do for us a perfect work. It looks as if we are situated so that we can get, now, or a little later $75,000 for our place. Do you know what that means to us? We have never had the money to buy a book we longed to read. They had to come from the public library. We have never this – and never that. If it hadn't been for American "vision," you could not have had seven unbroken years of study – and this blessed year in Europe. Say what you will, the golden age of Athens rested on the back of the slave. Only last week a letter from a nephew,[9] a sophomore at Vanderbilt, a truly brilliant mind in his line says that he will have to stop, perhaps for good. His father, because of an injury, must turn the family over to the boy, only 18.

There's a sister of Margaret's age seemingly born to be an artist.[10] Do you see what our $75000 would mean to those to. Emma a wreck in health, slaves all day in a government office. Every bit of me sympathizes with you, in all of this – and yet the tragedy of the whole business, that I should feel forced to write a panegyric on "Hard Cash."

Anyway, may the golden shower come. The Armstrongs sold their place (70 a) last week for $75000.[11] All of the land on that side of the road from Camp Alis – to mouth of the cove has now been sold. Our old place of the big brick house across from where we now are, sold for $800 an acre. They have been after us for a year and were here again Saturday trying to get our price. Enough of this. I should hate to see your three gleaming white bungalows climbing up our lovely slopes, and your four draggled-tail ducks swimming in our clear little mountain stream, dammed up for their feathery edification but —.

Your "Tall Young Man"[12] and sequels are the best of you: I read and reread. I shall see Mabel to-morrow, and in a day or so, will write the Citizen's decision. I think I can have made no mistake. I've tried to be very careful as to order etc. Those packages that had split open had become much disarranged, and sometimes it seemed to me <u>deranged</u> But I have had much joy in the work, and only hope that I have not failed altogether in my stewardship. Mr. R. and Margaret send love. I'm going in to see your mother in a few days. With much love,

M.R.

1. Refers to Mrs. Roberts's acceptance of editing the massive prologue of "Passage to England." Wolfe continued writing sketches for the unfinished manuscript until August 1925.

2. On July 27, 1925, Wolfe wrote his mother from London: "I have sent Mrs Roberts no more mss., partly because I have been travelling a good part of the time, partly because she told me some of the packages were damaged; and I have been unable to discover whether all I sent arrived. I have made a great many more notes and during the past ten days have been writing again. I shall send her three or four more batches before I sail; and I am bringing a valise full home with me, including my play" (Wolfe, *Letters of Thomas Wolfe to His Mother,* 97).

3. Wolfe was satirizing Asheville's obsession with real estate; "Meadow Lake Realty" was fictional.

4. Wolfe's mother and sister, Julia E. Wolfe and Mabel Wolfe Wheaton. Mrs. Hamlet Pettus was an old friend of Mrs. Roberts's.

5. Manuscript reads "father" even though Mrs. Roberts's father, Joseph Henry Hines, died when she was six months old and she never knew him. She clearly means her stepfather, Thomas Allbright.

6. After William Orton Roberts, J. M. Roberts's father, was swindled of his Tennessee acreage, J. M. and his sisters Emma and Hortense supported their parents as well as their youngest sibling, Mary Linn, who had tuberculosis.

7. The Robertses' hardships were unknown even to their children. "They hid it from everybody. Neither Buddie or I knew how hard their lives were" (Margaret Rose Roberts to Ted Mitchell, interview, August 7, 1994). In *Look Homeward, Angel,* Wolfe described how the Leonards "were fighting very stubbornly and courageously for their existence" (321). In 1995, Miss Roberts responded to her mother's letter as follows:

> This especially confidential letter to Tom, my mother would never have allowed to be published, but I have finally decided to permit it because I think it shows how valiant my parents were in fulfilling their dreams for the school in spite of almost superhuman financial problems. The basic reasons that my mother gave for these were all true indeed, but with some of her specifics I take issue. I claim the right to do this because I do not believe that there is a more severe critic of one's parent's public image than that of a shy, sensitive young daughter and I was it.
>
> She says the public wondered at the "shabby houses" that they lived in. This was not true. Although by necessity we moved fourteen times between 1911

and 1937, we lived in not a single house that I was ashamed of or that could be called "shabby." My mother, not the public, honestly felt as she did because any house to her was shabby that was not spacious inside and that did not have beautiful land around it with a view and most of ours did not always have such. Looking back, now, on all the moves we made, it must have been a terrible burden to her, but if it was, she never in any way let us know it. But instead, she made us feel that each of those moves was a new adventure.

Their clothes were shabby. This also was not true. Could a woman ever have looked shabbily dressed who always looked, as Tom truly said, "clean, like a scrubbed kitchen board"? [Wolfe, *Look Homeward, Angel,* 213]. Her clothes were very simple, without any particular regard to fashion – not for lack of money but because at that time and until the end of her life, she had no interest whatever in clothes. After she retired when she became active in her literary clubs, my aunt persuaded her, against her will, to buy a few beautiful clothes. Afterwards she said to my father, "I wish I had not bought them – I'm giving papers before my clubs in the hopes that they will be interested in what I have to say, not in the kind of clothes I have on." She always went with all three of us to the best stores in town to buy our clothes and saw to it that we selected the best that could be bought to suit our needs, without regard to cost.

The biggest joke of all was her claim that they had to go to the library because they lacked the money to buy books. Tom was not writing fiction in *Look Homeward, Angel* when he said, "She watched his face light with eagerness as he saw the fifteen hundred or two thousand books shelved away in various places" [215]. I can not vouch for his figures being exact, but I know that our large living room that also served as the school library was loaded with books and they were not cheap school editions. They were of the best. In our own copy of *The Vicar of Wakefield,* with full color plates, she wrote: "Boys, this is a beautiful book. Please treat it as such." Her desire for books was so voracious that naturally she could not afford to completely satisfy it and what she could not find in Asheville's Pack Library, she got Tom to borrow and mail to her from the Chapel Hill and Harvard Libraries! She would rather have had books than all the clothes in Asheville.

Let no one think that I have contested all three of these statements by my mother in any spirit of demeaning her. I have only tried objectively to set the record straight. My mother seemed always as much a saint to me as she seemed to Tom and in my eyes she could do no wrong. As I look back on it now, all those moves to different houses that we made must have been a superhuman burden to her on top of her full time teaching. May she rest in peace in Riverside Cemetery near the grave of Tom Wolfe, whom she continued to address in many of her early letters to him (as a young man) as "My dear boy."

(Margaret Rose Roberts to Ted Mitchell, October 12, 1995)

8. Maggie Tulliver is a main character in George Eliot's *The Mill on the Floss,* a favorite of Wolfe's.

9. Mrs. Roberts's nephew, William Marvin Roberts Jr.

10. Mary Frances Roberts.

11. The Armstrongs owned the dairy farm above the Robertses in Chunn's Cove.

12. Refers to a sketch from "Passage to England."

31

RETURNING FROM EUROPE LATE AUGUST 1925, Wolfe met Aline Bernstein (1881–1955) aboard the *Olympic.* Bernstein, a renowned New York City stage and costume designer, was nineteen years older than Wolfe and married. She became Wolfe's mistress for the next five years and the great love of his life (portrayed as Esther Jack in *The Web and the Rock* and *You Can't Go Home Again*). She supplied Wolfe with not only the emotional support and belief in his talent that allowed him to write *Look Homeward, Angel,* but financial assistance as well. Wolfe loved her with "a single and absolute love that rises above and dominates everything in my life."[1] Mrs. Roberts's letter condemning Wolfe's affair has been lost, but her brave request for forgiveness has not.

ALS, 2 pp., Harvard, bMS Am 1883.1 (545)
Grace High School letterhead

May 19, 1926.

My dear Tom,

As I feared, my mid-Victorian moralizing was too much for you. I have hoped against hope that you would write, but I fear that rushing in, as I did, where an angel should have feared to tread, has been more than you could tolerate, even from so old a friend, and one who loves you so truly. You know you come close after my own children with me. Will you not let that be a ground of pardon for any old-maid meddling that I may have done in your most private affairs.?

I am so anxious to know something of your year's work, but especially of your play-work. Won't you write to me?

Here I have a favor to ask. A miracle has happened. Miss Dolly[2] sails for Europe May 29. We have all felt that she should be the first to reap the benefit of the sale of the farm, (Sold for $100,000).[3] She has been sick since she was eighteen and has suffered untold agonies with a heroism equal to that of the martyrs. She is one of the few really educated women that I know, and it has all been gained by brain-hammering, lying on her bed.

Aline Bernstein, "the one person on earth who has the greatest claim to my love," at her work table; undated. By permission of the Thomas Wolfe Collection, Pack Memorial Public Library, Asheville, North Carolina

She is so frail now that it looks like gambling with death to face such a trip, but she is determined to have her fling.

This is to ask you if you won't sit down at once (we know your habits) and give her names and addresses of reasonably priced pensions, if you can remember any. She would be happy to see you, if you can go down to Penn. Station between hours of 3.35 P.M. and 5 P.M. May 28. Call for Mary Linn Roberts, at the Ladies' Aid. Go as close to 3.35 as you can to see her. She will rest there to be joined at five o'clock by a cousin, Fay Hunt, who is going with her. They sail on the Corona, Cunard line 12:10 P.M. May 29.

Perhaps you may be moved to be light on me with your wrath when I tell you that next Saturday I shall have been sick four weeks, and am feeling pretty weak and useless. Dr. M.[4] says certain nerves have been worn-out and refuse to function – that I have finally reaped the burrs of overwork.

Do write to me.

Your friend always,

Margaret Roberts

It's quite amusing how hard-up we are in the face of our new-found prosperity. Our financial situation just now has set me to do some moralizing or philosophizing. This life is a great game if one doesn't weaken.

1. Wolfe and Bernstein, *My Other Loneliness,* 190. Coincidentally, when Wolfe and Aline Bernstein met, she had a copy of *Welcome to Our City* aboard the ship. Wolfe had submitted the play to the Neighborhood Playhouse, which the Lewisohn sisters, Alice and Irene, sponsored and served on its board of directors. Although Irene endorsed the play, Bernstein carried the manuscript with her to Europe to gain Alice Lewisohn's approval. (The Neighborhood Playhouse later rejected *Welcome to Our City;* see letter 37.)

2. Mary Linn Roberts.

3. According to Margaret Rose Roberts, "the farm sold for $126,000" (Margaret Rose Roberts to Ted Mitchell, interview, August 7, 1994).

4. Charles Millender, M.D., a friend of the Robertses. His daughter was at Chapel Hill with John Munsey Roberts Jr.

32

ALS, 18 pp., Harvard, bMS Am 1883.2 (294)
June 1, 1926   *Hotel Albert letterhead*

Dear Mrs Roberts: – I was away in Boston when your letter came, during a vacant interval in the examination period at N.Y.U. I came back Thursday for a final examination

To my deep and real regret I missed Miss Dolly entirely, although I made specific plans to see her. I had addresses and names to give her which might have been of help.

But I made a mistake. Your letter gave May 29th as the day of her sailing, and May 28th as the day when she might be found at the Penn station – 3:30–5:00 I remembered the day as May 29, concluding she would sail at midnight.

I shall see you perhaps in a few days. I may come home, although invitations have not been marked by their warmth or frequency, nor am I driven by my own inclination.

In Boston I found my Uncle Henry's[1] children boiling with the bitterest feeling toward him. They have not been near him since the death of my aunt[2] in January. According to their story, my aunts death was actively hastened by lack of food, heat, and service. He burned coke or soft coal, because it was cheaper – my aunt, with an enormous heart lesion was forced to attend the furnace constantly, in order to keep from freezing. He brought her tainted meat, or cheap soups, lying about the prices, insisting he had purchased the finest steak. As she died, unable to speak, she pointed with her finger to one of her daughters and then to a small sum of money she had hoarded through many years $60.00. With her eye fixed upon him, he appropriated this money, insisting it was intended for him. He patched his own shoes, washed his own laundry, and, during the last year of her life, cooked food for her over the smoke of the furnace in order to save the gas. Now he has been captured by a middle class Englishwoman, 35 years old, who flatters him, drives him home, and fixes his curtains. Sniggering behind his hand he told me she "would be something more than a friend" before the year was over. Thus, the property that this selfish and terrible old man has hoarded – he is 74, and a good type of senile decay, will pass on to a common money-hunter – his wife dead, without comfort, his children driven into the world – one to an abominable marriage which tainted her blood and ruined her health — will be deprived of what small comfort his property could give.

From him I learned details of my Uncle Will's[3] two million and my mother's I-know-not-what: Two years ago I was forced into work for which I had no affection, at the peril of what talent I had. It may be said that I was not "forced," but I insist that money has been held over me like a bludgeon

Recently, what little help I have secured from home to eke out my salary (and, I confess, my own lack of economy) has been withdrawn. Meanwhile, I get insane attempts at falsification – dark hints at "the poor house" and "old age" and the insistence that everything has been done "for the children" or in order to secure "a few dollars for old age" My uncle, sniggering, told me he supposed my mother had not told me (she was too cautious) that she is building a $100 000 hotel[4] at Brevard. This a week after a letter telling of pinch and poverty.

These are the facts, and are prefatory to your letter. You are certainly wrong in supposing I took your letter badly. I honor the motive, and I trust in your friendship too much to wear a chip around you. But I will be forgiven, I know, and understood, I believe, if I say that a brief, but very intense and varied life, has told me that all advice is bad – even that of so wise and understanding a person as you are.

Further, if, in this affair,[5] you see only consequences of future unhappiness for me – what, pray, should unhappiness mean to me who called for wine, and was given the sponge, and whose bread as a child was soaked in his grief. Am I so rich, then, that I can strike love in the face, drive away the only comfort, security, and repose I have ever known, and destroy myself just as my mind and heart, aflame with hope and maturity, as they have never been before, promise me at length release.

Well, I'm in no debater's mood. Thank God, I have escaped, at any rate, from <u>odious</u> bondage, and I shall come home, and depart thence, free, because that ugly monster, money, which breaks the will and kills courage, has been banished for me.

RIGHT: "In Boston I found my Uncle Henry's children boiling with the bitterest feeling toward him." Henry Addison Westall at the time of his ordination as a Unitarian minister. By permission of the North Carolina Collection, University of North Carolina Library at Chapel Hill, and Eugene H. Winick, Administrator C.T.A., Estate of Thomas Wolfe

BELOW: "My aunts death was actively hastened by lack of food, heat, and service." Laura May Hill Westall. By permission of the Thomas Wolfe Collection, Pack Memorial Public Library, Asheville, North Carolina

I expect nothing from my family – now or hereafter. I have given my life to the high things of this earth – I am free to say that I consider any debt that has been made has been repaid by the effort and example of my life; and I assure you that, from now on, I shall strike a blow in the face of insolence, confessing no obligation where none is due, and repelling any hostility toward my life and my creation with all the energy and violence I command.

Of this you may be sure: – I believe you have been my constant friend, that you have never stooped to the common daily treachery of the village, that in your heart you have believed in me and trusted in me. Be assured, then, that you at least I shall want to see when I come home

I am sailing on the Berengaria June 23.

Until we meet, then,

With great affection,

Tom.

1. Julia E. Wolfe's brother, Henry Addison Westall (1854–1947). Portrayed as Bascom Pentland in *Of Time and the River* and Bascom Hawke in "A Portrait of Bascom Hawke" (*Scribner's Magazine,* April 1932).

2. According to her daughter, Elaine Westall Gould, Laura May Hill Westall died of malnutrition. (Elaine Westall Gould, *Look Behind You, Thomas Wolfe* [Hicksville, N.Y.: Exposition Press, 1976], 114). Laura Westall is Louise Pentland in *Of Time and the River.*

3. William Harrison Westall (1863–1944).

4. The hotel was never built.

5. Wolfe's affair with Aline Bernstein.

33

THE FOLLOWING UNDATED FRAGMENT offers few clues of where it might be placed. Wolfe's discouragement with New York and his plays may be in response to the final round of rejections of *Mannerhouse* and *Welcome to Our City* in 1926.

Ca. 1926?   *ALS fragment, 4 pp., Harvard, bMS Am 1883.2 (294)*

with me is not a virtue, but a fact that can not be concealed. My family have contributed little to my repose, painfully little to my happiness – not even a roof for shelter when I return

I am sick and far from all my world – even from New York and my plays. An inspiration has come to me to destroy all my mss – to withdraw forever from the envenomed flames into which long since I hurled my golden heart.

I shall sing some songs, and drink some wine, and read some books. But write them — [*illegible*] an end.

All facts are small before the fact of death. The suddeness and the cruelty of this past week's happenings have burnt me like an acid. I shall tell myths no longer. God saw a speck and killed an army. This, I am sure, is how things happen

Well, there's enough of this, too. I have a great need of some one to love – oh, the waste, the waste of that too in the past – all that was great and that sang in me But there's the next best thing – I am going back where someone loves me. My life unsought, unheard is dying like God's cry in a desert. God bless you   Tom

---

34

On June 23, 1926, Wolfe boarded the *Berengaria* and was reunited with Aline Bernstein in Paris. At this time he began writing notes and phrases for an autobiographical novel he tentatively called "The Building of a Wall." He jotted down ideas in a plain tablet and later in a hardcover composition book. After completing these notes, he began writing in large accounting ledgers supplied by Aline, who believed this was the only way Wolfe could keep track of what he had written. He eventually filled seventeen ledgers and in 1928 called the completed manuscript "O Lost." (He renamed it *Look Homeward, Angel* in 1929 after the sales force at Scribner's requested a more commercial title.)

ALS, 5 pp., Harvard, bMS Am 1883.2 (294)

Bath   England
July 19, 1926

Dear Mrs Roberts: – Here are just a few lines – a short record of my doings since I left you. I was in Paris ten days, in Chartres two days, in London a week, and here two days. I am on my way to the North of England – to Lincoln and York for a few days, and finally to the Lake District, where I settle down to work.

My trip has been fuller, richer, more fruitful than I had dared hope; I looked and looked so fiercely the first time that I return now to something which seems to be opening itself for me.

I have begun work on a book – a novel, to which I may give the title of The Building of a Wall – perhaps not; but because I am a tall man, you know perhaps my fidelity to walls and to secret places. All the passion of my heart and of my life I am pouring into this book – it will swarm with life, be peopled by a city, and if ever read, may seem in places terrible, brutal, Rabelaisian, bawdy: its unity is simply this – I am telling the story of a powerful creative element trying to work its way toward an essential isolation; a creative solitude; a secret life – its fierce struggles to wall this part of its life away from birth – first against the public and savage glare of an unbalanced, nervous brawling family group; later against school, society, all the barbarous invasions of the world. In a way, the book marks a progression toward freedom; in a way toward bondage – but this does not matter: to me one is as beautiful as the other. Just subordinate and leading up to this main theme is as desperate and bitter a story of a contest between two people as you ever knew – a man and his wife[1] – the one with an inbred, and also an instinctive, terror and hatred of property; the other with a growing mounting lust for ownership that finally is tinged with mania; – a struggle that ends in decay, death, desolation.

This is all I've time for now.

I wish I could tell you more of this magnificent old town, held in a cup of green steep hills, – climbing one of them, made on one plan from one material – the finest place really I've ever seen.

Write me, American Express Co, London. God bless you all

Tom

1. W. O. and Julia Wolfe, portrayed as W. O. and Eliza Gant in *Look Homeward, Angel.* "I hope I never own another piece of property as long as I live—save a house to live in. It is nothing but a curse and a care, and the tax-collector gets it all in the end," W. O. Gant tells Eliza, who looks at him "with a startled expression, as if he had uttered a damnable heresy" (Wolfe, *Look Homeward, Angel,* 12). However, according to the Buncombe County Register of Deeds, W. O. Wolfe owned a substantial amount of real estate, some jointly with Julia.

35

Signed postcard of Strasbourg. –
Porte de l'Hopital – La Rue d'Or
Et la Cathédrale; Harvard, bMS Am 1883.2 (294)

Ca. fall 1926

Dear Mrs Roberts: I'm on my way to Germany; expect to be back in New York next month Will answer your letter as soon as I get my breath. Left Oxford two or three weeks ago – Saw Billy Cocke several times. Think he's terribly lonely, but he'll get on – Right Stuff. Love, Tom

36

UNDER MARGARET ROBERTS'S GUIDANCE AND ENCOURAGEMENT, Wolfe's genius developed during his boyhood's "wild confusion of adolescence."[1] Still affected from having written about her in his autobiographical work-in-progress, Wolfe details how she became the mother of his spirit.

ALS, 8 pp., Harvard, bMS Am 1883.2 (294)
Harvard Club letterhead

Monday – May 30, 1927
Dear Mrs Roberts: – Your card just came – I wrote you four or five days ago care of Mabel, because I didn't have your postal (the only communication I have had from you since I came to America) What you say of the three letters that came back to you distresses me terribly: I get a little mail from time to time, and I hope I have succeeded in getting the thing straight finally at the office. If I am going to lose any letters, I want all the others to go – not yours. You say that no one <u>outside</u> my family loves me more than Margaret Roberts. Let me rather say the exact truth: – that no one <u>inside</u> my family loves me as much, and only one other person,[2] I think, in all the world loves me as much

My book is full of ugliness and terrible pain – and I think moments of a great and soaring beauty. In it (will you forgive me?) I have told the story of one of the most beautiful people I have ever known as it touched on my own life. I am calling that person Margaret Leonard. I was without a home – a vagabond since I was seven – with two roofs and no home;[3] I moved inward on that house of death and tumult from room to little room, as the boarders came with their dollar a day, and their constant rocking on the porch; my overloaded heart was bursting with its packed weight of loneliness and terror; I was strangling, without speech, without articulation, in my own secretions – groping like a blind sea-thing with no eyes and a thousand feelers toward light, toward life, toward beauty and order, out of that hell of chaos, greed, and cheap ugliness – and then I found you, when else I should have died, you mother of my spirit who fed me with light. Do you think that I have forgotten? Do you think I ever will? You are entombed in my flesh, you are in the pulses of my blood, the thought of you makes a great music in me – and before I come to death, I shall use the last thrust of my talent – whatever it is – to put your beauty into words.

Goodbye for the present. This is Decoration Day. I am decorated with weariness, but I am going to try to get it all down on paper in the next few weeks and then I may go abroad for a short time. My attic is getting hot – my

Holograph of "Mother of my Spirit" letter, May 30, 1927.
By permission of the William B. Wisdom Collection,
Houghton Library, Harvard University, and Eugene H.
Winick, Administrator C.T.A., Estate of Thomas Wolfe

friend, Olin Dows[4] (almost as great a saint as you are) came down from his 80 rooms and 2000 acres on the Hudson Saturday and asked me to finish the book in the country.[5] But I'm afraid of the big house and all the swells – he's had it alone all winter – but now his mother's coming from Washington (with all the legations) and his sister from Sweden: they're in for a big summer. But there's a lovely little cottage of two rooms, with a bath, deep in the woods, by the bathing pool, and he's offered this to me, together with as many acres of land as I need, forever, if I should ever care to stay there near him He paints, lives like a Spartan on vegetables, and is a Bertrand Russell[6] Socialist (much to his father's sorrow)

Write as soon as you get this. When I pluck up more strength, I'll write a good one. Excuse the gibberings. Goodbye. God bless you all. Tom

P.S. If you write again here, and your letters' returned, write me care of Aline Bernstein – 333 West 77th St – New York City (I'm in good standing, however and <u>already</u> paid up)

1. Wolfe, *Look Homeward, Angel,* 307.
2. Aline Bernstein.
3. Wolfe is referring to how he was sent back and forth between his family home at 92 Woodfin Street and his mother's boardinghouse, Old Kentucky Home, at 48 Spruce Street: "There was no place sacred unto themselves, no place fixed for their own inhabitation, no place proof against the invasion of the boarders. As the house filled, they went from room to little room, going successively down the shabby scale of their lives" (Wolfe, *Look Homeward, Angel,* 137).
4. Olin Dows (1904–1981) met Wolfe when they were students at Harvard. Dows had seen and greatly admired *Welcome to Our City* and grew to venerate Wolfe's talent. A lasting friendship soon developed. Dows is portrayed as Joel Pierce in *Of Time and the River:* "Joel revealed instinctively what every one who knew him well felt about him—an enormous decency and radiance in his soul and character, a wonderfully generous and instinctive friendliness towards humanity—that became finer and more beautiful because of its very impersonality" (512–13).
5. Foxhollow Farm, the Dows family's two-thousand-acre estate in Rhinebeck, New York. Depicted in *Of Time and the River* as "that magic domain known as Far Field Farm" (515).
6. Bertrand Russell (1872–1970), English mathematician and philosopher.

37

ALS, 9 pp., Harvard, bMS Am 1883.2 (293)
Early June 1927   *Harvard Club letterhead*

Dear Mrs Roberts: – Forgive my long silence and the shortness of this letter. I have poured my life, my strength, and almost all my time for almost a year into my book which is now nearing its end. I think it is the best thing I've ever done: certainly it is the only thing I have ever really worked on. I have learned that writing is hard work, desperate work, and that (as Ben Jonson said) "he who casts to write a living line must sweat." I have lived since I came back to New York in a deserted ramshackle building[1] that trembles when a car passes:

"Well, I suppose I have rich friends." Wolfe (right) at Foxhollow Farm, the Dows family estate at Rhinebeck, on the Hudson River. Pictured with Wolfe are (from left) Elsie Benkard, Olin Dows's first cousin; Olin Dows; Dows's sister, Margaret; and Dows's mother, Alice. Photo courtesy of James C. Cleary

I have lived in its huge dirty garret, without heat, without plumbing – without anything but light. My mother wrote me several weeks ago – I hear from at least one member of my family every two or three months – congratulating me on the possession of "rich friends." Well, I suppose I have rich friends – a few of all kinds, rich and poor, have shown me amazing devotion – but I have taken only what was necessary for the barest existence. I have lived closer to poverty this year than ever in my life. And I do not regret it. I have had all I needed. The world for me was ghost when I wrote. I don't know what the outcome will be. I have no power to peddle my wares, and I strike patronage a blow in the face. The other day word reached me that a rich woman who has supported a famous little theatre here for years (Miss Alice Lewisohn of the Neighborhood Playhouse) had told one of the directors last year that she would have done my play (<u>Welcome</u>) but that I was the most arrogant young man she had ever known. The news gave me pleasure: my proud foolish words to her of disdain and contempt came back to me and I felt that I had acted well – I who will never be dandled into reputation by wealth. I have forsaken all groups, I live, save for the affection of a few friends, as much alone as anyone can live. And I know I am right! I believe – they believe – I shall come through. I am swamped with offers of employment for the next year – at N. Y. U., with an advertising company,[2] in the movies – scenarios. I have accepted none of them – I hope I shall find <u>one</u> when the time comes. But I have done nothing, thought of nothing, but writing.

I wish I could tell you more of my book. I meant alone this: I think I shall call it <u>Alone, Alone,</u> for the idea that broods over it, and in it, and behind it is that we are all strangers upon this earth we walk on – that naked and alone do we come into life, and alone, a stranger, each to each, we live upon it. The title, as you know I have taken from the poem I love best: The Rhyme of the Ancient Mariner:

Alone, alone, all, all alone,
Alone on a wide, wide sea,
And never a saint took pity on
My soul in agony.[3]

My state is not bad – in spite of the fact that I am considered arrogant and proud (the protective coloration of one who was born without his proper allowance of hide) I am told, by someone who loves me, that I could have what I wanted of people – "the city at my feet", and so on – if I let myself out on them. Perhaps not – but, what's better, my friends like me.

I'm very tired; my health has stood the pounding beautifully. I don't know what I shall do when I finish. I may go abroad for a short trip. Haven't your card with your new address on it: I'm sending this to Mabel with the hope she can deliver it at once.

Good bye for the present. Write me soon. You are one of the few people that will never become a phantom to me. God bless you all.

Tom
Address Harvard Club

1. 13 East Eighth Street.
2. The J. Walter Thompson Company.
3. "The Rime of the Ancient Mariner" by Samuel Taylor Coleridge (1772–1834). Wolfe read and reread Coleridge's poems throughout his adult life: "And then Coleridge came—Perhaps I was not afraid to read in his experience, in his life a possible portent of my own (Wolfe, *Autobiographical Outline,* 63).

38

WOLFE WROTE THE FOLLOWING UNFINISHED LETTER about July 8, 1927, but did not mail it. Another letter, written on July 11, duplicated some of the material in his earlier version. Note how he transferred two unpleasant events—wearing his brother Ben's ill-fitting shoes and sister Mabel's sadistic taunting—into fiction.

Fragment, 21 pp., Harvard, bMS Am 1883.2 (294)

Ca. July 8, 1927   *Harvard Club letterhead*

Dear Mrs Roberts: — I read your letter this afternoon a few minutes after I had purchased second class passage on the <u>George Washington,</u> sailing Tuesday.[1] Thus, I will not be here to greet you if you come in August: I am returning in September: All this I decided at once on Sunday, after mulling the business hopelessly for months. I had thought before that I would finish the book here and go abroad in the autumn to stay for a year in Italy. Several considerations prevent me. First, I have exhausted my wits on a gigantic piece of work – and I shall not want to write more, I think, for several months. Second, I should be here in New York next winter to try to launch the thing and some of my plays Third, my going away for a long period of time would cause the deepest pain to the one person on earth who has the greatest claim to my love.[2] There is nothing in my life as important as this: — I was a lonely outcast, and suddenly I became richer – in the one true wealth — than Maecenas.[3]

I am going to Paris for a short time – then on to Prague, Budapest, and Vienna, all lovely and unvisited. I should be back in Paris for a few days in September. If you have come by that time I shall see you. I don't know what my address will be – I hate the American Express Company (a nasty crowded place full of my loud-mouthed brethren and insolent clerks — this is <u>Paris</u> only), but their checks are the most-convenient things I know of. Write me there – unless I tell you differently.

I have been in the country several weeks with my friend Olin Dows. I'm much restored physically, but my brain is falling apart like over-scrambled eggs. Hence this stupid letter. I refused to live in the big house with the swells; he gave me the gate-keepers lodge – a little bit of heaven with a little river, a wooded glade, and the sound of water falling over the dam all through the night. Beyond, the stream widened into the mighty Hudson – the noblest river I know of.

I had to dress up in my dinner jacket almost every night, which was good for me – because I'm somewhat afraid of people, and sometimes conceal my fear by being arrogant and sneering magnificently. On the Fourth of July, in the evening, I went with Olin to a neighboring estate of one of his friends – a young man named Vincent Astor, who is one of the richest young men in the world – his chief claim I believe to distinction. The young man likes to play with every kind of steam engine (he has a miniature railroad on the place) and to set off fire works. He set off several thousand dollars worth for our delight – they were the loveliest things I've ever seen and did incredible things — whistling like birds, bursting in cascades of color, changing their lights, and so on. The simple villagers – some hundreds or thousands – sat on the lawns, and all the swells upon the verandahs. How they stared at me! I looked very well in my clothes, but they knew I was an alien of some sort — I have a kind of notoriety among them, I believe, as Olin's wild Bohemian friend: whenever they met me, they asked if it were really true that I stayed up all night, and was writing a book – and what was it all about! But they were all very lovely – I'm afraid if I had to do it I'd find them dull. Astor's grounds were huge and beautiful (thousands of acres magnificently kept), his house was huge and ugly – a stone Victorian thing that belonged to his father — the rooms were also huge and ugly stuffed with ugly red plush furniture. After the fire works we went inside to the dining room and ate ice cream and chicken salad and punch with the assistance of eight or ten flunkies. I'm sure I'd go murderously insane and kill a few of them if I had them around long. Astor's wife is a tall blonde slender young woman – very elegant and beautiful, and cold. Olin told me it was the first social position in America: the big rooms, the people around her really gave one the sense of a court. (But I've heard them talk – opinions that would disgrace an English Tory.)

But I lived very simply at the lodge house – by myself – going to the big house once a day, or having one good meal brought to me, and poisoning myself on my own cooking the rest of the time. As for Olin, he is in many respects the finest young man I've ever known – a very great person.

What you tell me about bending my proud neck is right If I am a difficult person now, it is partly because of my childhood, when I lived in terror and could not defend myself. But I get a little better all the time: — I have spent years recovering from those first wounds. What you say to me about my family affects me only in so far as it comes from you, and hurts me a little because it does come from you. I think you should understand that there is no question of my casting my family off – it is a question of my family casting me off. You know of course that I've had no money from them in more than a year – save a $50 check from my mother Christmas (she gave it to them all, she said) and a $15 one from Fred And I hope you know that I am very fortunate even to get an answer to my letters — Mabel never writes: my last two letters have gone unanswered. As for my mothers losses, I do not think it matters at all – no one has ever had anything out of it anyway, and she has quite enough. I'm sure, to get along on <u>Harvard,</u> you know, came out of my father's estate — my mother promised to pay for <u>one</u> year, and then for <u>two,</u> but when the time came, everything came out of the legacy. I signed a paper and was left with nothing.[4] As to their other estimates of my extravagant expenditures — they included the milk I had in the cradle, the air I breathe, the food I ate, the cheap clothes I wore, and, I suppose, the pair of shoes belonging to my brother Ben that I was forced to wear for six weeks ("It's a pity not to use them!" said my mother) until I was crippled for weeks, and my straight boy's toes were permanently crushed and twisted into ugly bunches.[5] I have gone home of recent years and heard how they fought for my welfare — how first they insisted I go to college (which was due to <u>your</u> insistence and my father's desire that I be a Congressman, Governor, ambassador by my 21st year – to the glory of the name) Also, how my sister fought for me to go to Harvard. Well, I went on my own money and everyone's head and heart was against me

They have never admitted, I suppose, in public that I was anything less than the apple of their eyes, their heart's-core of love — but does not this rebound to their credit, and the patient sacrifice and toil they love to assume? Did my sister ever tell the public of her hatred for me (<u>hatred</u> is the word — I am not afraid to use it) during my child hood? Did she ever tell you how the sight of my face, brooding over a book or a vision would arouse her own restless nature to a Screaming fury: — how she would scream "bastard" at me, sneer at what she called my "queer, dopey, freaky little face," pout out her lip at me in mockery of my own, and let her head goggle and drag stupidly as my own did on its scrawny neck. How she would tell me I was "a Westall – not a Wolfe. There's none of papa in you" — when this was supposed to be the last insult – a synonym for selfishness, coldness, and unpleasant eccentricity?[6]

[Breaks off]

1. Wolfe sailed aboard the *George Washington* on July 12, 1927.
2. Aline Bernstein.
3. Gaius Cilnius Maecenas (d. 8 B.C.E.), Roman statesman and patron of young writers, among whom were Virgil and Horace. His munificence as a patron has made his name proverbial.
4. Wolfe persuaded his mother in 1920 to allow him to attend Harvard for one year by agreeing that the expense would be deducted from a legacy of five thousand dollars left to him in his father's will. When he remained at Harvard for two more years, no mention was made of deducting the additional expenses from the legacy. After

W. O. Wolfe's death in 1922, his estate had shrunk to the extent that the bequests of five thousand dollars to each of his children could not be paid. Wolfe signed a document waiving claim to his five thousand dollars, in return for the money he had received during his three years at Harvard. See Wolfe's letter to his brother Fred, January 22, 1938, in Wolfe, *Letters,* 704–6.

5. See Wolfe, *Look Homeward, Angel,* 227: "But his toes that had grown through boyhood straight and strong were pressed into a pulp, the bones gnarled, bent and twisted, the nails thick and dead."

6. "Convulsed by a momentary rush of hatred, she would caricature the pout of his lips, the droop of his head, his bounding kangaroo walk. 'You little freak. You nasty little freak. You don't even know who you are—you little bastard. You're not a Gant. Any one can see that. You haven't a drop of papa's blood in you. Queer one! Queer one! You're Greeley Pentland all over again'" (Wolfe, *Look Homeward, Angel,* 238). Wolfe's mother's maiden name was Westall. The Westalls were called the Pentlands in *Look Homeward, Angel.* Greeley Pentland was Mrs. Wolfe's brother, Horace Greely Westall, described as "degenerate, weak, scrofulous" in *Look Homeward, Angel* (15).

39

ALS, 4 pp., Harvard, bMS Am 1883.2 (294)
Harvard Club letterhead

Monday night July 11, 1927

My Dear Mrs. Roberts: –

I have written you an enormous letter – in answer to your last[1] But it's unfinished; I'm terribly tired, and off to Europe again to-morrow at midnight. Write American Express Company, 11 Rue Scribe, Paris. I'm going on to Prague, Budapest, and Vienna – but mail will be forwarded. I'm coming back to America in September, but hope to see you before in Paris. I'll finish the great letter on the boat and send it to you from the other side, with such help as I can give. I'm thrilled by your going more than by my own.[2] My books almost done; I'll revise it this summer: coming back to sell it, if I can. Will be at N. Y. U. They've given me everything I asked for – they were very kind. Radio wants me also. If I take this in addition to teaching I'll be very rich – perhaps $150 a week. Too much for me: if I sell book, nothing forever after but write.

Wrote Mabel long letter last night: call her up for more complete information

God bless you all – your going is like magic.

Tom

If you write Tom Wallis, tell him I found his phone call next day at club, and went to his hotel, but that he had departed. Love to you all

You should have seen me up the river with the swells. They thought me mad. Olin Dows a great person.

1. Mrs. Roberts's letter has not been located.

2. The Robertses were planning a trip to Europe that summer, but because of Mr. Roberts's ulcer hemorrhage, the trip was cancelled. Written in J. M. Roberts's hand on the back of the envelope accompanying this letter: "This was written in July 1927. We, Mrs. Roberts, Margaret and I were getting ready to sail for Europe the latter part of that summer but I came down with a severe hemorrhage from stomach ulcer which cancelled our trip – J M R" (*Harvard, bMS Am 1883.2 [294]*).

40

MRS. ROBERTS'S FOLLOWING LETTER is a moving document, extolling her loyalty and love for "the boss." Her deep devotion helps explain her reaction to Wolfe's portrait of John Dorsey Leonard in *Look Homeward, Angel.*

AL, 2 pp., Harvard, bMS Am 1883.1 (545)

129 Linden Avenue
Asheville, N.C.
September 21, 1927.

My dear Tom Wolfe,

I see by the paper that you are to land in New York this week. You are a heathen Chinee. That marvelously lengthy letter you promised to write on shipboard[1] is still in embryo, no doubt, and very likely you did not get mine.

Anyway, your conscience should so sting you that you will surely as soon as possible write a 40-pounder. I <u>must</u> know what you are doing in your head (and in your heart?) How is the novel coming on? What is the fate of your play?

What of your trip? Surely you must know how keen I am to know all of these things. So as soon as you get your classes to sweating over themes, do please steal a little time to tell me everything I need to know.

I do not know whether Mabel had heard of our latest trouble. If she had, you already know that Mr. Roberts had another hemorrhage of the stomach on August 6. It was a terrible shock because he was looking better than in years, and it came almost without warning. We were horribly uneasy for several days until all discharge could be checked. Now for several weeks he has been slowly improving and now sits around the house but has not been out.

We had everything ready to sail September 3, and hoped to see you before you sailed for home. How all our fortunes do lie in the laps of the gods! I suppose going abroad was too golden a dream for such as we anyway. But we are so happy to see the boss (ever tho slowly) getting back to a semblance of his former state that nothing else matters. He has been to me sun, moon and stars and I can't conceive of having to do without him.

[Written on left margin, p. 2]
Now, Tom, if you have a heart, show it by writing.

[On right margin next to "Mr. Roberts had another hemorrhage of the stomach on August 6"]
We go back to Baltimore Sept. 29

[Unsigned]

1. If completed, this letter has not been located. The fragment (letter 38) written shortly before boarding the *George Washington* may have been the first part of the "enormous Letter" Wolfe describes in letter 39.

41

ALS, 12 pp., Harvard, bMS Am 1883.2 (294)
September 25, 1927   *Harvard Club letterhead*

<u>Monday</u>
Sept 25

Dear Mrs Roberts: – I came back to New York Sunday a week ago; I have already started my work at N. Y. U. They have given me a very good schedule: all my work with two hours exception comes in the evening from 6:30–9:00 – I work only Mon, Tues, Wed, Thurs, and am through from Thurs evening until the following Monday at 6:30. In this way I hope to get some writing done. My book is about done; I am trying to engage a good typist[1] now to type it I came back from a magnificent summer, mainly in Germany and Austria (Bury me in Vienna!), and I am in splendid health and spirits for a year's work. My flesh and my blood is haunted with the ghosts of implausible food and wine, my eyes are stored with the images of a thousand deathless forms of beauty – books, pictures, men and cities – such glories as I did not know existed

I am saddened to hear of Mr Roberts' sickness, of the postponement (temporary, I hope) of your voyage God speed his recovery: give him my affectionate regards at once. You ask me to write you at Baltimore, but you do not give an address. Perhaps this will reach you before you go. Can you not, after his treatment, both come to New York for a day or two? I assure you that one may rest here quietly – much more it seems to me, than in many sweller places. I can not come to see you now – but I could watch over you if you came here.

Mabel and Ralph[2] have been here several days – they are going home, they say, tomorrow, although Mabel no longer seems to know from one minute to another what she wants to do. She looks much better since she came, but I have been horribly surprised at her condition. She has gone to pieces – her mind leaps from point to point without connection, she talks incessantly, hysterically, her eyes are dull and watery, her skin blotched and lumpy. She speaks vaguely of bad kidneys, bad heart, bad nerves, bad blood; she is inclined to blame her collapse on services to others – her sisters' children, her mother, her relatives – and so on, but Hell and Heaven, as usual, and all the Kingdom of God, lie probably within her, as within us all. Most of us, in my family, brought into the world a terrible inheritance of taut nerves, passionate intensity, and morbid introversion – but, used properly, these things should serve us well; surrendered to, they work our ruin. And it is fatal to seek Nirvana by drowning ourselves in the bottle. She was, and is, a person of great quality – the waste of life everywhere about me is apalling. For her husband, too, I have a feeling of great respect. He is perhaps not a great person, or a very intelligent one, but he has acted magnificently towards her. They have no children – that, I think, may be almost all the trouble. He looks sad and old. I have done all I could do to make their stay here happier – we have eaten and talked together, and they have seen the finest of my friends. I hope their minds have not been so far tainted by the universal American corruption – reverence for money – that they have been unable to appreciate the quality of a very simple, very great, very beautiful person.

I am simply stabbed with horror when I see the poison of the American villages shot through the veins of really good people.

I must go to class now[3] Write me as soon as you can You are my friend – the friend of my spirit, and much wiser than I am. Keep locked in your heart any of my wild words – however true! – that might later cause me pain.

God bless you all. I think I shall come through. It has taken me 26 years to escape, but I shall yet come to Carcassonne.[4]

Tom

Three publishers are going to read my book – as well as Ernest Boyd[5] — a well known critic and writer.

1. Eventually Wolfe hired former student Abe Smith to type "O Lost." Smith is portrayed as Abe Jones in *Of Time and the River*.

"I love Mabel for her big, golden heart" (Mabel Wolfe Wheaton). By permission of the North Carolina Collection, University of North Carolina Library at Chapel Hill, and Eugene H. Winick, Administrator C.T.A., Estate of Thomas Wolfe

2. Mabel and her husband, Ralph Harris Wheaton (1881–1973). Wheaton is Hugh T. Barton in *Look Homeward, Angel.* Despite an often turbulent marriage, the Wheatons remained married for forty-two years, until Mabel's death.

3. Wolfe was still teaching at New York University.

4. Figurative reference to Carcassonne, "The Medieval City." Located in the French Pyrenees, it is the largest fortified city in Europe still in existence.

5. Ernest Boyd did not find time to read the manuscript now titled "O Lost" and turned it over to his wife, Madeleine, who was starting a literary agency at this time. After reading one-third of the mammoth novel, she jumped to her feet, shouting: "A genius, I have discovered a genius!" (Madeleine Boyd, *Thomas Wolfe: The Discovery of a Genius,* ed. Aldo P. Magi [N.p.: Thomas Wolfe Society, 1981], 3). Wolfe caricatured Ernest Boyd in "Mr. Malone" (*New Yorker,* May 29, 1937).

42

AL. 2 pp., Harvard, bMS Am 1883.1 (545)

Feb. 28, 1928.

My dear Tom, As this is the last day of leap-year, I make bold to try one more time to persuade you to let us know if you still live and what is uppermost with you. How about THAT BOOK? Don't you know that I am consumed with the desire of knowing if it is being published. Do write everything. I suppose you think I am too old-fashioned to keep up with your meteoric flight into the realm of ideas. That is probably true, but tho my head fails to function in your rapid transit, never forget that my heart will always be as open to understanding and appreciating yours as it was when you were eleven.

Your character and your achievements, your difficulties and your overcomings are a part of my daily thoughts; I long for your spiritual and intellectual success (I don't mean that. These you have already achieved. I mean for the world's recognition of them.)

Tom, in your letter of last fall, you dropped a painful hint about Mabel (This was written when she & Ralph were up there.) Did you mean <u>what it seemed to me to mean</u>[1]? I wish you could come home Easter. It might be well worth your while. Write to me and if you desire, I will speak more plainly. I love Mabel for her big, golden heart.

[On left margin]
    What about that Book!

1. According to Mabel's niece Virginia Gambrell Wilder, Mabel's trouble hinted at here may have been an alcoholic or nervous breakdown (Virginia Gambrell Wilder to Ted Mitchell, telephone interview, April 23, 1996).

43

ALS, 7 pp., Harvard, bMS Am 1883.2 (294)
Harvard Club letterhead

Friday April 6 <u>1928</u>

Dear Mrs Roberts: —

Forgive this long silence: I finished my book and sent it to a publisher[1] for reading ten days ago. This means nothing more than it will get read, and that I will get an answer in another three weeks. I am completely, utterly exhausted – the last twenty pages were agony – but I have a feeling of enormous relief to know that it's done. I have done a rashly experimental thing – the publishing firm said it's the longest mss. they've had since <u>An American Tragedy</u>[2] – but, like Martin Luther, I couldn't do otherwise. Hereafter I'll keep more within prescribed limits.

The Dean of Washington Square College[3] (N.Y.U.), who is a young man, a millionaire, an idealist, and a sensitive romantic person, has just finished reading it. He wrote me a magnificently honest letter about it: he was terribly shocked at the pain, the terror, the ugliness, and the waste of human life in the book – he thought the people rose to nobility and beauty only at the end (in this he is terribly wrong!) But he said the book was unique in English and American literature, that if it is published it must be published without changing a word, and that he felt he had lived with the people in it for years.

Whether any publisher can be found who is willing to take the chance, I don't know But, for good or bad, I'm going the whole distance now

I shall not be back at N. Y. U. next Fall. They have been splendid – offered me raise, and finally told me the latch string was out at any time – that I could come back any time I needed the job.

If the book doesn't go, I'm going to begin hack writing – stories, articles, advertising – anything I can get. Anything is right, I feel, that will take me closer to the heart of my desire. I shall probably go abroad again this summer – where or for how long I can't say. Again, a great deal depends on the book.

But I shall probably see you all for a few days at the end of May.[4]

After the sap has risen in me a little more, I'll write you a longer and better letter. This is just a filler-in.

Let me hear from you when you have time. Give my love to all the family. And tell me something about mine. I write, but I don't always get answers.

How is Asheville? Still, I hope, repentant.

Tom.

1. The young firm of Boni and Liveright published Sherwood Anderson, Ernest Hemingway, and Theodore Dreiser. The firm declined Wolfe's manuscript because of its great length. Wolfe burlesqued Boni and Liveright as Rawing and Wright in *The Web and the Rock* (New York: Harper and Brothers, 1939), 488–96.

2. *An American Tragedy* (1925) by Theodore Dreiser (1871–1945).

3. Dean James Buell Munn.

4. Before Wolfe left to visit Asheville, he wrote his mother on June 7, 1928: "I think I'll come home for a few days—I'll drop in unexpectedly, perhaps, the first chance I have to come down—perhaps at the end of this week or beginning of next. Don't talk to me of staying at home and *resting.* There's no rest for me there—I've tried it before. I want to be alone for a time where no one can get at me. I want to see you all very much, but I'm not coming to see the whole damned town, including relatives. So don't try to drag me around or tell me I 'ought to go see' any one. I'll make *one* visit, and no more—to Mrs Roberts" (Wolfe, *Letters of Thomas Wolfe to His Mother,* 131–32).

44

ALS, 12 pp., Harvard, bMS Am 1883.1 (545)
July 3, 1928   *The Sebren Music Co., Inc. / "Ye Old Book Shop" letterhead*[1]

July 3.

My dear Tom Wolfe,

I wonder if I have waited one day too late. Somehow time flip-flops until keeping up with it calls for a flapper. I suppose that is why a worry of that type have evolved or devolved. Blessed boy, your visit is still stirring us. I have just reread Ibsen's "The Lady of the Sea," (a lá Ibsen centenary celebration which I am holding with myself) and I was struck with his calling the village of the play a "carp-pond." Now, you came as a Leviathan unto our little carp-pond and slashed the waters mightily and delightfully. "And still the wonder grew that one small head could carry all he knew."[2] Now, it is not so much a wonder to me that your head has carried so much, but that your heart and soul have digested so marvellously the huge masses that you have stuffed into that head. Rather, it is not simply a digestion but a transformation. All things with you have suffered a sea-change, and my faith never wavers. You will pass to us the rich fruit. It may not come this day, this month, this year, but Tom Wolfe's star is in the ascendent.

I enjoyed you more this time <u>this year</u> than ever before and have felt more the having you go.[3]

I am sorry that you must give up your plan of going to Vienna because your face and heart seemed so set for the life there, but perhaps the rich Americans will clear out and leave you a free (and cheap) field.

I am keenly anxious for that new novel to be born. I was much interested in Margaret's reaction to the sketch you gave us of how you meant to develop your idea. She is a simple, but not a silly, young girl, quite unsophisticated and yet rather unusual in her estimate of situations and people. She said: "Mother, I think even I (she has a decided inferiority complex) could understand the way Tom is going to make those characters play upon each other. It fascinates one to see how his mind works at such things." Well, it fascinates and awes her mother that a long-legged youngster, sprung from this "carp-pond," should be sailing into such tremendous seas.

Tom, I'm heartily ashamed of this paper, but I have at least one quality of genius, that of sometimes letting things get out before I realize, and so this is the last hope, in the way of paper. Ye old Bookshop, forced into bankruptcy, had an auction sale and we bought 130 books (some junky things in the lot), at 10½ ¢ a piece. I felt like a criminal but since they were going to somebody, we thought we might as well cheat the creditors as for the other fellow to do so. We are so happy to get a real book into the family that such an event as 130 at one time constitutes a celebration.

Well, you probably know as much about the political situation as we do. Al[4] of course swept the convention. There were the usual down-south fisticuff affairs – five in all, I believe. Wex Malone's[5] father was the mighty man in one – succeeded in getting his knuckles wrapped by a policeman's billy. Old time Southern oratory is not so prevalent as in the old days, but the blood gets "het up" just as quickly. The leopard's spots!

The boss man will vote for Smith. I am not a Socialist, but if the ticket qualifies in this state, I think I shall vote for it. If there is any good at all in platforms – even a simple, trusting person such as I has come to regard them all as largely mere gestures, – but if any platform really means anything, I believe more in most of what the socialist stands for than for the others. The Democrats came out squarely against our nefarious dealings in Nicaurauga etc. All of this did my heart good. But as the Nation says, they might have saved all the money and the heat and strain, and have instead let the usual small group meet in a hotel in N.Y. and quietly make their checkerboard moves until all was accomplished as they desired. I was born absolutely without a trace of cynicism in my makeup and I ache to have to feel any, but there seems to be nothing else to feel about our presidential conventions. We had a letter from Buddie just before Smith's nomination in which he detailed a good deal of underground news which the newspapers had, and were not supposed to publish. It was interesting. Tom, when I look at you and see your height and breadth, physically and mentally, I ache about Munsey. In his own field, he has great ability, very great ability, and I have faith to believe that he will go high, but how he is to do it without a physical break I don't know. As you told him in that wonderful letter which you wrote him at the time of marriage, now should be the time for his freedom.[6] He is brilliant, and I think his financial value ($60 a week) is some evidence of his mental ability. But I suppose it is just as wise to butt one's brains out against a stone wall as to grieve over so inevitable a thing. But the sight of you always floods my heart with such thoughts. Do thoughts get into your heart?

I remember your playful disgust at the way Mrs. Pettus praised you to your face – blarney-stone kissing, you seemed to regard it. Now, I can't see your face, and besides, I think I have a sort of right to say what I please about you, and you know I never have been far enough from my provincial rut to kiss the blarney-stone. So, please submit to my saying that I think I have never seen any face so added to by spiritual beauty as yours has been in the past two years.

That's an awkward sentence but I think you know what I mean. I have watched you intently, from your oratory in the days of the "Gettysburg Address" until your last day here. All along there has been a sure and rarely beautiful development, as the mind and spirit showed through the eyes and moulded the features, but in the past two years, a miracle has been performed, and your face, especially the eyes, has written the record. Lord bless you, boy, we love you, have faith in you, and know that all things must be well with you until you can take possession in full of your heritage. The publishers may be slow. They must hear the clink of the guinea, for which they cannot be blamed, but our Wolfe Caesar has fed on meat that had brought him to huge stature in mind and body, and both the publisher and the cook will before long awake to this fact and will realize that they must, the one by furnishing the printer's ink, and the other by "huge roasts of beef," keep the brute going. In your case, "Feed the brute," body and mind, must be the slogan of cook and publisher. As for me, I think I really learned how much you can stoke away and when you come again, I promise to do a first-class stoking job. We eat so comparatively little and so simply that I haven't thus far been able to realize the hugeness of the task, but don't lose faith. Come back to us again as soon as possible, and you shall have a baked pig[7] with an apple in its mouth, and all the accessories.

Now, as to the N.Y. trip, it looks very much as if we may go. Margaret has been accepted at Goucher, and if our plans carry, we will take her up in the car. If we get so close to N.Y. as that, it would be criminal for us not to go on.

Yet, not knowing in what condition Mr. Roberts will be in, we fear to say definitely. He has had a very painful and discouraging spell with his stomach since you left. Would it be possible for you to hold the opportunity open to us for a few weeks until we can see how he does? Being there would make our trip much easier and more delightful. Besides it would be quite a saving for us. We have no scruples in accepting your offer since you are good enough to make it, if you can arrange it so as not to inconvenience the other part-occupant or the old nurse.[8]

I think we can tell in about three weeks whether Mr. Roberts can risk the trip.[9]

Suppose I write you a little later.

I haven't seen any of your people since you left. I have meant to go see Mabel, but you know what a certain road is paved with. She does seems to be in so much better spirits this summer and I hope that now she may go forward in a calmer way. You are no ordinary family, but only you have found an outlet.

Mr. Roberts is starting to town and this letter must go. There is nothing in it but expenditure of ink that justifies a special delivery stamp, but be good enough to overlook the hasty scrawling and the flatness, and remember only that back here in Henderson's Desert is a family that follows your development with eagerness and joy – proud that they are privledged to follow the eagle's flight. That may seem grandiloquent talk, but it's gospel-true. You are an eagle, and don't forget now and then to let us have a word now and then as to the eagle's track.

Your friend,

Margaret R.

1. The return address on the envelope is 129 Linden Avenue, Asheville.

2. Describes schoolteacher in Oliver Goldsmith's *The Deserted Village.*

3. Describing this visit in Asheville with Mrs. Roberts to his mother, Wolfe wrote on June 25, 1928: "I should like to tell you more about myself, but during the last few years, I have discovered the value of silence. And I find that I can no longer chase around the neighborhood blabbing out the things I feel deepest. An insane desire to gossip and tattle comes from a lack of anything worth while in our lives: when we are bored by ourselves we try to live on the experience of other people. That is the thing I noticed about Asheville this last time. Everyone is touched with this disease a little— to my great surprise I discovered traces of it in my good friend, Mrs Roberts, and it made me cautious" (Wolfe, *Letters of Thomas Wolfe to His Mother,* 134). During this visit Wolfe invited the Robertses to stay in the apartment at 263 West Eleventh Street where he shared space with Aline Bernstein. (Although Bernstein lived with her family at 333 West Seventy-seventh Street, she used the Eleventh Street apartment for her theatrical design workshop.) However, once in Europe, Wolfe warned Bernstein not to allow Mrs. Roberts to examine the manuscript of "O Lost" that Mrs. Bernstein's old nurse, Margaret Stott, had in her keeping: "Stott has the mss. of one copy of my book. It is for you. Please do *not* let Mrs. R. see it" (Wolfe and Bernstein, *My Other Loneliness,* 203). The Robertses' visit to the Eleventh Street apartment never materialized: severe illness prevented Mr. Roberts from traveling anywhere (see letter 46). On November 2, 1928, Wolfe wrote Bernstein: "I am so disappointed that Mrs. Roberts never came" (Wolfe and Bernstein, *My Other Loneliness,* 286).

4. Al Smith.

5. Wex Malone, former student at North State School. His father was the manager of the Manor Hotel on Charlotte Street.

6. Wolfe's letter to John Munsey Roberts Jr. has not been located. However, Mrs. Roberts quotes from it in her memoir, calling them "Isolated sentences from a very personal letter dated Oct. 31, 1924" (26). The following quotes are all that survive of Wolfe's letter (punctuation and placement of paragraphs follows Mrs. Roberts's typescript):

Marriage means solidity, the institution of the family, conservatism, the total process of 'settling down.' And that is at it should be. But, my God, take your youth, your glorious, irreclaimable youth and go where the wind listeth, learn that the world is but your own big oyster, and be rebellious of everything established.

Only so, I think, by questing and asking and denying, by learning the glory of loneliness is it possible for one to reach the man within him. This is the Satanic period of our lives – Satan who was young, and the first great rebel – and only so, I think, do we reach ourselves and God at the end. . . . . .

I believe that I was older, <u>mentally</u> and <u>intuitively,</u> when I was sixteen than most men ever are – that's not modest but it's true – and I tell you I was a child then. Your beliefs, so firmly fixed, and so honestly arrived at, undergo, year by year, devastating changes; that which was eternal changes with the Autumn, that which was imperishable has died the death, and a new man emerges every season. . . . .

Love in our youth is not to seize and hold, but to pursue – it should be the will o'wisp forever eluding us, yet forever taking us to higher, better ground. . . . .

For a mother to <u>know</u> her son is, I solemnly assure you, one of the rarest and most beautiful things in the world. . . . . .

"All men," said Oscar Wilde, "kill the thing they love," but most of us do it, I think, not so much with a blow or a curse, as with the thoughtless and unwaiting impetuosity of youth and desire.

But memory is there, and enters at our hearts like a bitter steel, and stays forever,; and all our labor and our tears wash off no single stain; our deepest prayers avail us nothing then. I know that, too, from my heart.

7. Manuscript reads "pick."
8. Aline Bernstein and her former nurse, Margaret Stott. Stott was to look after Wolfe's apartment in his absence.
9. Mr. Roberts proved too unwell to drive his daughter to Goucher College; Margaret Rose made the journey by train.

45

Signed postcard of
"Paris..En Flanat";
July 19, 1928   *Harvard, bMS Am 1883.2 (294)*

Thursday July 19

Dear Mrs. Roberts: Thanks for the grand letter – I'll do my little best soon. Paris has been terribly hot – I'm getting out in day or two. Hope this finds the Professor feeling much better – Give my love to all – Tom

46

AL, 4 pp., Harvard, bMS Am 1883.1 (545)

129 Linden Avenue
Asheville, N.C.
September 8, 1928.

My dear Tom,

It is so good to see your hieroglyphics now and then. I wonder if you real-ize at all how much joy and mental stimulous we have had from you in all these years during which, in a crowded life, you have been willing to keep in touch with us. Anyway, always remember the hungry beggars who are happy to get any crumbs that may fall from your royal plate.

You seem not to have received my three cards and letter, the latter written to you while we were in Tennessee. To our keen disappointment, we have had to abandon the New York trip. While we were in Tennessee Mr. R. had a severe stomach attack (happy to say not a hemorraghe this time), from which he is just now recovering.

We dare not risk another hard trip now. Besides this, money is quite out of sight in Asheville, both literally and figuratively. Interest is so high that one would prefer to fall into the hands of the Isaacs of York. This makes us feel that we must borrow only the necessities.

Margaret Rose leaves for Goucher in two weeks. She is keenly eager and at the same time terribly afraid. We have been so close to her that both she and we feel as if the flesh is being sundered. In spite of the fact that she seems unusually young and unsophisticated, she is doing some thinking, enough, I think, to make college really mean something to her.

I saw Mabel for a few minutes last week, brought her home from town. You would be happy to see her so wonderfully improved, well and happy-looking. Your mother I have not seen. At an evening party recently a stranger woman said to the hostess: "Really, is he her son?" speaking of Fred and Mabel. Mabel says Fred has not failed to make the most of such a huge "guying" opportunity.

Tom, if you are in Paris again, won't you, if not too inconvenient, go to the Louvre, and buy two pictures, (photographs) of the head of Voltaire, the origi-nal being a head carved from wood. They are cheap, perhaps 25¢ or 50¢. I recently saw one and think no photograph can be so humanly vivid as this one is. You feel as if the man's eyes follow you. I don't want you to inconvenience yourself, but if you <u>are</u> <u>at</u> the Louvre I really am anxious for two of them. I will send you the money for them as soon as you come back. I have no assurance that this will reach you, or I should send it now.

Poor old Asheville sits by the river of Babylon and the many-stringed boom harps are dangling from very weeping willows. It seems that after sliding down here with more or less rapidity for these many months, she had at last broken her bones at the bottom. It seems certain that there will be much discomfort here this winter and among the really poor, actual distress.[1]

Mabel told Mr. Roberts that somebody stole money from your mother's room, something between two and three hundred dollars. Some more hard luck.

I am curious to know what you will do – go back to teaching or join The Great Advertiser. Anyway, let us have all the news about you – and <u>you</u> means also play, novels old and new, anything and everything.

I know it would be most delightful to meet Mrs. Bernstein, only I should be so awed by so gifted a lady that I would crawl deep down into myself and never dare to come out. It would be a human country mouse meeting the town mouse. My life is so circumscribed that my natural-born inferiority complex is in the saddle with me.

But with all our being circumscribed, Mr. R and I have a happy faculty of striking upon all sorts of delightful little experiences in the way of meeting human beings unexpectedly interesting in out-of-the-way places. It's a thing that adds greatly to the zest of living, and makes you realize that the world is not all Mencken's Boobery,[2] even tho these people could by no means qualify as Intellectuals. We had one such experience this afternoon <u>away</u> out in the country.[3] I'm always happening upon bits of delicious human nature that a writer could use to marvelous advantage.

Wee Cocke has won some new and great honors at Oxford. In case you see him, salute him with a holy kiss from the Roberts family. Our friends in Europe are much scattered. Ludwig is in Heidelberg, Milam in Slavokia, and Everett in Persia, and you, the Wandering Jew. The political pot boils, eye of newt and toe of frog![4] Don't forget us altogether and write a line whenever you can find time. You know how much you mean to me and all of us.

[Unsigned]

1. For a description of Asheville's impending ruin, see letter 66, note 3.

2. H. L. Mencken (1880–1956), American editor, essayist, and social critic, coined "booboisie" to describe contemptuously a segment of the general public he regarded as fools.

3. "One day Mother and Daddy were driving way out in the country and met a country man, and when they got on the subject of money, he told them, 'There's no use saving money. There's no pockets in shrouds'" (Margaret Rose Roberts to Ted Mitchell, interview, November 24, 1996). Wolfe adopts this comment in *Look Homeward,*

January 1929 99

Angel, 615: "there are no pockets in shrouds and we only need six feet of earth to bury us in the end."

4. *Macbeth* 4.1.14.

47

*Signed postcard of Napoli—Parco
Grifeo—Hotel Bertolini; Harvard,*
December 19, 1928   *bMS Am 1883.2 (294)*

Naples Dec 19

Dear Mrs Roberts – I have no card that can show you how beautiful – and how dirty – Naples is I'm coming home in a day or two with very gaudy – (and <u>bloody</u>)[1] – histories. Love to the Boss. God bless you all Christians and heathen – Tom

1. Injuries inflicted upon Wolfe during a drunken brawl at the Oktoberfest in Munich. See letter 49.

48

MRS. ROBERTS'S LETTER, written upon hearing that *Look Homeward, Angel* had been accepted for publication by Scribner's, must be measured against her reaction to the novel after reading it. Requesting that Wolfe allow her to nominate him for Asheville's civic award, she obviously had little knowledge of the novel's contents prior to its publication.

Ca. early January 1929   *ALS, 4 pp., Harvard, bMS Am 1883.1 (545)*

My dear Tom Wolfe,

We are walking on the clouds this morning. Fred telephoned us last night about the News, and I've been so excited since that I can scarcely keep my mind on anything but you and your <u>Deed.</u> Tom, Tom, it's true at last. Of course it had to come. That fact was established within you when you were measured for this present world. Good Lord, Boy. My heart thrills so that I can't think, and Mr. R. as sick as he has been, seemed gay and elastic. It had to come, but I never dared to hope that it could come to you <u>so young.</u> Why, you are only a short remove from that long-legged kid who moved me with his giving of the "Gettysburg Address." I think Emma asked me if I didn't think that speech too much for such a kid, and I said, "Nothing is too much for Tom." Cutting weeds was a great strain on you in those days, but cutting into ideas, your meat and drink. You were born that way.

You will have to release us from the bond of secrecy about the book at an early date, or I shall explode. I just want to shout it from the house-tops. So don't be <u>too</u> slow.

There seemed a hole in Christmas when we didn't get a card from you, – the first missing ever. But it came later, bearing the imprint of your character and tastes. Lord bless you, Boy, you have pushed open the gates. Nothing now can prevail against you.

Now, don't fly off the handle before you catch my point. I know you hate the "booster" spirit, Rotarianism and all its kin. But ———. Listen and don't champ the bits until you hear me. Asheville now has an opportunity to express herself for something besides the glories of commercialism and king Boosters. If possible, will you give her an opportunity to do so. She may fail to rise to the occasion, but <u>will</u> <u>you</u> cast the pearl before her, and let her have the opportunity of proving herself possessed of intellectual ideals. Now, this is the situation. There is a Civic award – Cup being presented by the Times to the citizen who has rendered the finest service to Asheville this past year.

The nominations must be made before the 16th. If your publisher would consent to the matters being made known, would you consent to your name being presented. It is so near to time that may be too late. If the book were already published! It's giving Asheville an opportunity to show her quality. Almost all of the nominations so far have been based on material grounds – one or two not. Write at once if you would consider it.

Now, Tom, tears of joy were in my eyes last night. Tears of entreaty are in my heart this morning. Don't be too too. You know I'm one of the last persons in the world to ask you to make an unworthy concession in order to please a publisher, but <u>please, please,</u> don't be too unyielding as to changes they want made. Concede as far as your artist's conscience will let you. Get the book published, as a wedge into the tough frame of this old world. I should think the stars would just be swarming about you so that they bump into each other, and knock off great swirls of stardust.

This is the last sheet of paper I possess, but you won't see the dirt on it. I have written three times and a P-card to the Harvard Club. Doubt if any reached you, but I think you know one thing – that our love and thoughts will always follow you to the uttermost parts of the earth.

Mr. R. had another hemorrage on Monday week before Christmas day. It's been a blow, but somehow we have to withstand. He is doing well, and sends you congratulations, every letter a capital.

Good-bye, with great love

Margaret R. ———

49

ON JANUARY 9, 1929, Wolfe negotiated a contract with Charles Scribner's Sons to publish "O Lost." Three days later he wrote a sixty-five-page letter to Mrs. Roberts thanking her for her buoyant letter of early January. Wolfe gave a full account of the events leading to the acceptance and publication of *Look Homeward, Angel* and described his latest adventures in Europe.

ALS,[1] 65 pp., Harvard, bMS Am 1883.2 (294)
Harvard Club letterhead

[On upper left margin]
This is a horribly long letter – I'm as limp as a rag – I pity the people who have to read it and I pity the poor devil who wrote it.

Saturday, Jan 12, 1929

Dear Mrs Roberts: Everything you write has power to touch and move me and excite me – my heart beats faster when I see your writing on a piece of paper, and I read what you write me over and over again, exultant and happy over every word of praise you heap upon me. Nothing you have ever written me has so stirred me as your letter which I got today – I have mounted from one happiness to another during this past week since I came back from Europe, and the knowledge that you are now so generously sharing with me my joy and hope just about sends the thermometer up to the boiling point. For several days now I have felt like that man in one of Leacock's[2] novels who "sprang upon his horse and rode madly off in all directions." I have literally been like that – at times I have not known what to do with myself – I would sit in the club here stupidly, staring at the publisher's glorious letter of acceptance; I would rush out and walk eighty blocks up Fifth Avenue through all the brisk elegant crowd of late afternoon. I am gradually beginning to feel ground again, and it is occurring to me that the only thing to do is to get to work again. I have the contract in my inner breast pocket, ready to be signed, and a check for $450 pinned to it, $50 having already been paid to my literary agent, Mrs Ernest Boyd[3] as her 10% share. There is literally no reason why I should walk around New York with these documents on my person, but in a busy crowd I will sometimes take them out, gaze tenderly at them, and kiss them passionately. Scribners have already signed the contract – I am to sign it Monday, but, with their customary fairness, they have advised me to show it to a lawyer before I sign it – I am therefore going with Mrs Boyd on Monday to see Mr Melville Cane, a lawyer, a poet, a member of Harcourt, Brace, and Co, and the finest attorney on theatrical and publishing contracts in America.

I have met him once, he read part of my book, and he has since been my friend and well-wisher. He told the person who sent me to him some time ago[4] that I represented what he had wanted to be in his own life, that I was one of the most remarkable people he had ever met. And when he was told yesterday that I had sold my book he was delighted. I am filled at the moment with so much tenderness towards the whole world that my agent, Mrs Boyd, is worried – she is a Frenchwoman, hard and practical, and she does not want me to get too soft and trusting in my business relations I wrote Scribner's a letter of acceptance[5] in which I could not hold myself in – I spoke of my joy and hope, and my affection and loyalty towards the publishers who had treated me so well, and my hope that this would mark the beginning of a long and happy association which they would have no cause to regret. In reply I got a charming letter in which they told me I would never have to complain of the interest and respect they have for my work. Mrs Boyd herself was almost as happy as I was – although she is agent for almost every important French author in America, and publishing and acceptances are the usual thing for her – she said the thing was a great triumph for her as well, as Scribners consider me "a find" and are giving her credit for it. It is all very funny and moving – seven months ago when she got the book and read parts of it, she got interested – it was too long (she said), but there were fine things in it, she thought someone might be interested, and so on. Now I am a "genius" – she is already sorry for poor fellows like Dreiser and Anderson – she told the publishers that "this boy has everything they have in addition to education, background, (etc, etc) "Of course, poor fellows," she said, "it's not their fault – they never had the opportunity"– and so on, and so on. Also, she pictures the other publishers as tearing their hair, gnashing their teeth, and wailing because they are not publishing the book. She gave it to one or two to read – they all said it had fine things in it, but was too long, they must think about it, etc. – and meanwhile (says she) Scribners got it She said she was talking to one of them (Jonathan Cape, his name is) a week ago – he said at once "Where is your genius, and when can I see him?" – She told him Scribners had it, and (groaning with grief, no doubt) he begged her to let him have first chance at the next one. We must salt all this down – her Gallic impetuosity, I mean – and I've got to come to earth and begin work. I've had to tell several people, and everyone is almost as glad as I am – the university people are throwing a job at my head – I can stop in June, if I want, they say. This is absurd. Of what earthly use would I be to them for only a half year – but they will give me more money, I think, than last year, fewer hours, (8 or 10) and almost no paper work. Now that this thing has happened, I feel kinder toward teaching than ever – of course, my $450 will not last forever, and even if the book goes well I must wait until 6 months after its publication (so reads a regular clause in my contract) for my first statement, and every four months thereafter. The University people are genuinely friends and well wishers – the Dean,[6] a wealthy and fine young man (of 38 or 40) would give me a job at any time – but I think this rather increases my value to them – it is a big swarming place, fond of advertising. The people at Scribners want me to set to work on revision at once, but they told me they thought I would have to find work later – no one knows how many copies the book will sell, of course, and besides, I must wait 8 or 10 months after publication for my first money (if there is any. But perish that thought) Mrs Boyd says the contract is fair, regular, and generous – giving an advance of $500 on a first book is unusual – of course that $500 comes out later from my first royalties. The contract offers me 10% of the retail price of the book up to the first 2000 copies; after that 15%. As the book is a very long one, it will have to sell, I think, for $2.50 or $3.00. You can estimate from this what it is possible to make – but for the Lord's sake, don't. This is a fascinating weakness I have succumbed to and everything is too uncertain. There are also clauses covering foreign translation and publication – and publication in any other than book form (that means serial and movies, I suppose, but that won't happen to me on this book) – but if it does, the publisher and author split the profits. Mrs Ernest Boyd is also recognized as my agent and business representative and all checks are payable to her. This may make my thrifty friends squirm – she also gets 10% of all my profits (I hope, naturally, her share is at least $100,000) – but its the best arrangement. How hard she worked to bring this about I don't know – nevertheless she did it, and I'll pay the 10% cheerfully – that's the regular agents' rate. Also, I think it is just as well that I am managed by a practical person who knows a little business. Although it is a business matter, and I ought not to get sentimental, I can't help having a warm spot in my heart for the old girl who brought it about. I might have done it by myself sooner or later, but she certainly helped enormously at the present. Finally, I want to start and continue my life by being decent and loyal to those people who have stood by me – whether for business or personal reasons. If we muddy and cheapen the quality of our actual everyday life, the taint I believe, is bound to show, sooner or later, in what we create. Mrs Boyd is so happy that Scribners took it – she said I should be very proud of that – she said they were the most careful and exacting publishers in America – others publish 50 or a 100 novels a year, but Scribners only 10 or 12 – although they bring out many other books. They are also trying to get the younger writers – they now have Ring Lardner, Scott Fitzgerald, and

Hemingway (to say nothing of Wolfe) They were reading sections of my book, they told me, to Lardner and Hemingway a week before I got home – I'm afraid somewhat coarse and vulgar sections

Finally, I must tell you that the ten days since I got home on the Italian boat have been the most glorious I have ever known – They are like all the fantasies I had as a child of recognition and success – only more wonderful. That is why my vision of life is becoming stranger and more beautiful than I thought possible a few years ago – it is the fantasy, the miracle that really happens. For me at any rate. My life, with its beginnings, has been a strange and miraculous thing – I was a boy from the mountains, I came from a strange wild family, I went beyond the mountains and knew the state, I went beyond the state and knew the nation, and its greatest university, only a magic name to my childhood, I went to the greatest city and met strange and beautiful people, good, bad and ugly ones, I went beyond the seas alone and walked down the million streets of life – when I was hungry, penniless, anemic countesses, widows of broken down opera singers – all manner of strange folk – came to my aid. In a thousand places the miracle has happened to me. Because I was penniless and took one ship instead of another I met the great and beautiful friend[7] who has stood by me through all the torture, struggle, and madness of my nature for over three years, and who has been here to share my happiness these past ten days. That another person, to whom success and greater success is constant and habitual and should get such happiness and joy from my own modest beginning is only another of the miracles of life. Ten days ago I came home penniless, exhausted by my terrible and wonderful adventures in Europe, by all I had seen and learned, and with only the hated teaching – now became strangely pleasant, – or the advertising, before me. The day after New Year's – truly a New Year for me – it began: the publisher's demand over the telephone that I come immediately to his office, that first long conference, as I sat there wild, excited, and trembling as it finally dawned on me that someone was at last definitely interested, the instructions to go away, and think over what had been said two or three days, the second conference, when I was told definitely they had decided to take it, the formal letter of acceptance, with the terms of the contract, and finally the contract itself, and the sight of the blessed check. It not this too a miracle? – to have happened to a penniless unhappy fellow in ten days? Are a child's dreams better than this? Mrs Boyd, trying to hold me down a bit, said that the time would soon come when all this would bore me, when even notices and press clippings would mean so little to me that I would not glance at them – so, she says, does her husband, a well known critic and writer, feel and act. But isn't it glorious that this should have happened to me when I was still young and rap-turous enough to be thrilled by it? It may never come again, but I've had the magic — what Euripides calls "the apple tree, the singing, and the gold"

Of my voyage in Europe this time, of all that happened to me this time, and of how all this began I can do no more here than to give you a summary: of my adventures on the ship, of my wanderings in France and Belgium and Germany, of all the books and pictures I saw and bought, of my new book,[8] now one third written, of my stay in Munich and the strange and terrible adventure at The Oktoberfest (with all its strange and beautiful aftermath) – how, insane with the brooding inversions of my own temper, disappointed and sick at heart because of the failure of acceptance of my book, lost to every-one who cared for me – not even leaving an address – sick with a thousand diseases of the spirit I fell foul of four Germans at the Oktoberfest and, no longer caring whether I killed or got killed, had a terrible and bloody fight in mud, darkness, and pouring rain, in which, although my scalp had been laid open by a blow from a stone beer mug, and my nose broken, I was too mad and wild to know or care if I was hurt or not – and became conscious only after the other people had been knocked senseless or fled and I had been choked unconscious, the one who remained, while his poor wife, screamed, fell on my back, and clawed my face to pieces to make me loosen my grip on his throat. Only then did I became conscious of the shouts and cries of the people around me, only then did I know that what choked and blinded me filling my eyes and nostrils was not rain, but blood; – then while I searched stupidly about in the mud for my hat which had been lost, all the people cried and screamed "A Surgeon! A Surgeon! Go For a Surgeon," and the police came and took me into custody, taking me immediately to the police surgeons and dressing my wounds. Of the beautiful and moving aftermath of this terrible and brutal affair, in which for the first time I went to the bottom of my soul, and saw how much power for bad and insanity lies in all of us, crying out inside me not because of my body's loss, but because of my soul's waste and loss, and the lovely people I had left so far behind me – I can tell you little of all this here. But it makes a strange and moving story[9] – the appearance next morning of this blind and battered horror, caked in blood and dirty bandages from head to waist at one of the greatest clinics in Germany, of the dry and prim Ameri-can medical-professor[10] working for 6 months in Munich with the greatest surgeon in Germany – how he came forward, took me in charge, took me to the greatest head surgeon in Germany[11] who made me come under his obser-vation and stay in his hospital 3 days, of how the nurses, innocent and sweet as children, nursed me and brought me food, of how they shaved my head, while the great man grunted German and went over my skull and more with his thick butcher's fingers, of how the American doctor came to see me twice a day, bringing books and fruit, and the enormous kindliness of his heart – of how finally he refused to accept a penny for his own services, backing away nervously, turning red, and saying in his prim professional way that he had a "son at home almost as tall as you are" – of how then he almost ran out of the room polishing his eyeglasses. Then, of how, still battered and blue, with a dueling students skull cap covering my bald head I went to Oberammergau, how one of my wounds broke open there, and I was nursed by the man who played Pilate (a doctor) and by Judas; and by a little old woman[12] there, – almost 80, whom I had known in Munich – almost as mad as I was, no husband any more, children dead, even the name of her village in America only a name she couldn't always remember – a vagabond at 78 around the world, hating the Germans she once loved, and loving only the Oberammergauers who had known her for forty years – she had written one book about them, and was at work on another – but she was afraid she was going to die and wanted me to promise to write it for her – when I refused to do this we had fallen out and she had left Munich in a temper at me. Now, all battered up, I was coming to see her again – she was the daughter of a Methodist minister, and despite her long life in Europe and the Orient she had never lost the stamp of it – she read insanely all the statistics concerning illegitimate children in Munich and Oberammergau, going almost insane when she discovered the guilt of her adored Passion Players Her treatment of me now was a mixture of old Methodist intolerance and "it serves you right" combined with love and tender mercy. Of how I left Oberammergau, of how she followed me up to Munich in a few days; of how the police almost drove me mad with their visits, questions, and inspections, of how the poor old thing became my accomplice, almost driving me mad with her advice and suspicions, seeing a policeman looking for me behind every bush, and rushing over to warn me at my pension at all hours of day and night, of how finally she saw the great Zeppelin over Munich early one morning and came to pull me out of bed twittering with excitement; of how from this time on she lived only for the Zeppelin, staying in her cold pension nearly all day long with the radio phones clamped to her ears, her old eyes bright and mad as she listened to news of the flight to America – of how a night or – two later the pension people had tried to get me when I was at the theatre, and of how the old woman had died that night with the phones to her ears still, of how they got me next morning and went over and saw her there, and old Judas and his daughter Mary Magdalene who had known her for thirty years – they had come up that morning from

Oberammergau, they were weeping gently and softly, they were taking her back, according to her wish, to bury her there (she had said it to me a 100 times), of how I had asked if I should go with them, and they had looked into my wild and bloody eyes, at my swollen nose, seamed head, and gouged face, and shook their heads slowly[13.] Then of how I knew I must leave this place which had given me so much, – as much as I could hold at the time – and taken so much. My lungs were already raw with cold, I was coughing and full of fever – I felt a strange fatality in the place, as if I too must die if I stayed longer. So that afternoon I took the train for Saltzburg, drawing my breath in peace again only when I got over the Austrian border. Then four days in bed in Salzburg and on to Vienna. The first days in Vienna, still in a sort of stupor from all I had seen or felt – full of weariness and horror; then slowly I began to read, study, and observe again. Then, just before I went to Budapest, Mrs Boyd's first warning letter about the book I had forgotten – Scribner's was interested; I should write at once. Forgot about it, believed in promises and the book no more – went to Hungary, went out among the wild and savage people of the plains, Asiatics now as they were when they came 1200 years ago under Attila. Then back to Vienna again and there a letter from Scribners[14] – at last, it seemed, something really hopeful. This whole story – strange, wild, ugly and beautiful, I don't know what it means – but the drama and the struggle within me at this time was much more interesting than the purely physical things outside. What it means, I don't know, but to me it is strange and wonderful, and my next book, a short one, will probably be made from it.[15] I have never written home or to you about this before – telling the bare facts – because it takes too long, and tires me out to tell it – you must say nothing of this to anyone – I will put it all down someday in a book, together with much more strange and marvelous, so that who can read may see.

Getting to present matters the letter in Vienna 6 or 7 weeks ago was the first indication I had of what has happened – the Scribners – the Scribner letter was signed by one Maxwell Perkins whom I have since come to know as a fine and gentle person, full of wisdom. Mrs Boyd tells me to listen to him carefully – he is one of those quiet and powerful persons in the background; the sole and only excuse, she says, for Scott Fitzgerald having been successful as he is. In his letter he said he had read my book, and while he did not know whether any publisher could risk it as it is, he did know it was a very remarkable thing and no editor could fail to be excited by it (I didn't tell him one or two had failed) What he wanted to know, he said, was when Scribners could talk with me. I was excited and eager, and as usual too enthusiastic – I wrote him at once, saying briefly my nose was broken and my head scarred (which was beginning early with a stranger, of course) but that his words of praise filled me with hope and eagerness. Said I'd be home Christmas or New Year's. Followed 2 more weeks in Vienna, 3 in Italy, then home from Naples. Called him up morning after New Year's. He asked me if I had the letter sent to Harvard Club[16] and I said No – it had probably been sent abroad. He asked me to come to Scribners at once. I went up – in a few minutes I was taken to his office, where I found Mr Charles Scribner[17] (simply there, I think, to take a look at me, for he withdrew immediately saying he would leave us alone) Mr Perkins is not all "Perkinsy" – name sounds mid-western, but he is Harvard man, probably New England family, early forties, but looks younger, very elegant and gentle in dress and manner. He saw I was nervous and excited, spoke to me quietly, told me to take coat off and sit down. He began by asking certain general questions about book and people (these weren't important – he was simply feeling his way around, sizing me up, I suppose) Then he mentioned a certain short scene in the book, and in my eagerness and excitement I burst out "I know you can't print that! I'll take it out at once, Mr Perkins."

Take it out? he said. It's one of the greatest short stories I've ever read.[18] He said he had been reading it to Hemingway week before. Then he asked me if I could write a short introduction for it to explain people – he was sure Scribner's Magazine would take it; if they didn't someone else would. I said I would – I was at once elated and depressed – I thought now that this little bit was all they wanted of it. Then he began cautiously on the book. Of course, he said, he didn't know about its present form – somewhat incoherent and very long. When I saw now that he was really interested I burst out wildly saying that I would throw out this, that and the other – at every point he stopped me quickly saying "No, no – you must let that stay word for word – that scene's simply magnificent" It became apparent at once that these people were willing to go far farther than I had dared hope – that, in fact, they were afraid I would injure the book by doing too much to it. I saw now that Perkins had a great batch of notes in his hand and that on the desk was a great stack of handwritten paper – a complete summary of my whole enormous book.[19] I was so moved and touched to think that someone at length had thought enough of my work to sweat over it in this way that I almost wept – when I spoke to him of this he smiled and said everyone in the place had read it. Then he went over the book scene by scene – I found he was more familiar with the scenes and the names of characters than I was – I had not looked at the thing in over six months. For the first time in my life I was getting criticism I could really use – the scenes he wanted cut or changed were invariably the least essential and the least interesting – all the scenes that I had thought too coarse, vulgar,

Maxwell E. Perkins, "very elegant and gentle in dress and manner." Department of Rare Books and Special Collections, Princeton University Libraries

profane or obscene for publication he forbade me to touch save for a word or two – there was one as rough as anything in Elizabethan drama – when I spoke of this he said it was a masterpiece, and that he had been reading it to Hemingway He told me I must change a few words. He said the book was new and original, and because of its form could have no formal and orthodox unity, but that what unity it did have came from the strange wild, people – the family – it wrote about as seen through the eyes of a strange wild boy. These people, with relatives, friends, townspeople he said were "magnificent" – as real as any people he had ever read of. He wanted me to keep these people and the boy at all times foremost – other business, such as courses at state university, etc, to be shortened and subordinated. Said finally if I was hard up he thought Scribners would advance money. By this time I was wild with excitement – this really seemed something at last – in spite of his caution and restrained manner I saw now that Perkins really was excited about my book, and had said some tremendous things about it. He saw how wild I was; I told him I had to go out and think – he told me to take two or three days but before I left he went out and brought in another member of the firm, John Hall Wheelock,[20] who spoke gently and quietly – he is a poet – and said my book was one of the most interesting he had read for years. I then went out and tried to pull myself together. A few days later the second meeting – I brought notes along as to how I proposed to set to work, and so on. I agreed to deliver 100 pages of corrected mss, if possible, every week.[21] He listened, and then when I asked him if I could say something definite to a dear friend, smiled and said he thought so; that their minds were practically made up; that I should get to work immediately, and that I should have a letter from him in a few days. As I went prancing out I met Mr Wheelock, who took me by the hand and said, "I hope you have a good place to work in – you have a big job ahead" – I knew then that it was all magnificently true. I rushed out drunk with glory; in two days came the formal letter (I wired home then), and yesterday Mrs Boyd got the check and contract which I am now carrying in my pocket. God knows this letter has been long enough – but I can't tell you half or a tenth of it, or of what they said.

Mr Perkins said cautiously he did not know how the book would sell – he said it was something unknown and original to the readers, that he thought it would be a sensation with the critics, but that the rest is a gamble. But Mrs Boyd says that to print such a gigantic mss from a young unknown person is so unusual that Scribners would not do it unless they thought they had a good chance of getting their money back. Everyone is drowning me with adoring now the Dean at N.Y.U. begs me not to get "ruined" like Thornton Wilder (I wish they would ruin me like Wilder to the extent of two or three hundred thousand copies) – but what the Dean meant is not to spend all my time in Society. This makes me grin, too – you know how "social" I am. I should love it, of course, if the book were a howling success, but my idea of happiness would be to retire to my apartment and gloat on them, and to let no more than half a dozen people witness my gloating. But I think if I ever see man or woman in subway, elevated, or taxicab reading it I will track that person home to see who he is or what he does, even if it leads me to Yonkers. And Mr Perkins and Mr Wheelock warned me not to go too much with "that Algonquin Crowd" – the hotel Algonquin here is where most of the celebrities waste their time and admire one another's cleverness. This also makes me laugh. I am several million miles away from these mighty people, and at the present time want to get no closer. All the Theatre Guild people, whom I know through my dear friend, have called her up and sent congratulations

But now is the time for sanity. My debauch of happiness is over. I have made promises; I must get to work. I am only one of the thousands of people who write books every year. No one knows how this one will turn out. You must therefore say nothing to the Asheville people about it yet. In course of time, I suppose, Scribners will announce it in their advertisements. As for the Civic Cup business – I am afraid that's out of the question. For one thing, no one knows anything about my book at home – whether it's good, bad, or indifferent – if anything is said about it, it must be later, after its publication. For another thing – and this troubles me now that my joy is wearing down – this book dredges up from the inwards of people pain, terror, cruelty, lust, ugliness, as well, I think, as beauty, tenderness, mercy. There are places in it which make me writhe when I read them; there are others that seem to me to be fine and moving. I wrote this book in a white heat, simply and passionately, with no idea of being either ugly, obscene, tender, cruel, beautiful, or anything else – only of saying what I had to say because I had to. The only morality I had was in me; the only master I had was in me and, stronger than me. I went into myself more mercilessly than into anyone else – but I am afraid there is much in this book which will wound and anger people deeply – particularly those at home. Yet terrible as parts are, there is little bitterness in it. Scribners told me people would cry out against this, because people are unable to realize that that spirit which is sensitive to beauty is also sensitive to pain and ugliness. Yet all of this goes into the making of the book, and because of this Scribners have believed in it and are publishing it. I will soften all I can but I cannot take out all the sting – without lying to myself and destroying the book. For this reason we must wait and see. If the people of Asheville some day want to heap coals of fire on my head by giving me a cup, perhaps I shall fill it with my tears of penitence – but I doubt this will come for a long time. The people of Asheville, I fear, may not understand me after this book and may speak of me only with a curse – but someday, if I write other books, they will. And my God! What books I feel within me and what despair since my hand and strength can not keep up with all my heart has felt, my brain dreamed and thought.

I have spent an entire afternoon writing this to you – it is a volume, but now I have worked off my wild buoyancy and must get to work.

Please keep silence abut the cup business. You understand why, don't you?

God bless you for your letter, and forgive the great length of this one, so filled with my own affairs that I have not yet sent my love to Mr Roberts. Give it to him with all my heart and tell him I want no better news from home than that he is up and hale again. I have told you about my own business at such length because I believed you really wanted to hear it all, and because I am so happy to share it with you. But God bless you all, and bring you all health and happiness. If you see Scribners advertisement you can speak of course, but please use your excellent discretion

I shall write you a short letter when I am calmer, telling you about N. Y. U. plans, and how my work on book is coming.

Love to all.

     Tom

P.S. Whatever of this you think may interest my family pass on, but tell them also, for God's sake, to be discreet. It made me so happy to be able to wire them good news the other day. Now, let's all hope something comes of it.

Again, God bless you all.

Note: I can hardly read parts of this myself, but you have had to puzzle my hen scratching out before, and perhaps you can do it again. I wrote it in a great hurry, and I was very excited – but I hope you make it out.

It's not a letter – it's a pamphlet. Maybe I'll ask you to give it back some-day in order to see how foolish I felt.

1. Written on envelope in Mrs. Roberts's hand: "Mabel, don't you dare to lose this letter."

2. Stephen Butler Leacock (1869–1944), Canadian economist and humorist.

3. New York literary agent Madeleine Boyd (1885?–1972). Portrayed as Lulu Scudder in *You Can't Go Home Again.*

4. Aline Bernstein.

5. Wolfe wrote Maxwell E. Perkins on January 9, 1929: "Although this should be only a business letter I must tell you that I look forward with joy and hope to my connection with Scribner's. To-day—the day of your letter—is a very grand day in my life. I think of my relation to Scribner's thus far with affection and loyalty, and I hope this marks the beginning of a long association that they will not have cause to regret" (Wolfe and Perkins, *To Loot My Life Clean,* 8). Perkins (1884–1947) is the most ac-claimed book editor of the twentieth century. He joined Charles Scribner's Sons in 1910 as advertising manager. He was made an editor in 1914 and editor in chief and vice president in 1932. In addition to the writers Wolfe mentions in this letter, Mar-jorie Kinnan Rawlings, Zora Neale Hurston, Erskine Caldwell, and Caroline Gordon were also among Perkins's authors.

6. James Buell Munn.

7. Aline Bernstein.

8. After completing "O Lost" in March 1928, Wolfe began working on a new novel, "The River People." Planned as a more conventional, commercial book, it would be based on Wolfe's experiences in Boston, New York, and Rhinebeck and his

wandering in various European cities. Wolfe portrays himself as writer Oliver Weston, and the plot revolves around the social circle of a wealthy young painter (based on Olin Dows) and his love for an Austrian girl (Greta Hilb, whom Wolfe met aboard ship returning home from Europe). The contrived plot did not hold Wolfe's interest, although he continued working sporadically on it for most of 1928. His starting attempts have been preserved at Harvard University.

9. On September 30, 1928, Wolfe was injured in Munich during a drunken brawl with German revelers at the Oktoberfest. He was hospitalized until October 4, spending his twenty-eighth birthday as a patient. His nose was broken, and he suffered several deep head wounds as well as small facial wounds. He described his experiences in "Oktoberfest" (*Scribner's Magazine,* June 1937) and gave it a fuller treatment in *The Web and the Rock.*

10. The American doctor Eugene F. Du Bois, who was working as a volunteer in the clinic of Dr. Friedrich von Muller. Du Bois refused to accept remuneration for his services to Wolfe.

11. Dr. Geheimrat Lexer.

12. Louise Parks-Richards, widow of painter Samuel Richards, who had studied at the Royal Academy in Munich. Mrs. Richards had first seen the Oberammergau Passion Players in 1890 and had remained fascinated with them. Her book, *Oberammergau, Its Passion Play and Players: A 20th Century Pilgrimage to a Modern Jerusalem and a New Gethsemane* (Munich: Piloty and Loehle, 1910), is an account in English of the Passion Play, with personal reminiscences and photographs of the actors and actresses.

13. Wolfe also wrote a similar account of Mrs. Richards's death to Aline Bernstein (see Wolfe and Bernstein, *My Other Loneliness,* 235–36). After Bernstein questioned the story, Wolfe admitted that it was his own fabrication: "As you indicate in your letter, the part about the old lady dying is a lie. I was still too shaky when I told my lie to make it convincing" (Wolfe and Bernstein, *My Other Loneliness,* 276). Richard S. Kennedy speculated that Wolfe "apparently wanted to test his fictional technique on two people who knew him well" (Wolfe, *Notebooks of Thomas Wolfe,* 1:204n26).

14. Maxwell Perkins to Thomas Wolfe, October 22, 1928: "Mrs. Ernest Boyd left with us some weeks ago, the manuscript of your novel, 'O Lost.' I do not know whether it would be possible to work out a plan by which it might be worked into a form publishable by us, but I do know that setting the practical aspects of the matter aside, it is a very remarkable thing, and that no editor could read it without being excited by it, and filled with admiration by many passages in it, and sections of it" (Wolfe and Perkins, *To Loot My Life Clean,* 3).

15. Possibly the unfinished and abandoned novel "The River People."

16. Maxwell Perkins to Thomas Wolfe, December 7, 1928: "Thanks very much indeed for your letter of November 19th. I look forward impatiently to seeing you, and I hope you will call up as soon as you conveniently can after reading this. Then we can have a talk" (Wolfe and Perkins, *To Loot My Life Clean,* 5).

17. Charles Scribner III (1890–1952), president of Charles Scribner's Sons.

18. Chapter 19, *Look Homeward, Angel* (262–69). Adapted by Wolfe and published as "An Angel on the Porch," *Scribner's Magazine,* August 1929.

19. Maxwell Perkins's notes have been lost.

20. Scribner's editor John Hall Wheelock (1886–1978) was responsible for guiding all of Wolfe's Scribner's books through publication.

21. Wolfe's notes made in preparation for his second interview with Perkins on January 7 are published in Wolfe, *Notebooks of Thomas Wolfe,* 1:301–2.

50

Two MONTHS BEFORE THE PUBLICATION of *Look Homeward, Angel,* a modified chapter entitled "An Angel on the Porch" appeared in *Scribner's Magazine.* In a letter now lost, Mrs. Roberts wrote Wolfe, fearing the upcoming publication of *Look Homeward, Angel* would reveal more of his family's dark secrets. ("An Angel on the Porch" describes W. O. Gant's dealings with the notorious madam of a local house of prostitution.) For the first time, Mrs. Roberts fully recognized the overtly autobiographical nature of the book Wolfe had been describing in his letters for over three years.

Written in Wolfe's pocket notebook 11, the following is a draft of his August 11, 1929 letter (see 51) to Mrs. Roberts. Some of the material in the draft below duplicates material in Wolfe's preface to *Look Homeward, Angel.*

Ca. August 1929   Notebook draft, 4 pp., Harvard, bMS Am 1883 (1226)

I hope you may be wrong in thinking what I have written may distress members of my family or anyone else Certainly, I would do anything to avoid causing any one pain – except to change the book fundamentally. I am afraid, however, that if anyone is distressed by what seemed to me a very simple and inoffensive story, their feelings, when the book comes out will be much stronger. And the thought of that distresses me more than I can tell you.

Nothing, however, may now be done about this. You say in your letter that you never knew many things about my life when I was a child and that many more you did not discover until years later. I am afraid there are still other things that you are yet to learn – a thousand words leap to my tongue, words of explanation, persuasion, and hope – but they had better rest unsaid.

Silence is best. More and more I know that the grievous and complex fabric of human relationship may not be explained by language. However our motives or our acts are judged or misjudged, we can only trust to the belief of other men that we are of good will

About my book the only apology I have to make is that it is not better – and by "better" I mean that it does not represent by any means the best of which I am capable. But I hope I shall feel this way about my work for many years to come. But there is much in this first book for which I hope I shall always continue to feel affection and pride

I can not go into explanations of the creative act. That has been done many times by other people, and much better than I could hope to. I can only assure you that my book is a work of fiction, and that no person, or no act or event has been deliberately and consciously described. But I think you know that fiction is not spun out of the air, it is made from the solid stuff of human experience. Dr. Johnson said a man would turn over half a library to make a book; so may a novelist turn over half a town to make a figure in his novel. This is not the only method, but this is illustrative, I believe, of the whole process.

51

ALS, 14 pp., Harvard, bMS Am 1883.2 (294)
Harvard Club letterhead

Sunday Aug 11, 1929

Dear Mrs Roberts: I have been away in Maine and Canada on a vacation, and I came back to New York only two or three days ago.[1] Maine was very mild and lovely – I was at a little place on the coast – rocks, magnificent Spruce forests, and the ocean. I escaped some of the hot weather in New York – we had fires at night most of the time in Maine[2] – but I'm afraid several weeks more of heat are still before us. It has been a very hot summer with little rain – I hope you have been more comfortable in Asheville.

I found your letter here when I came back. As usual, everything you say touches and moves me deeply – I wish my work deserved half of the good things you say about it: I hope that someday it will. The knowledge that you have always believed in me is one of the greatest possessions of my life – I hope it may be some slight return for your affection and faith to know that I have always believed in you, first, as a child, with an utterly implicit faith and hope, and later as a man, with a no less steadfast trust.

Life does not offer many friendships of which one can say this – I know how few there are, and yet my own life has been full of love and loyalty for whoever understood or valued it.

In your letter you say that many facts in my life you never knew about when I was a child, that much about me you did not understand until later. This does not come from lack of understanding: it comes because you are one of the high people of the earth with as little of the earth in you as anyone I have even known – your understanding is for the flame, the spirit, the glory

– and in this faith you are profoundly right. It is a grand quality to see only with that vision which sees the highest and the rarest. All that you did not see caused me great unrest of spirit as a child when I thought of you, and perhaps more now.

I hope you may be wrong in thinking what I have written may distress members of my family, or anyone else. Certainly, I would do anything to avoid causing anyone pain – except to destroy the fundamental substance of my book. I am afraid, however, that if anyone is distressed by what seemed to me a very simple and un-offending story, the feeling when the book comes out will be much stronger. And the thought of that distresses <u>me</u> more than I can tell you.

Nothing, however, may now be done about this. Everything that could reasonably be done to soften impressions that might needlessly wound any reader has been done by my publishers and me. Now, the only apology I have to make for my book is that it is not better – and by "better" I mean that it does not represent by any means the best that is in me. But I hope I shall feel this way about my work for many years to come, although there is much in this first book about which I hope shall continue to feel affection and pride.

A thousand words leap to my tongue – words of explanation, persuasion, and faith – but they had better rest unsaid.

Silence is best. More and more I know that the grievous and complex web of human relationship may not be solved by words. However our motives or our acts may be judged or misjudged, our words must speak for us, and we can ultimately only trust to the belief of other men that we are of good will.

I can not explain the creative act here. That has been done much better than I could hope to do it, by other people. I can only assure you that my book is a work of fiction, and that no person, act, or event has been deliberately and consciously described. The creative spirit hates pain more, perhaps, than it does anything else on earth, and it is not likely it should try to inflict on other people what it loathes itself. Certainly the artist is not a traducer or libeler of mankind – his main concern when he creates is to give his creation life, form, beauty – this dominates him, and it is doubtful if he thinks very much of the effect his work will have on given persons, although he may think of its effect on a general public. But I think you know that fiction is not spun out of the air, it is made from the solid stuff of human experience – any other way is unthinkable.

Dr Johnson[3] said a man would turn over half a library to make a single book; so may a novelist turn over half a town to make a single figure in his novel.[4] This is not the only method but it illustrates, I believe the whole method. The world a writer creates is his own world – but it is moulded out of the fabric of life. What he has known and felt – in short, out of himself. How in God's name can it be otherwise?

This is all I can say – I think you will understand it. Having said this I can but add that at the last ditch the writer must say this: "I have tried only to do a good piece of work. I have not wished nor intended to hurt anyone. Now I can go no farther – I will not destroy nor mutilate my work, it represents what is best and deepest in me, and I shall stand by it and defend it even if the whole world turn against me"

That, it seems to me, is the only answer he can make Perhaps there are two sides to this question but this, at any rate, is my side, and the one I believe in with all my heart.

And now forgive me please for so long and dull a letter. It is late at night, the weather is hot and enervating, and I am tired. But I hope I have been able to make clear what I feel about the book.

Practically all the galley proofs have been corrected, the book is being set up in page proofs, the Scribner's people have been magnificent in every way, and their hope and belief in the book grows. I have been blessed with the greatest good fortune – a year ago only a miracle could have made me believe in an association with such men and such a house. They have done everything to make the book a success – my heart is full of loyalty and affection for them Meanwhile I am getting ready for a new and better book. Mrs Ernest Boyd, my agent, has sailed for England, and will try to get an English publisher for the book while there. I may have news of much greater importance in another two weeks – but the thought of it is so breath-taking, and the possibility so remote, that I dare not talk of it, dare only hope for it, and keep my eyes on the earth and probability.

I hope this finds you all well and happy. Give my love to all, and forgive me for having again written about only my own affairs.

Ever yours,
Tom Wolfe

P.S.   By the way – one thing in your letter puzzles me, at the very end you say: "Please don't think we had anything to do with George's "tating" [this is how I read the word][5] in the North State"

I am mystified about this – can't make out the word I read as "tating". Will you please explain in your next?[6]

1. Wolfe rented a cottage at Ocean Point, Boothbay Harbor, Maine, for two weeks to correct galley proofs of *Look Homeward, Angel.* Aline Bernstein joined him there. In August he traveled alone to Quebec.

2. "The weather here has been splendid—rain only one day, and always cool. At night, several times, we have had to build fires" (Wolfe, *Letters of Thomas Wolfe to His Mother,* 149).

3. Samuel Johnson (1709–1784), known as Dr. Johnson; English lexicographer, essayist, poet, and moralist, the major literary figure in the second half of the eighteenth century.

4. See Wolfe's preface to *Look Homeward, Angel,* "To the Reader."

5. Brackets are Wolfe's.

6. Wolfe probably misread "toting" as "tating."

52

ON SEPTEMBER 7, 1929, Wolfe made a short visit to Asheville. He found the city full of interest in his forthcoming book. He visited Mr. and Mrs. Roberts but discussed little about the actual contents of *Look Homeward, Angel.* Mrs. Roberts later chastised Wolfe for not alerting her about the fictionalized portraits of her family in the novel.[1] (See letter 60.) Whether, as Wolfe later claimed, Asheville's hostile reaction was a complete surprise is open to dispute. (Five months earlier, while *Look Homeward, Angel* was still called "O Lost," Wolfe was already writing anticipatory replies to antagonistic critics for publication in the *Asheville Citizen.*[2]) After his visit, on the train returning to New York, he forlornly jotted down in his notebook: "Shall I ever come back to my home, ever again?"[3] Following the publication of *Look Homeward, Angel,* Wolfe went into self-imposed exile from Asheville for the next seven and a half years.

ALS, 2 pp., Harvard, bMS Am 1883.2 (294)
Harvard Club Letterhead

New York   October 17, 1929

Dear Mrs Roberts:

I sent you a copy of my book the other day. I hope it arrived safely. In it I wrote a few words which I ask you to accept as a sincere expression of the writer's feeling toward you.

My book is published tomorrow. Nobody knows whether it will survive the avalanche of books that are being published at this season, or not; but we all hope for the best luck. Naturally I am tremendously excited about it.

I can not add anything here to what I told you when I was at home: I have tried to do a good and honest piece of work, and I hope that my friends like it. I shall be sorry if they do not like it, but I shall go on in the hope of writing something someday that may be worthy of their praise. I think I can not say more than this.

"Shall I ever come back to my home, ever again?" Wolfe on the front lawn of his mother's boardinghouse, September 1929. By permission of the Thomas Wolfe Collection, Pack Memorial Public Library, Asheville, North Carolina

I send to you all my warmest, and most affectionate regards.

I shall write you a little later, after I know more about the fate of my book. With hope, and with love,

Tom Wolfe

Had dinner with Bill Cocke last night. He likes his work and his firm.

1. Neither did Wolfe alert his own family. His sister Mabel has stated: "I never dreamed—and this opinion I voice for my family: Mama, Fred, Effie, Frank—what would be in the book" (quoted in Nowell, *Thomas Wolfe*, 143).

2. See Wolfe, *Letters*, 176–77, "To THE EDITOR OF THE ASHEVILLE CITIZEN," and *Notebooks of Thomas Wolfe*, 1:327. Further proof of anticipated notoriety is evident in his letter to a former classmate at the University of North Carolina, Benjamin Cone: "I am thinking of wearing false whiskers and smoked glasses after the book comes out" (Wolfe, *Letters*, 194).

3. Wolfe, *Notebooks of Thomas Wolfe*, 1:370.

---

53 (Lost)

PUBLISHED ON OCTOBER 18, 1929, *Look Homeward, Angel* created an uproar in Asheville. The novel was condemned from street corner to pulpit and banned from the public library. Wolfe received anonymous letters "full of vilification and abuse, one which threatened to kill me if I came back home, others which were merely obscene."[1]

The letter that Mrs. Roberts wrote Wolfe immediately after reading *Look Homeward, Angel* is lost. In a memoir written circa 1940, Mrs. Roberts claimed the only sentence she could remember from that letter was the closing one: "You have crucified your family and devastated mine."[2]

The presentation of John Munsey Roberts as the violent and dull pedant John Dorsey Leonard greatly disturbed Mrs. Roberts, and as Wolfe's biographer Elizabeth Nowell explains, her loyalty to her husband was "naturally even greater than her loyalty to Wolfe."[3]

Shortly after *Look Homeward, Angel* was published, Mrs. Roberts complained to her daughter's college roommate:

> The book is about Asheville people, some of it true, and some fiction, but all convincingly written, and so localized that any inhabitant of Asheville can identify every spot and person. The author has made a vivid picture of Margaret's father as much unlike the man as it could possibly be. I think you need only to look at his picture, after your read the book, to know that he is not the man pictured in the book.[4]

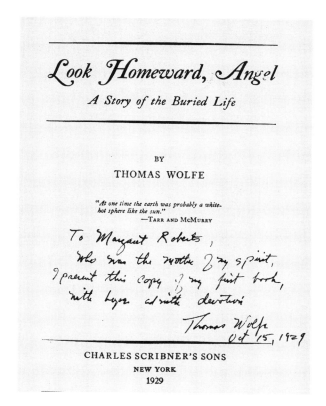

Title page of Margaret Roberts's inscribed copy of *Look Homeward, Angel.* By permission of the William B. Wisdom Collection, Houghton Library, Harvard University, and Eugene H. Winick, Administrator C.T.A., Estate of Thomas Wolfe

Mrs. Roberts obviously recognized the rancor that permeates *Look Homeward, Angel.* Of the few passages annotated in her inscribed copy, now preserved at Harvard University, she wrote on the flyleaf of the inside back cover: "Read p. 155. It perhaps explains a good deal as to how the book came about." Describing Eugene Gant's "feeling for the South," Wolfe wrote: "Finally, it occurred to him that these people had given him nothing, that neither their love nor their hatred could injure him, that he owed them nothing, and he determined that he would say so, and repay their insolence with a curse. And he did."

Although Wolfe sent a telegram on December 25, 1929 (see letter 57), and a letter on February 2, 1930 (letter 58), there would be no further communication between Wolfe and the Robertses for more than six years.

1. Thomas Wolfe, *The Autobiography of an American Novelist,* ed. Leslie A. Field (Cambridge, Mass.: Harvard University Press, 1983), 17–18.

2. Roberts memoir, 34.

3. Nowell, *Thomas Wolfe,* 154.

4. Ted Mitchell, "Margaret Roberts Writes to Her Daughter's Roommate," *Thomas Wolfe Review* 18:2 (Fall 1994): 70. In 1991, Margaret Rose Roberts described the deep loyalty that existed between her parents: "They had grown up in the same family since she was fifteen and she absolutely idolized my father. It might sound strange to you, but my mother and father were almost like one person. That's how close they always were" (Margaret Rose Roberts to Ted Mitchell, interview, February 13, 1991).

54

WOLFE DRAFTED A REPLY, handwritten in pencil in pocket notebook 12, to Mrs. Roberts's missing letter of October 1929.

Late October / early November 1929

AL draft, 5 pp., Harvard,
bMS Am 1883 (1227)

Dear Mrs. Roberts: When I got your letter a week or two ago I took it up to Mr Maxwell Perkins, who is the real head of Scribner's, and of whom you have heard me speak a great many times. He is a man of the finest and highest quality – brave, honest, generous, and gentle – and my friendship with him is one of the things I value most in my life. I gave him your letter to read and left his office while he read it there. When I came back, he said "This is the letter of a very magnificent person." That is also the way I feel. There are many things in your letter that caused me the deepest pain, but my feeling about you has been enhanced if possible, by the letter.

In view of the way you evidently feel about certain parts of my book – a feeling in which I want to say humbly I believe you are mistaken – your letter is very wonderful, and I will also say just and honest

I do want to say two things that touch upon statements in your letter:

First that in one of the passages you mention, there is not the slightest hint of "illegitimacy" and that if the entire passage is read calmly and carefully it will then seem that this is true.

You are entirely right in saying that I would not write such a book twenty years from now. More than that, I would not write such a book now. One of the people in my book says that we do not live only one life – maybe a dozen or a hundred. Since I began to write the book over three years ago I have lived at least one. And the sad part of it is that this life, including that other one that is brought out in my book is over, finished

At one place in your letter you seem to question my sincerity – "No one," you say "can make me believe you were not sincere."

55

WOLFE'S NEXT LETTER IS UNFINISHED and was never mailed. The first pages are badly worn. Wolfe may have carried it folded in his notebook or elsewhere upon his person for a long time (not an unusual practice for him).

AL, 7 pp., Harvard,
bMS Am 1883.2 (293)
Early November 1929   *Harvard Club letterhead*

Dear Mrs Roberts: I got your letter about two weeks ago. I have not been able to answer it before, because there have been a good many things to do in connection with my book, and because I allowed Freshmen themes to pile up on me until I [page torn]. I have been [page torn] my way out.

I can not answer your letter as it deserves to be answered, [page torn] because of themes and mid-term grades; and partly because [page torn] still excited trying to see how [page torn] book is selling, what the reviews [page torn] saying – and most of all, because I want to write you about your letter when I can write you calmly and at length.

But I want to say one or two things now: when I had read your letter I took it up to Maxwell Perkins, who is really the head of Scribners, and who is the very [page torn] brave, generous, and [page torn] you have heard me speak [page torn] him your letter to read, [page torn] his office while he read it. [page torn] I returned he said: "This [page torn] the letter of a very magnificent [page torn] person"[1]

That is also the way I feel [page torn]

What can I say to such people, or to anyone who insists on reading my book as a diary of literal events? The man who wrote The Times article[2] said that in my introduction I had raised the question whether the book was "autobiographical" or not, and then hastened to "beg the question by clever twists of phrases."[3] You know perfectly well that I have never begged any question, nor sought to evade an answer by "clever twists of phrases" What you will find if you read that introduction is a very simple, direct, and I hope very clear statement of the purpose and nature of fiction. If that statement is not clear, it is because I was allowed only one page,[4] and because my critical power is not great enough to define the word <u>fiction</u> clearly, but there is certainly no effort to beg a question or to evade an answer. But what answer do people like the Times reporter want? He states positively that I am Eugene and that the other figures in my book are people now living in Asheville.[5] The method of such people as this man is like the method of the petty lawyer who tries to intimidate and roar down his witness by shouting: "Answer <u>yes</u> or <u>no</u>" – as if any of the difficult, complex, and profound questions can be answered in such a way. Thus they bellow at you: "Is your book fiction or fact – answer yes or no"

"It is fiction," you reply "but –"

"Never you mind about that," he roars. "Answer <u>yes</u> or <u>no</u>"

"But fiction," you protest, "is very definitely related to —"

"None of your clever twists of phrases," he screams, "We're not going to let you beg the question in that way. Answer yes or no"

What can you answer? What reply can you make to such people? What can you do except to try to keep down the rage that rises in your throat, to keep from yelling:

"Damn your injustices!

[Ends here; remainder of page is blank.]

1. This material also appears in his pocket notebook draft (see letter 54).

2. Walter S. Adams. See his review, "Amazing New Novel Is Realistic Story of Asheville People," *Asheville Times,* October 20, 1929.

3. Ibid. Adams writes, "In the preface, Wolfe raises the question whether the work is really autobiographical and then hastens to beg the question with clever twists of phrases."

4. Wolfe's published preface in *Look Homeward, Angel* contains ten sentences. The original typescript, called "<u>Defensio Libris,</u>" had thirty-three sentences on five pages before it was cut for publication.

5. Adams, "Amazing New Novel": "This young man who is called Eugene Gant (in reality, Thomas Wolfe, the author)." Earlier in his review Adams states, "The book is written about Asheville and Asheville people in the plainest of plain language. It is the autobiography of an Asheville boy. . . . The author paints himself and his home circle, as well as neighbors, friends and acquaintances with bold, daring lines, sparing nothing and shielding nothing."

56

WOLFE MAY HAVE INTENDED the following fragment to be a portion of the previous letter (letter 55) or of a draft now lost.

Ca. fall 1929   *AL draft, 3 pp., Harvard, bMS Am 1883.2 (293)*

This has become a very long letter, but I know that at the end words can not help. If words could help, I might find an answer in a single sentence. But I can not.

What remains to be said is the most difficult and the saddest thing of all. I shall try to say it as clearly and as carefully as possible. My conviction about life amounts to this: that each of us is not one person, but many persons, and that each of us has not one life but many lives. It seems to me I have already had at least a dozen. My book said that we are strangers and never come to know one another. I believe that more firmly than ever now. The very difficult thing I am trying to say now is this – that people at home who have been distressed, angered, or wounded by my book, see me in a life in which I have ceased to live, see me in a form which is as remote from the person I am as the ghost in Hamlet. My book was called up from the lost wells and adyts of my childhood – for twenty months that experience blazed and was shaped and fused into a world of my own creation – my own reality. Now I understand that some people have read my book not for the reality that is its own, but for another reality which belongs to the world. Such people have seen in the book only a bitter attack upon people living in the town of my birth. Do you really think, Mrs Roberts, that any artist ever gave body and blood night after night to any creation, for the sole purpose of making a bitter transcript of life? Do you think that if the reality in my book was only the same reality that walks the streets, I would take the trouble of writing at all?

What I ask humbly is this: if I am to be shut out in exile, give me the hope of returning some day. If, because of my first book, the door is shut against me, at least give me the chance to redeem myself. For my part, I regard my work as just begun – only the first chapter written. It grieves me to think that that chapter has given offense, but at any rate I hope the other chapters will seem finer and more beautiful to those who were repelled by this one. I must in fairness state that I shall try to come close to life and to art with a much more blazing intensity and honesty than I have yet achieved

---

57

Telegram, Harvard, bMS Am 1883.2 (294)
Holiday greeting by Western Union

1929 DEC 25 AM 1 02
NEWYORK NY

MRS J M ROBERTS=

129 LINDEN AVE ASHEVILLE NCAR=

I SEND ON CHRISTMAS DAY THIS MESSAGE OF AFFECTION AND LOVE I WISH YOU HEALTH HAPPINESS AND GLORY ALL THE YEARS OF YOUR LIFE HAVE BEEN SICK BUT WILL FINISH LETTER THIS WEEK WITH WARMEST LOVE=

TOM WOLFE.

58

AFTER THREE SURVIVING DRAFTS and one unmailed letter, on February 2, 1930, Wolfe succeeded in completing a letter to Mrs. Roberts. More than three months had passed since the publication of *Look Homeward, Angel.*

ALS, 16 pp., Harvard, bMS Am 1883.2 (294)
Harvard Club letterhead

New York, Feb 2, 1930

Dear Mrs Roberts: Mabel writes me that you are still in bed after your recent operation, and I am writing you a short letter to wish you a quick and complete recovery to full health and strength. You deserve a full, magnificent, and happy life as much as anyone I have ever known, and I send you my earnest hope for its realization.

Two or three months ago I wrote you a very long letter in reply to your own, but that letter still remains, folded and unfinished, in my notebook.

It has been almost impossible for me to write letters, or anything else, during the last three months – partly because of classes and papers at N.Y.U., and partly because of telephone calls, invitations to speak, dine, or visit (which I now shy away from), interviews, and excitement. Now I am finishing my work at the university – I have resigned and will be finished there as soon as my term grades are in (I still have 200 quizzes and themes to read!) Scribner's have very generously made it possible for me to live modestly until my next book is done[1] – I have already begun it, and it is to be called The October Fair.[2] It deals with different scenes, with different characters, and with a different theme from the first: I hope, naturally, that it will be a better book than the first, and with all my heart I hope that people who thought my first book ugly and painful, will find beauty and wisdom in the second. That is a wish I shall always keep for my work, and I hope in some measure it comes true.

I am very happy to know that most of the reviewers have found beauty and wisdom in my first book, and many of them have found the people in the book magnificent and heroic. I have just finished reading a review by Carl Van Doren in which he says just that. The review is published in the Feb. issue of a little magazine called Wings: it is the journal of The Literary Guild of America, of which Mr Van Doren is the head. If you can get the magazine, I hope you will read the review.

I shall have time to write you the letter I want to write after next week. Meanwhile, will you let me say again one thing in reference to your own fine letter: I think you are mistaken in the estimate you put on some of the characters in my book and I know you are wholly mistaken in your interpretation of one of the scenes.[3] You are certainly right in saying I would not do such a book twenty years from now – I hope I will do one that is much better and much more beautiful, but such growth as that must come with time, and with maturity and wisdom.

But I do believe sincerely, Mrs Roberts, that any bitterness in my book – and I would not deny that there is bitterness in it – is directed not against people or against living, but against the fundamental structure of life, which seems to me, or at least seemed to me when I wrote the book, cruel and wastefully tragic. I may be wrong in that feeling, but at any rate, it was deep-seated and real.

The other thing I want to say is longer and more difficult, and I must write you about it later at length, but here it is indicated in outline: that all creation is to me fabulous, that the world of my creation is a fabulous world, that experience comes into me from all points, is digested and absorbed into me until it becomes a part of me, and that the world I create is <u>always</u> <u>inside</u> me, and never <u>outside</u> me; and that what reality I can give to what I create comes only from <u>within.</u> Its relation to actual experience I have never denied, but every thinking person knows that such a relation is inevitable, and could not be avoided unless men lived in a vacuum.

I began to write the book in a little room in London and I finished it in a New York sweatshop garret; and from beginning to end the theme was that men are alone and strangers on the face of the earth, and never come to know one another – this theme came as a result of years of wandering, and was as true of men in London, Budapest, or Naples, as of men in Asheville, Idaho, or Alaska. You said in one place of your letter that you knew I was sincere, no matter what anyone said. I thank you with all my heart; but how could you ever doubt it? Have you ever known me to be lacking in sincerity, to be evasive, dishonest, or to have my eye glued on the main chance? One man wrote in to Scribner's saying that the rumor was Wolfe had written the book because he needed money badly. What damnable nonsense! Doesn't every word, every sentence, every page, and the whole great length of the book show that such a work could never be written from a desire except the desire of the artist to create a vision of life that burned inside him? If I had wanted money don't you suppose there are a million easier, cheaper, shorter, and easier ways of getting it? The fact that the book has had a modest commercial success is one of the most astonishing things about it, but surely you must understand it was not published for this reason, and that dozens of hack writers make more money on one of their books than I could make on six of mine.

Finally, Mrs Roberts, will you please believe me when I tell you sincerely and earnestly that when I began this book in London, and finished it in New York, I shaped and created its reality from within: my <u>own</u> world, my <u>own</u> figures, my <u>own</u> events shaped themselves into my <u>own</u> fable there on the page before me, and that I spent no time in thinking of actual Smiths, Jones, or Browns; nor did I have any idea of putting them in my book; nor do I see yet how such a thing is possible? If anyone thinks it is, let him take notes at street corners, and see if the result is a book.

I have written you more than I intended at present: let me in concluding entreat you to remember that I have written only <u>one</u> chapter of my <u>whole</u> book, and that if you do not think the first is worthy of me, I shall try to do something that will deserve your faith and affection in those that follow. Let me also say now that the saddest thing about all of this to me is not that some people have misunderstood the intention and meaning of my first book, but that some people I still love and honor have misunderstood me. I will not say a word against them – the really sad thing is that we lead a dozen lives rather than one, and that two or three of mine have gone by since I was a kid in Asheville If people now draw back when they see the man, and say: "I do not know him. This is not the boy I knew" – I can only hope they will not think the man a bad one, and that they will be patient and wait until the boy comes back. And I think he will, after the man has made a long journey.

Good-bye for the present. I send you again my warmest, my deepest affection, and my most devoted wishes for your health and happiness. I think you are one of the grandest people I have ever known.

Tom Wolfe

P. S. I hope you have seen some of the reviews of my book. They have been on the whole very wonderful – the best reviews, I understand, a first book has had in several years. I hope you have read some of the most important ones – those in the New York <u>Times, World, Herald-Tribune, New Republic, The Bookman, Plain Talk,</u> and others; as well as the statements made by Hugh Walpole, Thomas Beer, F. P. A., the columnist, and many other people.

I hate to speak of all this, but all of these people have found beauty and heroism in my book, both in the events and in the people; and I hope you will be interested in what they say, in what they think and feel.

If I am to be honest I must create my vision of life as I see it; but I hope that in my future work everyone I respect and like will find beauty and wonder in everything I do.

Forgive me for talking so much about the book – it is my first, and naturally close to my heart.

Again, I send you my warmest and most devoted remembrance.

1. Scribner's paid Wolfe a $4,500 advance on his next novel; it was paid in monthly installments of $250 beginning February 1, 1930.

2. "The October Fair" became a portion of *Of Time and the River.*

3. Perhaps the material in *Look Homeward, Angel,* 232–35, which Mrs. Roberts refers to in letter 60.

59

THE PLACEMENT OF THIS UNDATED LETTER as Wolfe's final communication with Mrs. Roberts for six years is conjectural. There is no clue to indicate whether it was written before or after Wolfe's letter of February 2, 1930. It is not listed on Margaret Rose Roberts's inventory of Wolfe's letters owned by her mother. Unable to conceal his deeply wounded feelings, Wolfe may have written this as a more immediate response to Mrs. Roberts's "You have cruci-fied your family" letter, but he may have decided not to mail it. It remained in his personal papers that eventually went to Harvard University after his death. Whether or not the letter was sent, its note of finality marks the end of the first phase of the Wolfe/Roberts saga.

ALS. 7 pp., Harvard, bMS Am 1883.2 (296)
Ca. 1929–1930   *Harvard Club letterhead*

Dear Mrs Roberts:

I have always thought you one of the best friends I have ever had. I used to think your letters the finest. I still think you at heart a very grand person.

During the years since I left school I can not say that life has "taught me" – it has rather conditioned me. I am much more of an <u>idealist</u> than I ever was – for, contrary to general belief, the monotony, brutality, hardness, and mechanism of modern life does not harden the dreamer – it makes him more fanatic than ever.

But it gives him clearer vision. Your letters seem sentimental and false to me. I do not think you any longer think of me – you think of a boy you once knew. I am sorry he no longer lives – but you must not blame me for his death I think you are being a little too consciously the "fine woman" in your letters. And you talk of my family – your effort to see "both sides" – I consider nat-urally a cruel injustice. You talk of the "fine big heart" of a family that cheated me of part of my inheritance, that cursed and jeered at me as a child, and that has not written me for several months. You rely I suppose, on what people call "experience" or "life" for the terrible fallacy that "there are two sides to every-thing" There are not, you know. On anything that matters there is only one.

But in defending our lives and attacking others we are too passionate – we could write volumes when words are enough. It is no use. It is too long, too weary – we agree, we differ – it's all one.

Life's not to be made right with the dictionary, and I am already sorry for writing as I have. Let us say then: You were, you are, a great, a grand person. I was a boy, a particle of fire. I am no longer a boy, and I cannot reweb this passionate life even for those I love. I shall have time, I hope, during the remainder of my life to wreak out my spirit in a dozen books. I hope you may live to read them.

You had me – you lost me. I had you, I loved you. I lost you, I love you. No more. No more. Words are no good.

God bless you.

Tom Wolfe

THE LETTERS

∿ Part II

I feel new strength and hope: I am standing on the shores of a new land, and if the old world is behind me, my heart somehow is full of hope about the new one I shall explore; because I found out that although "you can't go home again," the home of all of us, of every mother's son of us, is in the future.

Thomas Wolfe to Margaret Roberts
(March 7, 1938)

MRS. ROBERTS'S SIX-PAGE LETTER marks the first communication with Wolfe since her "You have crucified your family and devastated mine" response to *Look Homeward, Angel.* While visiting her daughter, Margaret Rose, in New York City, she saw Wolfe's signature reproduced upon the dust jacket of *The Story of a Novel* and resolved to end their estrangement. Although unable to disguise her hurt, she extended an amicable invitation to Wolfe to call on her.

ALS, 6 pp., Harvard, bMS Am 1883.1 (545)

130 Morningside Drive
Apartment 33, New York.
May 11, 1936.

My dear Tom Wolfe,

You will be amazed, perhaps greatly displeased to see this scrawl after so long a time since my last word from you – your Christmas telegram in [*left blank*].[1] I would have written you then but I was so wounded in my feelings and so weak in my body (you may not have known how desperately ill I was from October until March, and then how very weak from March until June recovering from a very serious operation performed in Cleveland,)[2] that it was not until June that I tried to muddle through a letter to you. But it was so far from what I wanted – that I decided not to send it, or rather, drifted to that decision. I wanted so desperately to show you that I loved you in spite of the bitter stabs you had given to those as dear to me as light itself, and at the same time I wanted to pour out the flood of bitterness that filled me because you had, as I felt so unjustly, held them up to the scorn and ridicule of our little world. I should not call it bitterness. It wasn't that. It was just <u>hurtness</u> – hurt because the boy I loved so dearly had done this thing to the man I have always worshipped, and to others of a family that have been not merely "in-laws" to me, but rather sisters, close sisters, and a father. From the time when I was left absolutely penniless at 16, and hungry to learn, they were the ones who helped me to be able to shove forward in my head and heart and pocket book. Without them I could never have occupied even the small mental patch of ground that I have. You see, when you hurt not only Mr. Roberts, but Emma, and Mrs. Pattison,[3] and even Grandpa R –,[4] I felt wounded in the house of a friend.

After I failed to send that letter, I have thought after reading each new book, that I would write, but as the time went by I realized that time had made it more difficult instead of less to say what I felt, and also I realized that you were now too much absorbed in your fierce "borning" of your books to be perhaps even interested in hearing from me.

But, somehow, the rereading of your letters last winter, especially the big one in which you told of your wild joy when you knew "Look Homeward, Angel" was actually to be published – it was a letter that would wake the dead – I thought again I would write. But I didn't. Then when the other day in Margaret's room I saw that big, familiar "Thomas Wolfe" sprawled on the cover of "The Story of a Novel," I resolved to risk disturbing you.

We have read everything except this "S. of a Novel." Have puzzled, wondered, been amazed by their beauty and power, been disturbed by much that you have written, and delighted by much. Some meat too strong for my digestion; – but no letter can be long enough to go into all this.

I have written because I suppose being actually in New York, the scene of your struggles and triumphs, my mind has gone back, first to the boy I loved, and next, to the eagerness with which I read your letters detailing the progress of your book – back to joy in seeing you grow; back, too, to the tide of misery caused to us by what you did to us. As you say in "Time and the River," "it's all there."[5]

I have not changed in thinking that the wounding was needless. Time has not in the least made me forget the day, when, too weak to walk steadily, I crept to the door when I heard the postman shove inside the screen what I was sure was your book. By some unhappy fatality as I crept back into the bed, the book opened at the chapters dealing with us – and curiosity drove me forward. And you had just been with us so recently, had talked pleasantly with Mr. R. – and had not warned me!

I am not so dumb as not to believe that an artist has a right to get his material where he pleases and twist it as he pleases, but I maintain that he has no right to twist or invent, in making a pen-picture and then write under it the name of a living person, as for instance when you make Mr. R. a contemptible snob in the Junius Horner-groceryman's daughter incident – a story perhaps current among the boys, but which was entirely unknown to any of us.[6] Again, – but what's the use!

I haven't yet read "The Story of a Novel." I knew Margaret had it, so I did not read it when it came out serially. We have just come up from Asheville, and I mean to read it within the next day or so. I am wondering if you still think all you did to us and others whom you harm so dreadfully was kind, or necessary, or wise. You have too much power, too much beauty, as I see it, to need to butcher those who thought you counted them as friends, and – but what's the use again?

the
story of a
NOVEL

by

THOMAS WOLFE

author of "Of Time and the River"

How does a great novel come into being? What is its genesis? How does it develop? What are the sensations of a literary artist as characters take form beneath his pen? These and similar questions often come to the mind of every reader of fiction — and they have never been answered with such frankness, honesty, and conviction as in this brief "credo" of an outstanding American novelist. Here is the soul of an artist laid bare, with all his hopes, fears, doubts, and aspirations. But it is not only about Mr. Wolfe's own books — it is about all writing and about American writing especially — a book that every one directly interested in the art of fiction must read, and that every one of the many thousands who enjoyed Mr. Wolfe's novels will find permeated by the same "insatiable and enormous eagerness in life and living" that placed the stamp of genius on his novels.

The subject matter of this book created a literary sensation when it appeared in *The Saturday Review of Literature*. It inspired an editorial on Mr. Wolfe and his writing in *The New York Times*, John Chamberlain devoted his column to it, and it attracted favorable comments from critics all over the country.

The Story Of A Novel

Thomas Wolfe

---

the story of a NOVEL

From Death to Morning

Fourteen Stories by

THOMAS WOLFE

"These stories are Mr. Wolfe's peculiar property; they belong to him with the certainty of style and introspection — no other can match them; and they show the most striking literary personality of our day."

PERCY HUTCHISON in
The New York Times

"What stories they are! . . . They are cumulative evidence of his right to be classed as one of the great American novelists, if not the greatest."

Philadelphia Ledger

"Reading the work of this genius is like listening to Wagner or watching the aurora borealis. It is an experience beside which the mill run of most fiction seems trivial and insignificant."

The Chicago Tribune

"In these days when some of our best writers are tired or short of breath it is thrilling to contemplate and to read the teeming novels of Thomas Wolfe."

BURTON RASCOE in *The New York Herald Tribune*

OF TIME AND THE RIVER

"He gives you an experience you can't just file away under Miscellaneous. . . . For decades we have not had eloquence like his in American writing. . . . At his best he is incomparable. . . . *Of Time and the River* is a wonderful, flashing, gleaming riot of characters, caricatures, metaphors, apostrophes, declamations, tropes, dreams."

CLIFTON FADIMAN in *The New Yorker*

LOOK HOMEWARD, ANGEL

"As interesting and powerful a book as has ever been made out of the circumstances of provincial American life. It is at once enormously sensuous, full of the joy and gusto of life, and shrinkingly sensitive, torn with revulsion and disgust."

MARGARET WALLACE in *The New York Times*

by Thomas Wolfe

Published by CHARLES SCRIBNER'S SONS

Dust jacket, *The Story of a Novel*, 1936. Collection of Ted Mitchell

May I say here that Mr. Roberts has at no time tried to influence me not to answer your letter. He has left me absolutely free. It would really have been worth your while to have observed the fineness in the man through the whole unhappy business. But you knew him many years intimately and saw only a snob, a pedant, a dullard, and, what seemed worse than anything to me, a man who was brutal to a frail wife. (No human being could ever have been more gentle, more considerate than he has been to me in every relation of life.)

If I threw the June letter of [*left blank*][7] because it was muddled, this one surely deserves no better fate. But because we are so near to you that fine, happy old memories keep coming to the surface; because your letters reread moved me more deeply than I know how to tell you; because of that sprawling signature on the back of "S. of a N. – "; because Buddie and Margaret think that I should have appreciated your power and beauty, and squelched the personal, – should have allowed the artist in you to predominate over the friend in you, — because of all these things, but, above all, because, wounded to the quick as I, and we, were, I have never forgotten to love you at all times from the time when you were twelve to now – and to rejoice at your success. I have been angry and hurt, but I have felt that sometime as you grew older, you would, with your powers, learn how to go up and on without treading others down as you did us – and through it all, I have loved you, and, of course because I did love you, resented more and suffered more because of what you did to the others I love.

I have written too much, and too, I don't know what. Instead of praising your books in detail, I have still been rebellious but, anyway, if you will, we shall be at home to you at this address until July 1. Margaret took a larger apartment that we might be with her. Penelope[8] spends the week-ends with us. Mr. Roberts has had a pretty wretched time with his stomach since November – has just come in from seeing a doctor. I tried to telephone Mabel as we came through Washington but they said her phone had been taken out.

This is our first stay of any length in New York. We are dropping hayseed everywhere, so that Hoover's "grass growing in the streets of New York" may become a reality.

Yours, in memory of old days,

Margaret Roberts.

1. 1929 (see letter 57). Apparently Mrs. Roberts had forgotten Wolfe's letter of February 2, 1930, or believed the telegram arrived afterward.

2. "A toxic goiter that almost killed her; mother was ill with it when *Look Homeward, Angel* came out" (Margaret Rose Roberts to Ted Mitchell, interview, August 13, 1994).

3. J. M. Roberts's sister, Hortense Roberts Pattison.

4. J. M. Roberts's father, William Orton Roberts.

5. *Of Time and the River,* 690.

6. "Leonard surprised this youth one afternoon in Spring, on the eastern flank of the hill, in the thick grass beneath a flowering dogwood, united in sexual congress with Miss Hazel Bradley, the daughter of a small grocer who lived below on Biltburn Avenue, and whose lewdness was already advertised in the town" (Wolfe, *Look Homeward, Angel,* 234). Miss Hazel Bradley is believed to be Hazel Dillon, a printer's daughter. See Mauldin, *People and Places of Thomas Wolfe's "Look Homeward, Angel,"* 52.

7. 1930.

8. Penelope Pattison, Hortense Pattison's daughter.

61

TLS, 6 pp., Harvard, bMS Am 1883.2 (293)

May 20th, 1936.
865 First Avenue,
New York, N. Y.

Dear Mrs. Roberts:

I had hoped to answer your letter sooner, but I was just on the point of going away for a few days vacation when I received it and I decided to wait until I came back. I have been working hard and got pretty tired. I find that you reach a point in writing when you cannot go on farther no matter how much the heart and soul may want to, the body and brain will not respond. So I went down to Pennsylvania for a few days, I wonder if you know the State? It is one of the most beautiful places I have ever seen. It has almost every variety of landscape and the finest farms in the world. I went with a friend, we avoided main highways as much as we could and drove along the back country roads. We drove a thousand miles in four days and saw some astonishing and beautiful things in the country of the Pennsylvania Dutch. They are a wonderful people. Everything in that part of the country has an air of thrift and of tidiness, of solid and prosperous substance. In the city here, you see such shocking contrasts of wealth and poverty and often you hear such sad and tragic stories of human suffering and injustice and oppression. Going out to a place like the country I have just come from, restores your faith, not only in nature but in man. We got as far as York Springs, the little village a few miles from Gettysburgh, near which my father was born. I went out to the little country grave yard where his father and mother and a good many of his people are buried, and talked to a lot of people who remembered them all and visited some relatives of mine who live in York Springs[1]. Isn't the beauty of this country simply astonishing? I had never seen the West until last summer and

I remembered that you and Mr. Roberts lived there for some time. I loved the West, I felt instantly at home the minute I got off the train in Colorado. The people were wonderful to me, there is something so spacious and free and generous in their hospitality. I had just come from Denmark. You must admit that from Denmark to New Mexico at one jump, is a pretty large order. It is a wonderfully valuable and informing experience that seems to crystalize things I have been feeling and thinking about America and Europe for years now. I wish I could see you and tell you about it.

I am back at work now. It is going to be another very long, hard pull. I am already beginning to be haunted by nightmares at night. I am probably in for several thousand hours of hell and anguish, of almost losing hope, utterly, and swearing I'll never write another word and so on, but it seems to have to be done in this way and I have never found any way of avoiding it. I am both fascinated and terrified by this new book.[2] It is a thing which has been going in my mind for years and it is not one of the books that have been announced. It is a much more objective book than any I have yet written. Sometimes I am appalled by my own undertaking, and doubt that I can do it. The best friend I have in the world, who is also the best editor this country has produced, and who has never been wrong in his judgement yet, told me at once, when I described the book to him, that there was no doubt that I could do it, that I was the only one who could do it, that he had known for years I would have to write this kind of book some day, and by all means to do it at once with all my might. I think it is a good thing for several reasons; in the first place, if I succeed, it will meet the objections which some of the critics have passed about my being an autobiographical writer. In the second place, I think that one of the things that is likely to happen to the artist when he gets a little older, is that he may tend to become cautious and conservative and to stick to the thing which he has learned or is learning to do. There is a good deal to be said for this, but I do think it is a pity if a man is to lose the enthusiastic eagerness, the desire to experiment and find out new ways, the fearlessness of conception and effort which he has in his twenties. I don't want to lose it and my friend tells me I never will, and that there is no question about my being able to do this thing if I see it through. I wish you knew him, his name is Maxwell Perkins. He is not only a wonderful friend, he is also a great man and a great person with the finest qualities of character, spirit and intelligence I have ever known. He has often asked me about you and I know he would like to meet you.

This last year has been a very extraordinary one. I have seen some wonderful things and met a great many people. I took too much time away from work, but I was desperately tired and had in fact been writing steadily for almost five years and I have found that a man's energy and the way he uses his talent is like a reservoir, when it gets depleted, you have got to let it fill up again. Well, I think it is full again, full to overflowing. I hope and believe that I may have learned something from all the mistakes and errors of the past and that I will be able to work hereafter without quite so much useless waste and confusion and agony of spirit. I don't think by any means that I can wholly avoid these things yet, but I do think you learn something from every piece of work you do and that every piece of work you do adds something to your stature, increases the power and maturity of your experience and helps you to use your talent with greater certainty.

By the way, I got a very nice letter a week or two ago from a woman who knows you and Mr. Roberts and the children. I haven't got the letter where I can lay my hands on it at the moment but she lives in London Terrace, so I suppose you will know who she is. She seems to be an awfully nice person, invited me to come to see her and her husband and described in the most appetizing way, a meal she would cook for me. Probably we can all get together some time, if you know the person I mean.

I am sorry you didn't see Mabel when you came through Washington, I know she will be disappointed when I tell her you couldn't find her. Yes, I think they did have their telephone taken out, but they are still living there. They have had a terribly hard time and she has suffered a great deal, but somehow, I always believe that she has it in her to pull herself together in a time of crisis or necessity and meet the situation no matter how hard or bitter. Mr. Wheaton, as you know, is a fine man in many ways. He has devotion and loyalty and great staunchness of character, but I think, and this of course, is confidential, that he is a most tragic individual case of the effects of this tragic depression. I am sometimes accused by the communist writers here in New York, of lacking what they call 'social consciousness' and of not showing in my writing sufficient resentment towards the present system. Well, there are several answers to that. When I am told that I do not appreciate or understand the lot of the worker, I remember and am proud to remember that I am the son of a stone cutter, that I come from people in Pennsylvania and in the hills of Western North Carolina, who have had to work hard and long for two hundred years or more by the sweat of their brow, the strength of their hands, to earn their daily bread. I am not talking of the more prosperous members of the family whom you may have known in Asheville, yet even they, my mother's brothers and my mother herself, knew poverty and want in their childhood in the years after the Civil War, and my father worked all of his life. So I think you will agree with me there is no particular reason for me to be very much impressed by the assertion of young gentlemen calling themselves Communists, whose fathers provide them with a comfortable allowance which enables them to indulge their political fancies without knowing a great deal about some of the things or people of whom they write.

What I am really telling you, and I think you agree with me in your own feeling, is that by instinct, by inheritance, by every natural sympathy and affection of my life, my whole spirit and feeling is irresistably on the side of the working class, against the cruelty, the injustice, the corrupt and infamous privilege of great wealth, against the shocking excess and wrong of the present system, the evidences of which are horribly apparent I think, to anybody who lives here in New York and keeps his eyes open. I think that the whole thing has got to be changed, and I'll do everything within the province of my energy or talent to change it for the better, If I can, but I am not a Communist, and I believe that the artist who makes his art the vehicle for political dogma and intolerant propaganda is a lost man. I think almost every great poet and every great writer who ever wrote and whose works we all love and treasure has been on the side of the oppressed, the suffering, the confused and lost and stricken of the earth. Do you know of a single exception to this? But really isn't this just another way of saying that every great man or any good man, is on the side of life and although I am myself the son of a working man, I go so far as to say that an artist's interests, first and always has got to be in life itself, and not in a special kind of life. His devotion, his compassion, his talent has got to be used for man and for the enrichment of man's estate and not for just one class or sect of man. Finally, I think that in so far as any artist would turn against a man because that man is rich or would have no understanding or tolerance of the lot of a man who belongs to a certain class, the artist who would feel this way is by just this much, a smaller man than he should be.

To get back to Wheaton. I think he has been crushed by the catastrophe of recent years. Furthermore, although I never had much feeling one way or another about great corporations until this thing happened, I think the way he was treated by the great corporation that employed him after he had given his life, his strength, his youth and all his best energies since his fourteenth year, was simply damnable, and I for one, do not propose to sit around silent and acquiescent in a society where such a situation exists and where such things happen. Wheaton knows how to do nothing except to sell cash registers. His father died when he was a child and it was up to him to contribute to the support of his mother and his sister without delay. He left school at the age of thirteen or fourteen, went into the cash register factory, learned the business

Mabel Wolfe Wheaton and Ralph Harris Wheaton. "Wheaton looks just the same as he always did. He dresses well, still makes a good appearance, talks in his grave and dignified way, but the man is really lost." By permission of the Thomas Wolfe Collection, Pack Memorial Public Library, Asheville, North Carolina

and finally became an agent as you knew him in Asheville. Now he is no longer a young man, he has been in poor health for many years, his reserve of physical strength and energy is very short and he was kicked out ruthlessly, brutally and without notice by the employers to whom he had given his life and who for thirty years or more had profited by his efforts. I suppose the cold blooded answer to this would be that he profited too, and that he was paid well for his services and that when the period of his usefullness waned as far as the company was concerned, they owed him nothing more, they were free to dismiss him as they choose. I say to hell with all such reasoning, it is probably in accord with the ruthless code of business procedure, but it is not in accord with human life, with human justice, with human decency, do you think so?[3]

Wheaton looks just the same as he always did. He dresses well, still makes a good appearance, talks in his grave and dignified way, but the man is really lost. It is almost as if his life had been run over by a steam roller, or as if he had been hit at the base of the brain with a blunt instrument. I don't think he has even been fully aware of what happened to him, and it is a tragic thing to contemplate but, I sometimes doubt very seriously if he will ever be able to pull himself together, find employment and go back into the full flow of life again. In the face of this situation, it has been up to Mabel to keep the whole thing going, to keep body and soul together for both of them. Frankly, I think she has done amazingly well. The whole thing has been a terrible blow to her, the loss of everything they owned, the uprooting of her whole life in Asheville where as you know, she knew everyone, and to which she was so much attached. I don't think she has ever gotten over it, for her it was really almost like being sent into exile in Siberia. She has cracked under the strain time and again, but she has always pulled herself together and kept things going. She is running as you know, a kind of lodging house in Washington. She really rents a number of small apartments in a block of buildings above some stores, and then she lets the rooms in these apartments to government clerks, girls working in department stores and other people with small incomes. Of course the strain, the anxiety of this kind of life on a person of her temperament is terrific, furthermore, as you know, in spite of her railings and tirades against this or that, she would give any one, as the saying goes, the shirt off her back, if she thought some one needed it. As a result, she is constantly being victimized by unscrupulous and dishonest people who will stay in her place for months and then go away without paying her any of the money they owe her; so many of the other people with little gray lives and no particular color or personality of their own, will swarm about a person like Mabel as flies swarm about a sugar bowl, feed upon her vitality, use up her time and exhaust her energy. Of course, I suppose this cannot be helped. She is the kind of person who gives herself out as naturally as the sun shines and I don't think this will ever change. But it has been a severe strain just to get enough money out of it to pay expenses and have a little bit over for the support of herself and Ralph. And here this year, the landlords raised the rent again to such a degree that it looked as if it would be impossible for them to continue and come out even, so I suppose that's one of the reasons she had the phone taken out. Anyway, they are still there in Washington. The address is – 920 – 17th Street, N. W., and I know if you are in Washington, she would be delighted to see you.

I think I have myself learned a good deal about men and living in the last year that was surprising and astonishing and sometimes pretty painful and unpleasant. For the first time I received some considerable amount of public notice and I confess there are now times when I long for the comparative obscurity of a few years back and wonder whether such success as I may have attained, doesn't take with it a pretty heavy price. For one thing I found out to my utter astonishment that anyone in the world can sue you and for no earthly reason save that there are apparently a lot of people who think it would

be rather nice to sue you and see if they cannot badger, worry, threaten, torment or wheedle you into giving them some money, simply because they don't
have any intention of going to work and earning it for themselves. I assure you
that this can happen, that it is happening all the time, that it has happened to
me and that so far as justice, right or fairness is concerned, the law from what
I have seen of it, seems to have no concern with these matters at all. Rather it
becomes a question of who can twist the terms and phrases of the law to his
own advantage. Of course, I suppose in the end, if you carry it through you
can usually win out, particularly if the person suing you has taken money from
you, has concluded contracts and agreements of which you have never been
informed, has been dismissed utterly and forever from your employment, has
in fact, not one square inch of earth on which to stand. I say you can win, but
in the end, no matter what happens you always lose, don't you? You have to
go and employ a lawyer, you have to be hauled into court for an examination
before trial, you get gray hairs worrying and fretting over it. And finally, you
pay them some money, so that you can get peace of mind and go on working
and not be bothered and exhausted by it any more.[4] I have been through the
whole thing. I have had people, members of some poor and humble families
whom I liked, with whom I had enjoyed pleasant and friendly relations, walk
off with my manuscripts, sell them and pocket the money.[5] I have read my
name in the paper as a speaker at public dinners, of which I knew nothing and
to which I had never given my consent. Only the other day, I received a great
batch of essays with a letter saying that the promoters of this essay contest,
were delighted that I had consented to be one of the judges, but I had never
heard of the thing before. Some of the success has been very pleasant, some of
it grotesque, some very comical, and some of it appalling, but I have hung on
grimly and I am back at work again and of course, as long as I can work, I am
all right. They can take what little money I have left, I suppose I can earn more
money, they can even walk away with my manuscripts, I can certainly write
more manuscripts, but if they take away my power to work, then they have
taken everything. But I think that this probably won't happen.

I did not mean to write you so long a letter. But I was so glad to hear from
you after all these years. I want to see you and Mr. Roberts. If you want to talk
to me about some of the things you speak about in your letter, I will talk to
you about them, if you think it will make for clarification and better understanding, but if it causes greater pain and confusion in the lives or hearts of anyone, I'd rather not say anything.[6] I do believe from your letter that you want
to see me again and all I can say sincerely and honestly is that means a great
deal to me. About so many other things – could I just say this: that I know I

have done things that I ought not to have done, and left undone things that I should have done, but that my hope and faith is that I grow a little in knowledge and experience and in understanding all the time, and that I shall, accordingly do better in the future. I am digging in here for a great burst of work and may not pause for a week or two but I shall call you up and hope you will be able to arrange a time for meeting,[7] and perhaps you can also meet Mr. Perkins, if you feel like it.

Meanwhile, thanks again for your letter and with all good wishes to all of you,

Sincerely yours,
Tom Wolfe

P.S. – I haven't had time to correct this letter carefully — so please excuse errors, and the worn-out typewriter ribbon!

1. Wolfe visited his first cousin Edgar E. (Jim) Wolf, the son of his father's brother, Gilbert John Wolf. (The Pennsylvania branch of the family spelled their name without the final *e*.)

2. "The Vision of Spangler's Paul" was consolidated with other material and published posthumously as *The Web and the Rock* and *You Can't Go Home Again*.

3. Ralph Wheaton's misfortunes with National Cash Register are recounted in Wolfe's "The Company" (*New Masses*, January 11, 1938). The material also appears in *You Can't Go Home Again* as chapter 8, "The Company." Wheaton is fictionalized as Randy Shepperton, and National Cash Register as the Federal Weight, Scales, and Computing Company.

4. Madeleine Boyd was confronted with her embezzlement of German royalties for *Look Homeward, Angel* in 1932; Wolfe fired her. Later, destitute, she sued Wolfe for royalties on *Of Time and the River* for which she had no claim; the case was settled out of court, with Wolfe paying her $650 as a gift to be rid of her.

5. Kathleen Hoagland and her mother often had Wolfe to their home. Kathleen's brother, Muredach J. Dooher, was the manuscript dealer described here who cheated Wolfe.

6. Wolfe described his current relations with the Robertses in a letter to his mother, on May 28, 1936: "Mr. Roberts and Mrs. Roberts are in town, by the way, visiting Margaret. Mrs. Roberts wrote me the other day, after all these years. Her letter, I am afraid, still showed resentment about what she thinks I said about members of her family in 'Look Homeward Angel'; nevertheless, she said they still cared for me and wanted to see me while they were here. I wrote back and told her that I would like to see them, that I was glad to know they wanted to see me; but that as far as the matters she discussed in her letter were concerned, I would rather not talk about them if it was going to cause pain and confusion and misunderstanding to anyone. She wrote

me another letter in reply to this one and asked me to let her know when I could come and have dinner with them. I suppose I will go and hope that everything turns out for the best" (Wolfe, *Letters of Thomas Wolfe to His Mother,* 265). Wolfe here sounds less than eager at the prospect of meeting Mrs. Roberts face-to-face and, in fact, did not accept her invitation to dinner. She was stung by Wolfe's snub and, after one more letter, did not write him again for another year.

7. According to Margaret Rose Roberts, "She wrote to Tom and said when she saw that signature scrawled across the book she couldn't bear to leave New York without seeing him as she hadn't seen him for seven years. So she wrote to him and asked if he could come to dinner. Tom wrote back that he was so happy she wanted to see him again, and that he was going down to Pennsylvania for a few days to look up some of his ancestors, but as soon as he returned he would phone her. And he told her that Mr. Perkins had always wanted to meet her, and he hoped they could arrange a dinner together. Tom told her, 'I'll be so happy to see you again providing that we can let bygones be bygones and not open up any old wounds.' Well, that was Tom's way of escaping from things he didn't want to talk about, and my mother was not like that. She said to us, 'You know perfectly well I can't talk to Tom after seven years without making any reference to what happened.' And so she wrote him a short note which said, 'I'll be so happy to have you come. We'll sit down together and talk the way we always have, and let the chips fall where they may.' That's why Tom never came. He couldn't bear the thought of a confrontation" (Margaret Rose Roberts to Ted Mitchell, interview, November 5, 1990). The short note Miss Roberts refers to has not been preserved.

62

ALS, 1 p., Harvard, bMS Am 1883.1 (545)
Apt. 33, 130 Morningside Drive
Postmarked June 11, 1936   *New York*[1]

My dear Tom,

It has just occurred to me that, on reading the last paragraph of my letter, you may have feared that we meant to lure you in here and scalp you. Believe me, our intentions are entirely pacific, inspired by memories of the happy early days.

This note's real purpose is not to break in on your fury of composition which I know that you cannot and will not let either angels or devils do, but merely to try to keep certain dates before. The time is somewhat complicated for us by other people's actions, which we cannot control. As it now is, to have the most satisfactory visit, could you possibly come before June 20, and not on this Friday, Saturday, or Sunday? Nor next [*left blank*]. Of course, if you

LEFT: Mr. and Mrs. Roberts with their granddaughter, Martha Elizabeth, in front yard at 14 Fairway Drive, summer 1936. Courtesy of Jerry Israel, Asheville, North Carolina

J. M. " Buddie" Roberts Jr., wife Verna, and daughter Martha Elizabeth, in front of 14 Fairway Drive, summer 1936. Courtesy of Jerry Israel, Asheville, North Carolina

could come once, or many times after June 20, well and good, but, as things are, there will be much less satisfaction to you and to us, I know, if we are hampered, as we should be, in this first visit after the strain of long silence.[2] But of course I know you cannot interrupt your work. Just do the best you can.

Most sincerely, Margaret Roberts.

[On left margin]

Your letter was surely interesting. I can well understand the part about Mabel and Mr. W – and all else.

1. Determined from return address on back of envelope.

2. "Verna and Buddie were going to be there with their daughter, Martha Elizabeth" (Margaret Rose Roberts to Ted Mitchell, interview, July 24, 1994). Martha Elizabeth Palmer remembered meeting Wolfe on another occassion: "I always thought my father was 'ten feet tall', physically a big man, but Tom Wolfe was taller and bigger. . . . He ate so many boiled shrimp (with bacon) that there was little left for me" (Martha Elizabeth Palmer to Ted Mitchell, December 2, 2004).

63

ON MAY 3, 1937, Wolfe arrived in Asheville for his first visit to his hometown since the publication of *Look Homeward, Angel* in 1929. Although most of the feathers he ruffled had been smoothed, many of the victims of *Look Homeward, Angel* were slow to forget or forgive what Wolfe had written about them and their families. George W. McCoy attended North State School in Asheville but did not meet Wolfe until he entered the University of North Carolina during Wolfe's senior year. When he dealt with Wolfe, McCoy was state news editor of the *Asheville Citizen.* In 1953,[1] he described Wolfe's reunion with Mr. and Mrs. Roberts in their home near Asheville:

> When Tom came home in May, 1937, he told me he would like to visit Professor and Mrs. Roberts, but hesitated to do so without an invitation. Mrs. Roberts also told me she would welcome Tom if he came to her home, but she hesitated to extend an invitation since he had not kept the appointment to have dinner with her and Professor Roberts when they were in New York the previous year.
>
> The situation appeared to call for the offices of a third party and I became a willing volunteer. Having persuaded Tom to go, we drove to the Roberts home at 14 Fairway Drive[2] in Beverly Hills near Asheville. There he was warmly welcomed and the long period of estrangement was ended. After the amenities were completed, I withdrew, leaving Tom and Mrs. Roberts to talk about every subject from Dan to Beersheba, with one exception. I learned a long time later that the subject of *Look Homeward, Angel* was not mentioned.[3]

Wolfe rented a cabin from his boyhood friend Max Whitson in nearby Oteen, planning to work all summer in it, hoping for seclusion. In July Mrs. Roberts asked Wolfe if two young admirers of his work from Nashville, Tennessee, could call on him before the summer ended and he returned to New York.

Postmarked July 23, 1937   *ALS, 2 pp., Harvard, bMS Am 1883.1 (545)*

My dear Tom,

Knowing what your purpose is in being in Asheville, I hesitate to break into your time, and I would under no circumstance do it for my own sake.[4]

But you will recall, I think, what I told you the two young people living in Nashville who <u>literally</u> adore you. They have bought every line you have written, and I judge know your books literally by heart.[5]

When we were in Nashville last summer, they heard we were from Asheville and came to see us to ask if we knew you. I think they had a faint hope that being your fellow townspeople we might in some way bring them in touch with you in New York, to which they were going for their vacation for practically nothing except to try to see you. Of course after our experience with you in New York last summer I felt helpless to try to help them in any way (A wise child remembers its burn).

I can assure you of this; there is absolutely no lion-hunting, scalp-taking in their seeming pursuit of you. It is a case of entirely sincere hero-worship.

Now that you are in Asheville, they want to come over with the hope of seeing you, and want to know if they could come over next Sat. If your

The Roberts home at 14 Fairway Drive, where they reconciled with Thomas Wolfe in 1937. Photo by Ted Mitchell

mother is taking anybody, or if Mable is, for rooms, or rooms and meals, they would like to stay there. (They are engaged, but not married.)

They would just as soon come later in August if you expect to be here.

I can't entertain them because we are moving over the week-end, but they don't want me to. They will go to a hotel if neither your mother nor Mable are taking outsiders now.

I hope you realize how I have hesitated to write this to you, because I realize that every interruption is anethema to you when the fury of writing pursues you. But it has been hard to resist their earnest enthusiasm.

We have taken it for granted that whenever you had time to see us, you would let us know.

Please tell Mable that I can hardly expect her to understand why I haven't been to see her since she moved back. I think she would, though, if she could all the wind currents that have blown me hither and yonder this entire year.

Please pardon this intrusion, but call me phone 1963–W at once, so that I can invite these young people. They want to come at your convenience but are afraid you may leave unexpectedly.

I venture to hope that you can spare the time for them, and I venture to ask that you will for old time's sake.

Margaret R.

This is pretty rough paper and penmanship to send to a distinguished author.

1. George W. McCoy, "Asheville and Thomas Wolfe," *North Carolina Historical Review* 30 (April 1953): 200–217.

2. Now 46 Fairway Drive.

3. McCoy's source is J. M. Roberts. However, Margaret Rose Roberts was convinced the subject of *Look Homeward, Angel* had been broached: "Mother was not the kind of person who could have gone on for seven years and *not* discuss what happened. I'm certain they talked about it" (Margaret Rose Roberts to Ted Mitchell, interview, November 5, 1990). Despite these contradictory accounts, conversations about *Look Homeward, Angel* between Wolfe and the Robertses—if any—have not been documented.

4. Wolfe was immersed in writing "The Party at Jack's" in his cabin at Oteen.

5. E. E. Miller and his fiancée, Eula Person.

64

TLS, 3 pp., Harvard, bMS Am 1883.2 (294)
[Oteen, North Carolina]

July 26, 1937

Dear Mrs. Roberts:

I did not get your letter until Saturday night when I was in town and went out to Mabel's house. And as it was then rather late I did not call you but decided to write you and call you up when I am next in town. Of course I have no telephone out here and that is why I have not called you earlier. I know you must understand that I should have tried to see you or communicate with you before if I had not been so busy. I have been away from home so long and there have been so many connections to make, so many threads to pick up, so many people, family, relatives, friends, acquaintances and even people I had never seen before to talk to. A great deal of it of course, has been very pleasant and a great deal of it has been exhausting and perhaps useless but unavoidable. In addition I have got to work again and have been trying to push on in spite of all this social activity and these interruptions. From now on I hope to have more time for work and for seeing old friends. But that is the way things have been thus far and I know you can understand it.

And of course I'd be delighted to meet the two young people from Nashville, and I think the meeting could be arranged at almost any time. I don't believe this coming Saturday is a good time because I have tentatively promised my sister Effie[1] who was up here last week and whom I have not seen for eight years to take the bus and come down to visit her over the week end in Anderson, South Carolina. This date was subject to change but we had tentatively decided upon it and my brother Fred had made plans to meet me in Spartanburg, introduce me to some of his friends there and then drive me over to Effie's. If this arrangement is carried out this coming Saturday would not be a good time for the visit of your friends from Nashville. The only other engagement I have in mind is also a tentative one. My friend Hamilton Basso[2] who lives at Pisgah Forest has written me and suggested that he come over some week end early in August and drive me up to visit our friend Sherwood Anderson[3] who lives near Marion, Virginia and who has invited me to come to see him. I am waiting for more definite information from Ham Basso because I believe he is mistaken in thinking Sherwood Anderson is at home. Sherwood told me when I saw him last in April that he had accepted an invitation to attend the Writers' Conference at Boulder, Colorado and give some lectures there. I accepted the same invitation two summers ago and had to

Wolfe in the cabin at Oteen, July 10, 1937. By permission of the Thomas Wolfe Collection, Pack Memorial Public Library, Asheville, North Carolina

report out there by the first of August and remain until about the middle of the month. So I doubt that Anderson will be back at Marion before the end of August.

Anyway, excepting the trip down to South Carolina this week end I have no definite engagements and it seems to me you might arrange the meeting with your friends at almost any other time. The only other thing that worries me is the feeling of personal responsibility. I wish you would do what you could to ease that up a bit. It is very flattering of course to be the object of anyone's adoration but it is also a very hard and trying role to live up to. And I am so genuinely so profoundly grateful for the good will and belief of people. It seems to me that the knowledge that something one has written has meant so much to anyone ought to make a writer proud and happy and is more than anything else the reward for which he lives and works. But I was a very tired man when I left New York and I am not rested yet. I have really had no real rest or release from pressure for the last eight or nine years – none at all since Look Homeward Angel was published – and the last two years since the publication of Of Time and the River have been terrific ones. If I survive them, they will add enormously to my store of experience and to the materials of my work. But the reason I am here at present – in my cabin and on my hill is that I followed a profound and powerful instinct which told me that this was the thing I ought to do – that now I needed desperately a period of contemplation and repose, when I could let the accumulations of the last ten years soak in, digest it, and meditate for my future purpose. And that I think is really what I am here for; it's so good to be back home again, so good to see old friends and to restablish old connections.[4]

But I do want to try to take things a bit more casually for a time – I don't want to disappoint your two young friends but I should like to feel relieved of the strain and pressure of having to try to live up to their image of me. I know that you can arrange the whole thing simply and without complication – get them to understand that I am no longer a wild eyed boy or a flaming youth or anything like that but just a man who has done a lot of work and a lot of living at high pressure and is now trying to relax and think it over. If they will take me like this I am sure we will all be more comfortable and have a better time. At any rate I know you can fix the whole thing tactfully; I am sorry these young people are going to make the trip all the way from Nashville just to meet me. I wish they too just "happened in" so to speak – it gives me a feeling of tension and anxiety to know they are going to the expense and trouble of such a journey just to see me. But since they are I want them to enjoy themselves; I wish they'd come out here and spend the day with me – on some Sunday if it could be arranged. Then if they like we could go in and visit Mama and Mabel or any other members of the family. As to where they are going to stay you will have to decide that later. Mabel and Ralph have been living in a very nice house on Kimberly Ave. But they have just rented it for the summer and they are moving to a very much smaller one and I don't know until I see it how much extra room they have. As for Mama's house, there is certainly room there, but it is frankly in a dilapidated state – an old house in a state of disrepair which has long since passed its palmy days. Of course it is Mama's home and she loves it and sees it with a different eye, but these are the facts and I don't know whether it would be advisable for the young people to stay there or not. However we shall see; all these things can be arranged. I'd keep them here if there was room. But we can easily find a place for them somewhere.[5]

This is all for the present. I think this gives you all the essential information and I leave the rest to you. You can arrange the date at almost any time that is convenient with the exception of this coming week end. I shall call you up and talk with you further about it in a day or two when I come into town. Meanwhile with all good wishes to you and Mr. Roberts,

     Sincerely yours,

       Tom Wolfe

[Handwritten by Mrs. Roberts below Wolfe's signature]

You should have them write to me at once when they can come and let the date be fixed with them a good bit ahead so that there will be no disap. for them.

1. Effie Wolfe Gambrell (1887–1950), portrayed as Daisy in *Look Homeward, Angel*.

2. Hamilton Basso (1904–1964), Scribner's author and journalist. Basso had met Wolfe in the Scribner's office in 1935 and, after a friendship developed, shared an avid correspondence with Wolfe. Basso saw a great deal of Wolfe during the later years of his life.

3. Short-story writer and novelist Sherwood Anderson (1876–1941) had long been one of Wolfe's literary idols. On July 8, 1935, he wrote Anderson: "It seemed to me ever since I first began to read your books when I was a kid of twenty that you got down below the surface of our lives and got at some of the terror and mystery and ugliness and beauty in America better than anyone else" (Wolfe, *Letters*, 472).

4. Wolfe soon found it nearly impossible to work in the cabin as friends, family, and curiosity seekers flocked to see him. He later told newspaper editor R. P. Harriss: "I've been down home at Asheville, and I found that being forgiven was almost worse than being damned. Did you ever have just too much hospitality?" (R. P. Harriss, "A Memoir of Thomas Wolfe," *Baltimore Evening Sun,* September 16, 1938).

5. E. E. Miller and Eula Person found accommodations at Julia Wolfe's Old Kentucky Home boardinghouse. Along with the Robertses and Hamilton Basso, Miller and Person visited Wolfe at Oteen on Sunday, August 15, 1937.

65

October 2, 1937   *ALS, 1 p., Harvard, bMS Am 1883.1 (545)*

Oct. 2.

My dear Tom,

I think, considering the fact that you were so generous of your time, you will be pleased to read this letter and know that seeing you meant so much to them. I had an equally delighted letter from the young woman, Miss Person, but I have misplaced. As I told you, I felt horribly guilty in thus pushing in upon you, but, in spite of my sense of guilt, I can't be sorry so far as we individually are concerned, for the day will live with us as a gleaming one. I think we both realized your power of mind and spirit more vividly than ever before, except, of course, the wonderful days of your boyhood and young manhood, when, it seemed to me, there was none like you in many ways.

However, I also know, in spite of the pleasure your visitors got from that Sunday that it was such inroads upon your writing time that drove you away from Asheville.[1] We were so hard at work and so neglectful of the papers that you were gone a week before we knew it. Peace be to you for your work, wherever you may be.

Meeting Mr. Basso was an event of importance in our very simple lives, for which many thanks to you. Please do not feel under any obligation to use up your writing time in writing in return – and here's to hoping that you will somewhere find freedom for what your mind says you must do. Yours in memory of the old days of your brilliant boyhood,

M.R.

[On left margin]

I suppose your clipping bureau has sent you Joseph Sell's (of the Manchester Evening News) opinion that on you, Josephine Johnston, and E. Caldwell rests the future of the Amer. novel.

1. While still in Asheville, Wolfe wrote a correspondent, "It's pretty hard to tell you what I shall do about staying here in Asheville. I wanted to come back: I thought about it for years. . . . But my stay here this summer has really resembled a three-ring circus. I think people have wanted to be and have tried to be most kind, but they wore me to a frazzle. My cabin outside of town was situated in an isolated and quite beautiful spot, but they found their way to it" (Wolfe, *Letters,* 653). Once back in New York, he wrote John Munsey Roberts Jr. on November 5, 1937: "Anyway, that cabin of mine with its beautiful hill, which I thought was going to be a haven of peace and rest was about as restful as a subway at rush hour. I had them all out there from Bill Cocke to the undertaker. But as for peace and quiet, I've got more if I had moved my cot out and parked it in Times Square" (*Harvard*).

66

On December 31, 1937, Wolfe signed a ten-thousand-dollar contract with Harper and Brothers for a novel, "The Life and Adventures of Bondsman Doaks." He was elated with his new editor, Edward C. Aswell (1900–1958), a fellow southerner (from Tennessee), also a Harvard graduate, and six days younger than Wolfe.

At the beginning of 1938, Wolfe launched into intensive work on his new novel. He began devising ways that the unpublished portion of his second novel, *Of Time and the River* ("The October Fair"), could be consolidated into his "Bondsman Doaks" book. He began assembling new and old material that would take his protagonist, Joe Doaks, through the Depression in both Libya Hill (his new fictional counterpart for Asheville) and New York. The manuscript eventually became a massive biographical chronicle with a new title,

"The Web and the Rock." Uncompleted at Wolfe's death, the giant manuscript was published posthumously as *The Web and the Rock* (1939), *You Can't Go Home Again* (1940), and *The Hills Beyond* (1941).

In February Wolfe wrote Mrs. Roberts asking her to help locate newspaper accounts detailing the fall of Asheville's Central Bank and Trust Company. He planned to use Asheville as the setting for a book about his growing social concerns as well as the end of prosperity in the 1920s and 1930s. *You Can't Go Home Again* would chronicle the ruin of Asheville at the outset of the Great Depression and the scandals surrounding the failure of Central Bank and Trust that ended the city's days of glory. This material was edited and published posthumously in *You Can't Go Home Again* as Chapter 7, "Boom Town"; Chapter 8, "The Company"; Chapter 9, "The City of Lost Men"; and Chapter 25, "The Catastrophe."

TLS, 2 pp., Harvard, bMS Am 1883.2 (294)

114 East 56th Street
New York, New York
c/o Miss Elizabeth Nowell
February 14, 1938

Dear Mrs. Roberts:

I have wanted to write you for a long time, but many things have happened to keep me busy, including courts and lawyers, and a long and ugly business of trying to recover manuscript which a man had taken, and which he had not returned.[1] I won the thing the other day, completely and overwhelmingly – that is, if one ever does win anything when the lawyers have taken out their pound of flesh. Anyway, for the first time in three years I am out of the woods – out of the legal woods, at any rate, the long, exhausting and complicated series of legal difficulties with which I shall not weary you with here, but which all boil down to the same thing in the end – to the organized national industry of shysterdom, parasitism, and shaking-down – in my case, of being shook – to which everyone apparently who is unfortunate enough to receive any degree of public notice is in one way or the other susceptible.

I wrote you and Mr. Roberts a Christmas card, but it was returned, apparently with the address unknown – I simply addressed it Asheville, North Carolina, because I did not know what address, if any, that new place of yours has. But I am going to call up Munsey tonight at the AP to get your exact address: I saw him and Verna and their beautiful little girl several weeks ago – I went out and had supper with them, and after that we talked until the usual knocking-off hour of four in the morning. Your little boy looked well and handsome, and no one is going to accuse him of anemia. We had a good time, and I think Munsey is happy in his work here.

Now, I want you to help me if you can. And I know that I can depend on you to keep this confidential. I am also writing to my cousin, Jack Westall,[2] with a similar request for information and help; and I think I may also write young Taylor Bledsoe, because he indicated to me last summer that he might be able to give me some information if I ever needed it that would be useful. What I want is this:

I am writing a long book, and I want to put everything that I have in it: and this time the book is not about a town, nor about any certain group of people, but it is about America and what happened here between 1929 and 1937.[3] I think you will agree with me and see what I am driving at when I tell you that what happened in Asheville in that period seems pretty important and significant in the light it throws on what happened to the whole country. So, to get down to brass tacks: first of all, do you know what is the best and completest newspaper account of the events – the bank trials, the affairs of the city, etc. – which occurred between 1930 and 1932? And do you know where I can get a copy of them? I would be willing to buy them, if I could do so at a fair price, or if you know anyone who has kept such a record, and would be willing to let me have it for several weeks, I would make every guarantee to preserve it and to see that it is returned to its owner safely. And if anything else occurs to you, if there are any people you think I could write, or any other information that might be useful, I should be grateful if you would let me know about this too.

There is so much that I would like to tell you now of what has been happening to me, and so much that I would like to tell you about this book. But if I ever got started here I would never finish. All that I can tell you here is this: I began life, as so many young men do, as a lyrical writer, and my first work was largely concerned with the affairs and preoccupations of youth and of the world in terms of its impingements on my own personality. Now I am older, and I shall never write that kind of book again. I am no longer so much concerned with my own life, I am rather passionately concerned with the life around me and with the broader social implications it has. At any rate, for better or for worse, I am now committed utterly to this book – like old Martin Luther, "I can't do otherwise" – there is no other way. Therefore, please help me if you can. And please write soon.

Meanwhile, with all good wishes to you and Mr. Roberts for your health and happiness,

     Sincerely,

        Tom Wolfe

P.S. I had letters from the nice young couple from Nashville who came out with you and Mr. Roberts to see me at the cabin last summer, but in the process of moving from one place to another last fall I mislaid the letters and now I do not know how to write them. But if you write them I wish you would tell them what happened and say that I send my greetings to them. Basso and his wife are somewhere on the continent of Europe – in France, I believe: I saw him in September before he sailed, and he asked to be remembered to you and Mr. Roberts. This is all now; please write soon.

TW/GJ[4]

1. A lawsuit Wolfe filed against manuscript dealer Muredach J. Dooher for withholding manuscripts Wolfe had given him to sell and later asked him to return. The trial on February 8, 1937, marked the last time Wolfe and Maxwell Perkins saw each other. Although Wolfe had severed his relationship with Scribner's in January 1937, Perkins volunteered to testify at the Dooher trial because he had been present during several discussions with Dooher.

2. Julia Wolfe's nephew, James F. "Jack" Westall.

3. When Asheville's real estate boom collapsed in 1926, Central Bank and Trust Company held millions of dollars in real estate loans secured by excessively depreciated paper. Alarmed that foreclosure on loans would bankrupt local businesses and ruin Asheville's economy, bank officers convinced city and county officials to leave over six million dollars in cash deposits at Central Bank while they operated on the proceeds of short-term notes. Although North Carolina law required city deposits to be secured by sufficient collateral, Central Bank instead delivered depreciated real estate notes at inflated pre-1927 prices. State bank examiners declared Central Bank insolvent in 1928 but did little except notify municipal officials. The state bank examiner's report was kept secret, and Central Bank continued to operate. The bank remained open between 1928 and 1930 only by falsifying its books and through deposits from Asheville and Buncombe County. When the bank was forced to close its doors in November 1930, panic spread throughout the region. City officials were forced to resign, and a Buncombe County jury began returning indictments against those who participated in the Central Bank swindle. Two of the indicted officials, Asheville's former mayor and a Central Bank officer, committed suicide. Tried and convicted, Central Bank's president was sent to prison. For Wolfe's rendering of the bank scandal, see *You Can't Go Home Again*, 359–72.

4. Gwen Jassinoff, a typist Wolfe hired while living at the Hotel Chelsea.

67

February 21, 1938   *Signed postcard, Harvard, bMS Am 1883.1 (545)*

Dogwood Road, Charlotte St. Extension,
Asheville N.C.
Feb. 21.

My Dear Tom,

I think I shall have no difficulty in finding what you want, but it may take us three or four or five days. Will work as fast as possible and will write as to what we have accomplished.

The address you ask for is: E. E. Miller
1714 West End Avenue
Nashville, Tennessee

I do not have the girl's address but a letter to him will be for both. I have for a long time had a letter from them which they wrote me about you but I didn't know when you left or where you went. Will do our level best to get what you want. M.R.

68

TLS, 2 pp., Harvard, bMS Am 1883.2 (294)

114 East 56th Street
New York, New York
c/o Miss Elizabeth Nowell
March 1, 1938

Dear Mrs. Roberts:

I was delighted to get your postcard this morning and to know that you would be able to help. I also had a long and very interesting letter from Jack Westall just a few days ago about the same matter, and he also said he would be glad to help, but wanted to know specifically just what I had in mind. I tried to tell him, so far as space and time permitted me, and thought I might repeat it for your own benefit.

He wanted to know just why I had emphasized the date, 1930–1932: as he went on to explain in his letter, the whole thing was a culmination of things that went far back in the past, twenty years or more, and as he said, it would be important to know the whole story.[1] I agreed with this absolutely, and told him please to let me have any information that was at all pertinent; but I explained to him that my book was in no specific sense of the word "about

Asheville," that it was a book on a tremendous scale about America and that what was so important and significant to me in the thing that happened at home was its reference and relation to the whole scheme. Of course, the true Asheville citizen takes a certain melancholy pride, I think, in the fact that what happened to Asheville was in a sense unique: I think, however, you will agree that its uniqueness was only one of degree, and not of kind – as I told Jack Westall in my letter, it seemed to me that Asheville was pretty typical of the rest of the country with three extra degrees of fever.

I explained to him also that the present time frame of the book was between the period 1929 and 1937: I know that this conflicts somewhat with actual historical fact so far as Asheville is concerned, but I cannot see that this matters very much: I explained to him I was not writing an historical account, but a work of fictional imagination – in a lot of ways, it seems possible to attain a higher and more intense degree of truth imaginatively than by merely being faithful to exact dates and literal circumstances.[2]

I realize, of course, that the peak time, so far as Asheville is concerned, was around 1926; but I have chosen 1929 deliberately for the opening of my book, because it represents a time when the great national boom had reached its highest fever pitch of intensity – anything and everything, of course, that can contribute to the whole picture, from beginning to end, is meat for my grinder: of course, as I believe we said last summer, the tremendous thing is the human thing, the great human tragedy, the social drama in all its inner weavings, and its whole web-like complexity. In the end, it is this – what actually happened to the lives of the people – that I am after, it is important to me, down below the story of the banks and speculation and real estate and politics and all the rest of it. And, believe me, I know what happened to people, because I know the people. It is still happening, too, it is happening to my mother yet – they are trying to take her house, the little remnant of her property away from her[3] – and it has happened in so many ways to so many other people I know: I have rebuilt this in my brain, and woven it into my imagination – now, I want any of the literal facts, of the actual record that I can get. It is going to be a tremendous job – the whole thing – but I think it may be worth it in the end.

This is all now. I hope this finds you and Mr. Roberts well. I have not seen Munsey since I wrote you, but shall look him up one of these days soon. About myself, there is not much to report except that I am working. I do thank you most gratefully for your willingness to help.

With all good wishes to you all,

Sincerely,

Tom Wolfe

1. "The year 1930 saw the toppling of a house of cards piled up for about 15 years" (Jack Westall to Thomas Wolfe, February 16, 1938; *Harvard.*).

2. Wolfe's fictional account of Asheville's ruin was not too far removed from "actual historical fact." In *You Can't Go Home Again* he wrote: "Already the town had passed from their possession. They no longer owned it. It was mortgaged under a debt of fifty million dollars, owned by bonding companies in the North. The very streets they walked on had been sold beneath their feet. They signed their names to papers calling for the payment of fabulous sums, and resold their land the next day to other madmen who signed away their lives with the same careless magnificence. On paper, their profits were enormous, but their 'boom' was already over and they would not see it. They were staggering beneath obligations to pay which none of them could meet—and still they bought" (142–43).

3. One of Wolfe's objectives for making his 1937 trip to Asheville was to determine if he could help his mother untangle her financial troubles with Wachovia Bank. Like many others in Asheville, Julia Wolfe had speculated wildly and successfully on real estate during the 1920s. After the stock market crashed in 1929, she found she had overspeculated and could no longer pay her mortgages or taxes. Wachovia Bank sued her for the foreclosure of deeds of trust she had executed to secure payments. A year after Wolfe's death, the boardinghouse Old Kentucky Home and four additional lots belonging to his mother were sold by Wachovia Bank at public auction.

69

AL, 2 pp., UNC

Dogwood Road
Charlotte St. Extension
Asheville, N.C.
March 5, 1938.

My dear Tom,

You must be puzzled by our long delay, or think we have failed you altogether. I thought when I first wrote you that getting the papers would be comparatively simple, but there has been some difficulty, and still is, though I think now that the papers can be had, though only by your having time to wait for them.

We thought surely that Mr. Hendricks, editor at that time of "The Advocate" would have a complete file of the A – and also of the Taxpayer's League "Bulletin," which I think would be worthwhile for you. He did not have the papers, but talked for two hours to Mr. R. – telling him all sorts of the stuff of which novels are made, and which never came out in any of the papers. His head is full of that period material, and he is very reliable. Mr. R. thinks you would find a gold mine in Hendricks if you could come down here quietly. Then he (Mr. R–) saw Mr. Toms,[1] owner of the Advocate. He is willing to let you have the Ad-files, with of course, the strict understanding that they be <u>carefully</u> returned in good condition because he has just the one complete set. Mr. R. felt under circumstance, that it was necessary to tell Toms who wants them but Toms pledged himself to strict secrecy. Since he Toms was being willing to thus place in somebody's hands his only file, Mr. R. thought it was only fair that he should know to whom he was entrusting them. Mr. R. told him that you would do whatever was reasonable about a rental price, but Toms did not say he expected anything. That can be arranged.

But here comes the hitch! Toms is trying to get a radio station here, and if he does, he will, for some reason, need his complete file for some three or four months. He will know, in the course of two or, at most, three weeks whether the Radio commission will grant him the station. If he fails to get it, then you can have the files immediately after the two or three weeks interval, but, as I said if he succeeds, then he will need them for three or four months. Let me know how long you can wait.

Mr. Toms says if you could talk with Wickes Wamboldt,[2] you could get your head stuffed to bursting. Mr. Hendricks and Mr. Wamboldt know more than any fifty people, I should judge, about all that has been printed, and the dozens of stories that never got into print, and yet are authentic. As you say, each community thinks itself the hardest hit in such matters, but, Tom, I really doubt whether any community of any size ever had as many tragedies brewing at one time, so many tragic events as there were here in those two or three years. A thousand novels were here, yet all centering with the perfectest unity around the politico-bank situation. After my long delay, anxious to get this in next mail, and it must go to the box now, if I do. Your letters as to your ideas about your future writing wonderful. For simple, straight forward writing, yours on peace in this week's Nation wonderfully fine.[3]

Let me hear from you at once if you can wait on Toms.

1. Harold Thoms. Both Wolfe and Mrs. Roberts spell Mr. Thoms's name incorrectly throughout the following letters.

2. Wickes Wamboldt, former mayor of Asheville.

3. Anonymous, "How to Keep Out of War," *Nation* 146 (April 2, 1938): 376–78. Frieda Kirchwey, editor of the *Nation,* wrote to Wolfe and others for statements as to "How to Keep Out of War." Wolfe wrote a section of the article (377–78). See Wolfe, *Letters,* 734–36.

70

Ca. March 1938   *AL, 2 pp., Harvard, bMS Am 1883.1 (545)*

Dogwood Road
Charlotte St. Extension
Asheville, N.C.

How much like old times to say –
  My dear Tom,

  I suppose you have received my card, which, however, my husband carried
two or three days in his pocket. First, to the business in hand we thought it
wise, to avoid burying you under duplicates, to find out just what Jack Westall would send. He agreed with Mr. Roberts that he had certain selected things
he would send of which he would give us a list; then we could send whatever
else we could find. We should get that list from him today or tomorrow. The
files of the "Advocate," which was the organ of the Taxpayers League, and also
the Bulletins of the League will be a rich mine for your purpose. Jack W. says
he has a complete file of this during the period you want, tho, as I said, his
idea seems to be to send you only certain select things. I am pretty sure we can
supplement this and hope to be definite in a day or so. We kept a complete
file, but I have a pretty definite remembrance that in packing and sorting to
move here, in a sort of dazed misery caused by trying to sort out the junk
of twenty-five years' accumulation that I desperately hurled these, along with
other long hoarded potential treasures into the bonfire. I shall try all other
sources first, and if I fail, I'll then start digging in our masses of stuff. We have
our things stored in three different places, part still in Beverly Hills, part in
the barn, built since we came here, and part in the attic of this look-out post.[1]
And of course, tragically what you want is always in the most remote corner
under the highest pile of boxes. Nevertheless, if we don't get the papers elsewhere, we will make the attack on this stored stuff on all flanks.

  It will be intensely interesting to follow up what you do with it after you
get it. I notice John Dos Passos seems to have a similar plan of development
in his new book "U.S.A.T."[2] Well, whatever you do, I know you will do it
tremendously – and we shall see what we shall see.

  I am enclosing a letter from "Red" Miller, the young Nashville man, written soon after they left.[3] I also had one from Eula, which I did not save. They
were both lifted into the seventh heaven by seeing you, so, even though you
did give us too much time, perhaps it was for the best. I know we enjoyed it
completely.

You speak of Mr. Basso. You may recall that he spoke as if he would really like to come back with his wife to see the little house when he returns in the spring to N.C. We should be happy to have them come, but I always have a great hesitancy about imposing ourselves upon persons who are too often pursued cruelly by headhunters.

I suppose you are as Buddie said, "holed in," busy with your new book, and worked to death. I hope you are too busy to be eaten up by the national deviltries, that seem determined to destroy our poor old world. It looks as if a Titanic Fate had the world by the heels, and were swinging violently, each time more violently smashing its head against iron walls.

[Written on margin, p.2]

Have faith that we will do our best to get what you want. I regret keenly to tell you that Taylor Bledsoe[4] is at the asylum in Morganton. They hope he can be cured.

1. The garage apartment the Robertses built while the main house at 10 North Dogwood Drive was under construction.

2. *U.S.A.* trilogy by John Dos Passos (1869–1970), which consists of *The 42nd Parallel* (1930), *1919* (1932), and *The Big Money* (1936).

3. An excerpt from E. E. Miller's letter: "Mr. Wolfe is an even greater man than he is a writer. Before meeting him I did not think it possible that anyone could measure up to Look Homeward, Angel, nor did I believe that he would ever succeed in equaling that performance as a writer. But I now think it not only possible, but inevitable, that he will even surpass all his former work" (E. E. Miller to Margaret Roberts, September 6, 1937; *Harvard*).

4. Taylor Bledsoe, a former student at North State School.

71

TLS, 4 pp., Harvard, bMS Am 1883.2 (294)

114 East 56th Street
New York, New York
c/o Miss Elizabeth Nowell
March 7, 1938

Dear Mrs. Roberts:

Thanks very much for your letter with the enclosed one from Mr. Miller. By the way, I do not think that his address is included, because I cannot find it looking through your letter and his. If you remember to send it to me, along with the young lady's,[1] the next time you write, I will be grateful. They will probably be surprised to hear from me after so long a time, but I do want to answer the very nice letter they sent me.

Your letter is full of good news except, of course, poor Taylor Bledsoe. I felt, of course, last summer that there was something wrong; and yet, I liked him. He seemed to have a genuinely good heart and good feeling: I do hope he can be cured.

I wonder what is wrong with the set-up, anyhow. I suppose Asheville is no worse than other communities in this respect, and that the average of catastrophe is no higher there than anywhere else. And yet, that was one of the most disturbing revelations that I got last summer, going back as I did after an absence of eight years and with the sharp and fresh impressions that such absence gives to one. It seemed as if the whole landscape was strewn with the shipwrecks of people I had known: I inquired about person after person only to be told that they were at Dix Hill, or had just returned; or at Morganton,[2] or that they had gone completely to pieces through drugs or drink, or a combination of both. And looking back over my childhood and early youth in Asheville, it often seems to me now that the people who went down, who became these shipwrecks, were not the worthless litter of humanity, but often the best, the brightest, and the most intelligent we had.

It occurred to me that if such things happen to such people there must be something wrong with the background that produced them, something in the life around them that did not give them enough to employ their talents, or waken the deepest interest in their lives. Am I wrong about this? I want to keep a clear perspective, and I think the answer may be that my own life in so many special and intimate ways is bound up with the life of Asheville: I know so many people there, in a sense, when I go home, I inherit the life of the whole community.

Here, in this vast city, it is, of course, different: the number of people that one knows or can know is relatively small: I know that one can find every kind of human wreckage here, because I have seen it myself, but it does seem to me, among most of the people that I know best, such catastrophe does not happen with the appalling frequency it does at home. The big wicked city that one hears so much about is also a very busy and hardworking place. It would be ironic, wouldn't it, if one eventually discovered that he had to come here to keep out of mischief?

Anyway, the whole problem to my mind is a pretty serious one: if there is anything in it, I would like to find out why – it seems to me that that, too, is a legitimate subject for fiction. For example, often when I have heard the learned economists talk about the boom – how and when it began, how it got going, why it collapsed, what was fundamentally wrong with about it – I have kept silent, because there were so many human and spiritual things about it as well that never get mentioned. I think that one of these things – remembering my own childhood – is a deep and intense hunger in people for "something to happen" – waiting for something, they are not sure what, but something that is full of excitement, movement, color, sudden wealth.

Whatever use I make of anything you or Mr. Roberts, or Jack Westall, give me, I assure you it will be the best and most serious use. It is going to be a tremendous labor, but when I am done with it – at any rate, when I have set it down – I shall not only be delighted but I shall appreciate it if you will look it over to find out if I have done the job. I've bitten off a tremendous hunk to chew on this time – maybe more than I can – but as you say, we shall see.

At any rate, I can assure you the book is in no special autobiographical sense of the word about a special community and special persons. I still feel scared and a little hollow inside when I think of what I have done and am doing – but I have now given my inventive and imaginative powers full play, I have contrived a kind of legend or tremendous fiction – and the beauty of it is that in this free medium, I find for the first time in my life that I am myself much more free than I have ever been – that is, I can create in a free medium, and use everything I know or have seen or experienced or found out about. The book covers a tremendous panoramic sweep of places, people, events and times – I may be a doddering old man before I am done with it, but meanwhile, I am giving it everything I have. So everything you do, together with all the trouble and labor I know this entails, it is deeply and genuinely appreciated.

I don't know whether I shall come home this summer – if I do it will only be for a short visit, I have to work now at the top of by bent, and last summer I found out that one's home town is not always the best place to do it. But I can't tell you what a tremendous experience that was – I'd like to tell you all about it someday, for in a way I think it may have been one of the great turning points in my life. It crystalized a feeling, a conviction, a discovery that I had been slowly coming to for years. And I suppose that discovery and conviction might be best summarized by these words: "You can't go home again"[3] – by that I don't simply mean back to your home town – I mean back to your childhood, back to the image of the father you have lost, back to the whole cosmos of your youth, and all its colors and associations, back to time and memory, back to romantic love, back to so many other things that were once the whole world to you.

It has been a hard and grievous discovery, and so much time has been spent in mourning for the dead; but now that I have made it, I feel new strength and hope: I am standing on the shores of a new land, and if the old world is behind me, my heart somehow is full of hope about the new one I shall explore; because I found out that although "you can't go home again," the home of all of us, of every mother's son of us, is in the future.

That trip to Asheville crystalized that discovery, and I believe was one of the most important things that ever happened to me. For years, I had thought about my long absence from Asheville; I felt a sense of exile until it began to eat in me, haunt me in dreams. It became so oppressive and overwhelming that that return was inevitable – and it was a cleansing flood. I know you won't misunderstand me: I was more deeply touched and moved than I can tell you over the overwhelming reception I received, the great kindness and friendliness and interest of almost everyone I saw. And it is comforting to know that whenever I want to I can go back to my own town, and find friends there who will be glad to see me.

But my discovery that "you can't go home again" went a whole lot deeper than this: it went down to the very roots of my life and spirit – it has been a hard and at times terrifying discovery because it amounts to an entire revision almost of belief and of knowledge: it was like death almost because it meant saying farewell to so many things, to so many ideas and images and hopes and illusions that we think we can't live without. But the point is, I have come through it now, and I am not desolate or lost. On the contrary, I am more full of hope and faith and courage than I have been in years: I suppose what I am trying to tell you here is a spiritual conviction that will inform the whole book – you could almost call that book "You Can't Go Home Again" – although I don't think I shall call it that.[4] But I do want you to understand that it is not a <u>hopeless</u> book, but a triumphantly <u>hopeful</u> one. I've tried to tell you a little about it now, and I hope you see something of what I have in mind. Like you, like Mr. Roberts, like the late Mr. Shakespeare, I, too, believe in the brave new world, and I hope now that I am on the way to find it.

Meanwhile, until I hear from you again, with all good wishes to you and Mr. Roberts,

Sincerely yours,

Tom Wolfe

P.S. I heard from George McCoy about the fellowship at Harvard, and I wrote the committee a letter which I sent to him first for his approval. I did my level best for him, I meant every word I said. I hope he gets it: he deserves it, and God knows, a profession that has so many people of no honor and no integrity in it – I speak out of my own sad experience, and could give melancholy evidence to support the truth of everything I say – certainly has need of more people like George McCoy. So I hope his application is granted. I haven't seen your young son recently, but I am going to call him up one day soon. And this is about all the news: I live here in a very old Victorian style hotel[5] with enormous rooms and a lot of other strange critters like myself. Mr. Edgar Lee Masters[6] also lives here and has for years: I see him from time to time, in fact, he set me up to a glass of beer yesterday afternoon – but for the most part I just work. I wish you'd tell me how to sleep as you used to. It is not a question of health, it is just a plain damn question of writing – and that is a plain damn question. I work everyday from ten in the morning until about six at night, but after that I can't stop thinking about it: it goes rumbling and roaring around in my head, or what serves me for a head – the result is there is usually no sleep until long after midnight. I don't know what to do about all this, it has always been the same – at least everytime I start to work: the only satisfaction I get from it is the rather gloomy one that I must be really at work again. I don't think, otherwise, it means an early catastrophe – as "The Tempest" says – "His complexion is perfect hanging"[7] – I may be wrong, but something tells me my time is not yet. And now good-bye.

T.W.

TW/GJ

1. In an undated letter, Eula Person attempted to strengthen Wolfe's confidence in his writing: "Whenever you get tired and discouraged, please remember that there are hundreds of people like me who devour your books eagerly, <u>desperately</u> and want more, more" (*Harvard*).

2. Dix Hill and Morganton, state mental health facilities.

3. After returning from Asheville in 1937, Wolfe attended a dinner for Sherwood Anderson and his wife on December 1 in New York. Also attending was Ella Winter, the recent widow of the journalist Lincoln Steffins. Wolfe befriended the lonely widow and frequently dined with her. Over one dinner, Winter recalled, "He started telling me about his horror at going back to his home and what he found there, and I just said, 'But don't you know you can't go home again?' He stopped dead, and then said: 'Can I have that? I mean for a title? I'm writing a piece . . . and I'd like to call it that. It says exactly what I mean. Would you mind if I used it?' I laughed and told him that I didn't 'own' it any more than I'd own any other thought" (Nowell, *Thomas Wolfe,* 410). From that time on, Wolfe became obsessed with the phrase.

4. Wolfe's final manuscript totaled more than 4,000 typed pages and over 1,200,000 words. Wolfe and his typist, Gwen Jassinoff, prepared a long outline to identify the manuscript for when it would be turned over to Edward Aswell on May 17, 1938. Wolfe labeled Part IV of the outline "You Can't Go Home Again."

5. The Hotel Chelsea at 222 West Twenty-third Street. Wolfe rented room 829, a two-room suite with an anteroom for his typist.

6. Edgar Lee Masters (1869–1950), author of *Spoon River Anthology.*
7. *The Tempest* 1.1.25: "his complexion is perfect gallows."

72

TLS, 5 pp., Harvard, bMS Am 1883.2 (294)

114 East 56th Street
New York, New York
c/o Miss Elizabeth Nowell
April 6, 1938

Dear Mrs. Roberts:

I was mighty glad to get your letter and sorry to know that you have been put to so much trouble and bother to get the material I asked for. I shall appreciate it all the more on account of the labor you have expended, and I can repeat my assurances that I shall take the greatest care of anything that is intrusted to me and see that it gets returned in good condition to its owner when I am done with it.

It is an immense undertaking that I have embarked on, a week or so ago I was so tired that I simply could not force myself another foot; so I went out into the country for several days, all of which did a lot of good, but I have about reached the conclusion that when a man gives himself completely to a tremendous piece of work, there is just no such thing as rest, and he had better reconcile himself to it.

I saw an extraordinary Russian film the other night called "Lenin in October,"[1] which brought out that point very compellingly. In a scene where Lenin is in hiding in the furious days just preceding the Revolution, Lenin is pictured as saying to one of his associates who has been appointed to guard him and who has been on the job day and night without rest: "You ought to get some sleep." The man says that he will get some sleep after the Revolution. "After the Revolution," says Lenin, "we won't sleep at all." And maybe that is the way it has got to be.

It is curious how many hard and thorny things we find out about life, and how strangely palatable they become to us. It is all so different from what we imagined it was going to be when we were children, and curiously in so many ways it is so much better. I suppose like so many other boys I pictured a future life of brilliant works crowned by success and fame and ease, and surcease from labor; but it does not work out that way at all. Work gets harder all the time because as one digs deeper one goes into the rock. And there is no rest – those periods of delightful relaxation as a kind of reward for work accomplished that

I used to look forward to with such eagerness simply do not exist. Now I would say that almost the worst time in a writer's life are those periods between work – periods when he is too exhausted and feels too empty to attempt a new piece of work, or when a new piece of work is still cloudily formulating itself in his mind. It is really hell, or worse than hell, because writing itself is hell, and this period of waiting is limbo – floating around in the cloudy upper geographies of hell trying to get attached to something. It just boils down to the fact that there is no rest, once the worm gets in and begins to feed upon the heart – there can never after that be rest, forgetfulness or quiet sleep again: somewhere long ago – God knows when, or at what fated moment in my childhood – the worm got in and has been feeding ever since and will be feeding till I die: after this happens, a man becomes a prisoner, there are times when he almost breaks free, but there is one link in the chain that always holds; there are times when he almost forgets, when he is with his friends, when he is reading a great book or a great poem, when he is at the theatre, or on a ship, or with a girl – but there is one tiny cell that still keeps working, working; even when he is asleep, one lamp that will not go out, that is forever lit.

It sounds pretty grim, but like so many other grim discoveries, it is not so grim once you recognize it, accept it, make up your mind to it. In fact, when I think of all the dreams I had as a boy – my idea of "happiness," "fame," and so on – I do not know that I would have them back again, even if I could recapture them; and as for this thing I used to call happiness, I am not so sure but that it, too, is a very hard and thorny thing, and not the smooth and palatable thing I thought it was. And I am perfectly sure that whatever it is, if it exists at all, it cannot exist without work – which would have been strange doctrine indeed when I was twelve years old: as far as I am concerned, there is no life without work – at least, looking back over my own, everything I can remember of any value is somehow tied up with work.

What to do? Like you, I have become in the last few years tremendously involved with the state of the world – as my consciousness of life has enlarged, my consciousness of self has dwindled – there are things now that so afflict me in the state of man that I think I would take up arms against them, or give my life to stop them – but what to do? There is hardly a day goes by now but what people – for the most part, I think, sincere and genuine people – call me up or write me, and ask me to sign my name to a petition or proclamation of some sort, to go to Washington with a group to protest to the President about the state of things in Spain; to appear with a group at the French Consulate and protest to the French Consul about the state of things in Spain; to serve on committees of protest about the condition of the sharecroppers in the south

– about the imprisonment of Tom Mooney – about the violations of civil liberties in various places – about the Scottsboro boys – about the Moscow trials – for or against the Stalinites or Trotskyites – but what to do? What to do?

To reject these pleas for help and demonstration often seems callously indifferent and self-centered, particularly when so many of them are about things with which my mind and conscience are now seriously involved, but in the name of god, what is a man like myself to do? The observation of Voltaire in Candide that at the end of all the best thing is for a man to tend his garden used to seem cynically and selfishly callous to me, but I am not so sure now that it does not contain much deep wisdom, and much humanity, as well. Perhaps the best thing that a man can do is just to do the work he is able to do, and for which he is best fitted, as well as he can. And perhaps his greatest service to other men can be rendered in such a way as this.

I am solicited and persuaded on all sides now by worthy people to take sides and to make proclamations on all manner of things – there are so many writers and leagues of writers who are involved in all of this, but although I admire their energy, and do not question their sincerity, I do not know when these writers write – or how they can possibly find time to write: one does not write books by carrying placards in front of the French Consulate, or having interviews with President Roosevelt. It is hard enough for me to get anything done anyway, because everything comes out with such a tremendous superflux, and calls for such infinite boiling down and rearrangement – but it seems to me the best course for me is so stick at it somehow, somehow by the grace of God to get it done, somehow to get it all wrought into a single and coherent vision of life, not just as a series of explosive and isolated protests.

I think I have this ploughed to the bottom now as far as this present work is concerned: it has been going on for years and it has been hell because it involved, perhaps for the first time in my life, the creation of a whole universe of the imagination into which I could pour all the materials I had gathered. Now I think I have accomplished it, I have the whole thing launched and floated in my mind, and I believe I am the master of it: an enormous labor of completion and fulfillment is before me, but if I stick to it I shall get there.

There is not much news to tell you: Purdue University has invited me to come out and make a talk at some kind of university celebration in May; and I have agreed to go.[2] The pay seems high – $300 – and ought to leave me something over when my expenses are paid: I explained to them that I could not take time off now to prepare a formal speech, because I was not a public speaker anyway, but that if they would let me come out and talk informally about writing I might be able to say something interesting to them. Since writing is my life, and since in one way or another it is with me all the time now, I think I may have something worth saying. At any rate, they agreed very readily to my proposal, so I suppose it is all set.

Just do the best you can for me about getting the material I asked you for, and I will try to deserve it by the use I make of it. I have heard nothing further from Jack Westall, and hope he can also help. You can assure the Advocate man that I will take the best of care of anything he lets me have. Do you know Wicks Wamboldt's address? I might write him to see if he could help me.

I suppose it is wise, as you say, to go about the business as discreetly as possible; but I do want to assure you again, and everyone else, that I have no intention of doing a job on Asheville: God knows, after what I have known and seen and lived through myself in the last few years I am in no mood to exult and mock at the afflicted and tormented soul of man, particularly when it comes as close to home as this does. Time and again last summer I could have groaned in anguish at the things I saw: most pitiful and moving of all, perhaps, was the pretense – people with naked terror in their eyes still whistling to keep up their courage, still speaking the old words, the old spurious phrases that had lost meaning they may once have had because they referred to something that was gone forever. And I think the people knew it. I could give you an account of a meeting of the Associated Civic Clubs at which I was present – a concerted effort or "drive," as it is called to raise funds for a Convention Hall – it could be howlingly funny if it were not for the underlying tragedy and pathos of the situation.

There has been a good deal of talk about "the lost generation," meaning the young men who came up during and after the last war, but I wonder if the real lost generation is not these men of middle or advanced middle age, who keep saying the old phrases, trying to whoop it up in the old way over something that is gone forever: it made me think of a pep meeting in a morgue, a kind of cheering squad of ghosts. And, in the name of God, what are these men going to do? They have only one language, only one set of values: the language and the values were false to begin with, but now that they know that they were false, they have not even the conviction of their previous delusion to give them hope.

I am not lost because I accept and am ready to meet the future that is before us; but what are people to do when they cannot accept it, cannot face it, are looking forever backward at the image of a world that is gone. Do not think that I could be happy at the tragic spectacle, or take pleasure in flaying the hide of something that is already quivering and raw.

I wish I could come home, quietly, as you suggest, and talk to some of the people you mention, but you know what happened last summer. A prophet may be without honor in his own country, but he is also without privacy. I shall get out of town during the hot weather and go somewhere to work; but I simply cannot go through another summer like the last one, as interesting and overwhelming as it was, particularly now that I have plunged into this thing and must go on.

I keep wanting to see Munsey and will someday before long: at night, however, which is the only free time I have, I am often so tired that I feel like doing nothing except staying at home.

Let me hear from you as soon as you are conveniently able. Meanwhile, I send you and Mr. Roberts all my good wishes and best regards.

Sincerely,
Tom Wolfe

TW: GJ

[Handwritten postscript]

P.S. There is a popular song called "Roses in December" – well someone ought to write one now called Snow in April. It is the sixth day of the month, and as I look out my window at the present moment the whole world – the roofs and buildings of New York – are white and blind with snow: it looks like a blizzard, the first we have had in this nothing-of-a-winter.

April, April, laugh thy girlish laughter![3]

1. "Lenin in October" (1937), directed by Mikhail Romm and Dmitri Vasilyev.
2. On March 31, 1938, Professor F. A. Cummings of the Department of English at Purdue University wired Wolfe, asking him to speak at the annual Literary Awards Banquet at Purdue on May 19, in West Lafayette, Indiana. Wolfe was pleased with the honorarium of $300 and accepted the offer. He decided to make Purdue the first stop on his trip west, planning to travel through the Northwest to soak up local color.
3. "April, April" by Sir (John) William Watson (1858–1935), English poet.

73
April 1938   *ALS, 2 pp., Harvard, bMS Am 1883.1 (545)*

Thursday, April
Dogwood Road
Charlotte St. Extension
Asheville, N.C.

My dear Tom,

At last! I haven't written because until now there was nothing definite I could tell you. You will recall that I told you Mr. Toms said he could not be sure of what he could do for at least two weeks. This is the first time I could be definite.

In a nutshell – and I must write briefly in order not to miss the first mail out – Mr. Toms says if you can take them now and return them in 30 days – well and good. If that space is too short to be adequate to your use, then you would have to wait until 90 days from now. He will want you to put up a $1000 bond (says he thinks any professional bondsman would make bond for you for $5⁰⁰), pay the transportation charges, and whatever rental fee you think fair. So far as the bond is concerned, he says he would not take $1000 for the file of papers, therefore he feels justified in asking for a bond. It isn't that he doesn't trust your promise to be careful with them, but of course all sorts of things could happen.

If you want to try the thirty day period, let us know at once, and we'll get them on next express out, or whatever way is cheapest.

Be sure to state just what period you want. You said in your letter [*left blank*]¹ Do you hold to that? If you have any preference as to the way they should be sent, please state. I'm sorry for all this delay but it seems about the best we could do. I didn't mean to give you the impression that we had gone to a lot of trouble, but simply was apologizing for our delay.

If for any reason you decide not to take Mr. Tom's proposition, we shall continue to try to find papers.

Wickes Wamboldt's address is:

57 Beverly Road, West Asheville

He is honest, intelligent, and, except Mr. Hendricks, knows more than any (honest) person here about the whole wretched mess. (Mind your P's & Q's (with capitals) if you write to Mr. Wamboldt. He is the type of man to be very much hurt by certain of your writings. – just couldn't see why such should be put on paper. I have never heard him express himself, but I think I know he would be like that. He is a real man, and can give you what you want.

This letter must go to postman now. Your letter is wonderful. We have read and reread "What to do? What to do?" Yet how much better off you are than I, whose daily battle cry in this welter of world misery is "What to think." Ans. just what you want us to do. Do hope you are not already in hot summer,

Glorious here. Until we hear, goodbye,

M.R.

[Written on top and left margin of p. 1]
You will have to get papers back in 30 days from Apr. 27. It is possible that after two weeks from now, Mr. Toms thinks he might be able to give you an extension of <u>two</u> weeks, but can't promise that now, until he sees further. You will recall I told you he is trying to get a radio station and will need his files, and all this causes the uncertainty.

74

TLS, 4 pp., Harvard, bMS Am 1883.2 (294)

114 East 56th Street
New York, New York
c/o Miss Elizabeth Nowell
May 3, 1938

Dear Mrs. Roberts:

Thanks very much for your letter and for the information in it. I am deeply sorry to think you have been put to so much trouble in this matter, but I want you to know how much I appreciate it.[1]

Now about Mr. Toms' proposal. Frankly, I am afraid what he suggests is out of the question. It may be possible, as he says, to secure a thousand dollar bond at no greater expense than five dollars to myself. But that is not the point. The point, it seems to me, lies in the responsibility he asks me to assume, and the value he attaches to his papers. It may be perfectly true that he "would not take a thousand dollars for them." But it is also true that probably no one else would give a thousand dollars for them. Certainly, I would not, and I would not, therefore, care in any way, however hypothetical, to involve myself for any such amount. What he has may be very rare and very precious. Not having seen it, I cannot judge. But I have also learned, from past experience, that there are many people who put an utterly unreasonable value on something that may be of very little worth.[2]

For example, after "Of Time and the River" appeared, I received a long and rambling letter from an apparently illiterate man in Florida, who announced that he was a "doctor," who would like to build a new house and office, and take some graduate work in medicine, and would, therefore, very generously sell me his life story (which would make me fabulously rich and famous, of course) at the knock-down price of twenty-five thousand dollars.

I was also besieged, tormented, interrupted, and interfered with last summer by hordes of people who could obviously do very little more than write their own names, if their literary talents went so far, but who were generously trying to cram down my throat wads of manuscript, life stories, "great ideas," and so on, that would make me immensely wealthy – and would result in "a greater book" than "Gone with the Wind" – God knows why that immortal piece of bilge was invariably selected as the almost ne plus ultra in literary achievement, but invariably it was.

There is also the kind of person – seven million, two hundred and sixty-seven thousand, by the most recent and conservative count – who, unsolicited, send manuscripts of poems, plays and novels, and what-not to a defenceless author, and offer to split the staggering royalties, fifty-fifty, if he will only "write it up good" for them – I presume, in his off moments from carousing around with the Bohemian literary gang, on a quiet week-end.

All this is pretty brutal, but I have suffered from it for years – there was one painted hag last summer who wormed the location of my cabin from my sometimes too garrulous mother, hunted me out, and then demanded that I read a manuscript of one thousand, four hundred and sixty-two handwritten pages, rewrite and revise it for her, tell her "what to do with it," find a publisher for her – all within two weeks' time. The plain truth is, the more worthless the material, the more deluded is its possessor in his estimate of its priceless value.

I had thought perhaps that I might be willing to pay as much, say, as twenty-five dollars, for the loan of the papers for a few weeks – which certainly strikes me as being munificently and extravagantly generous for a file of newspapers in an obscure weekly sheet, in a small town. Mr. Toms has other notions, apparently, and while not disputing his own personal sense of their value, I simply cannot agree with him. Moreover, his frantic haste for their return is decidedly perplexing: if they had any value, to get them back within ten days or two weeks, or thirty days, would be absurd. I am a serious and hardworking man, I am engaged upon a tremendous piece of work – whatever value such information as this might be, it would only be a portion of the whole, and I cannot agree to such unreasonable demands. So we will have to call this portion of it off.

As to Wickes Wamboldt, I am perfectly willing to write him, and should be grateful for any information that he might give, but if he has as many sore toes to be stepped on as you say he has, perhaps I had better not try. Frankly, I am a little tired of taking it on the chin from these small-town liberals, these leaders of enlightened thought, these Buncombe county Communists or Socialists who are all for social reform, world revolution, and what-not, but who are all undone when you mention casually some good old Anglo-Saxon four-letter word that can be found repeatedly in Shakespeare or in the King James version of the bible.

When I was a child, the poet, the artist, the creative man was held up to me as an ideal of the highest and the best in human life – the man who bravely and truthfully wrought out his vision of the world, at no matter what the cost to him, according to the dictates of his conscience and his talent. In later years, when I tried to do the same thing myself, it was shocking and bewildering to find out that I was most bitterly denounced and execrated by some of the very people who had held this ideal before me – to find out that it is noble to tell the truth, so long as the truth is not too close to home, and does not refer to the wart upon Aunt Nellie's chin.

I am not bitter, but I am through with apology. The only apology I have now to make is to my conscience, to the knowledge wherein I may have failed, to the things to which I may have been unfair, to the things in which I did not fulfill myself and my work as completely as I should. I lived out my exile for more than seven years and then went back, and I saw what I saw, I know what I know. I know now that you can't go back – there is no turning back: with that knowledge also came a deeper feeling of compassion and of understanding for stricken people. But no apologies – they are not needed, they are not due. I was a citizen of Asheville, and I am now a citizen of mankind – there is my loyalty, and that is where it must go.

I know you can help me in this thing more than anyone I know at home, for I believe you understand better than anyone else what I am after. There is nothing very complex or mysterious about it; I know some other people who, I think, may help out, too, and who may have kept the records that I want, and I shall write them. When I was home last summer, I was given to understand that it would be very simple to provide them, but of course, as so often happens, results are harder to achieve than promises. If I cannot get them – I shall have to do without; but I have done without before, and I shall get along.

I do not want to harass you or Mr. Roberts with a matter that has already, I know, cost you so much of your generous time and care – but if you will keep trying and let me know what you find, I shall be grateful, and, as I said before, I think the result may be worth it in the end. Do not offend Toms – simply tell him that I appreciate his position, but did not feel that I could obligate myself in so large a sum; and that I appreciate his interest and his offer.

This is all now. I have been pretty tired, for I have gone through a long, hard winter here with publishers, law suits, and finally, with the thing I want to do – work. But I have just come back from a delightful week-end in central New York state, to Hamilton College, where I met some delightful people – including the son[3] of Elihu Root,[4] who is a professor there, and who lives in the old Root house – and a very fine man, Professor Saunders,[5] at whose home I stayed – who is the world's greatest authority on the peony.

It was a new and remarkable experience – I saw some beautiful country and some wonderful flowers – and I discovered that at Hamilton with people like Saunders and Root (Mr. Root is one of the greatest authorities on the daffodil) – you cannot even take peonies and daffodils for granted – was it Wordsworth who said: "A primrose by the river's brim, a simple primrose was to him" – and was it a primrose? Well, if it was, you could not even take a primrose by the river's brim for granted up at Hamilton – you would find out that it was anything but simple – that it was, in fact, a product of cross-culture between a very rare and little known breed that grows only in the upper reaches of the Himalayas mountains, and another which is occasionally found in portions of the Belgian Congo. Well, the world is sometimes a hard place – but you have to admit it has its points.

I am going out to Purdue University in about two weeks to talk to a student gathering there, and then I am going to take a short vacation. When I get back here in June, I am going somewhere out of town, and get back to work again. If I do not hear from you before then, I hope to hear from you when I come back.

Meanwhile, with all good wishes to you and Mr. Roberts,

Sincerely,
Tom Wolfe

TW:GJ

1. Wolfe wrote his mother on April 21, 1938: "I have written both Jack Westall and Mrs. Roberts several times, but although they have promised to send me the material I want within a few days, nothing has come of it yet. I suppose a good many of us are inclined to be longer on promises than on performances, but since what I ask for probably will cost someone a little time and trouble, I have no right to complain" (Wolfe, *Letters of Thomas Wolfe to His Mother*, 289).

2. On May 7, 1938, Wolfe described the situation with Mr. Thoms to his mother: "I at last heard from Mrs. Roberts about the result of her efforts to get a record of the

bank trials for me, and it didn't pan out to very much. The man they were going to get them from—I think his name is Toms, and he has or had something to do with The Advocate—was willing to let me have them for ten days or two weeks if I would post a bond of $1,000! This seems to me to be one of the most fantastic and outrageous proposals I have ever heard—to demand that anyone involve himself for such a sum of money all for the privilege of looking over the files of an obscure little newspaper in ten days' time. Of course, I wrote Mrs. Roberts and thanked her for her trouble, but told her that any such arrangement was out of the question. . . . Mrs. Roberts also told me at the beginning that she had 'everything,' but it was packed away in such a way that it would take a few days to get it out. I don't know what happened to this, but I have never heard anything more about it" (Wolfe, *Letters of Thomas Wolfe to His Mother*, 290–91).

3. Edward Wales Root, a professor at Hamilton College in Clinton, New York.

4. Elihu Root (1845–1937), American lawyer and statesman. Root was secretary of war in the cabinet of President William McKinley and secretary of state in the cabinet of President Theodore Roosevelt.

6. Dr. A. P. Saunders, professor of chemistry and former dean at Hamilton College. Saunders was a horticulturist who specialized in the propagation of rare peonies.

75

Postcard, UNC

Dogwood Road, Charlotte St. Ex.
Asheville, N.C. June 22, 38

Dear Tom,

Contrary to appearances, I am neither dead nor sleeping, but I surely have made slow progress. For my harvest, thus far I have <u>one</u> paper, but I have not given up hope and I hope you won't. I asked you in my letter how long you could wait to get them, but you have not answered. I feel so provoked to think that I kept mine so long, and think in a fit of moving time weariness threw them away. We have been so sorry for Mabel and Ralph because of his serious illness.[1] You should see our place now. Think it is going to be an ideal home spot. Today, "so calm, so cool, so bright"[2] is a perfect Asheville day, far remote from the deviltries abroad in the world. Keep up hope. Hope to do what you would

Love, M.R.

1. "It may or may not shock you to know he has Syphilis. He and Mabel both took the 'Wasserman Test'" (Julia E. Wolfe to Thomas Wolfe, March 31, 1938, transcription, Thomas Wolfe Collection, Pack Memorial Public Library, Asheville, North Carolina).

2. Transposition of a phrase from "Vertue" by the English poet George Herbert (1593–1633): "Sweet day, so cool, so calm, so bright, . . ."

76

FOUR HOURS BEFORE WOLFE LEFT FOR PURDUE on the evening of May 17, 1938, Edward Aswell arrived at his suite at the Hotel Chelsea to collect the gargantuan manuscript of *The Web and the Rock* and found Wolfe and Gwen Jassinoff still busy sorting it out. Only a half-hour before the train was to leave for Indiana were the manuscripts bundled and the packing finished. Aswell found himself limping under the weight of the enormous packages Wolfe had handed over to him.

Wolfe's Purdue speech, "Writing and Living," was a triumph.[1] He gave a well-prepared account of his writing career and revelations of his developing social consciousness. Following a weekend in Chicago, he boarded the *Burlington Zephyr* for Denver, where he had a reunion with friends he met in 1935 at the Boulder Writers' Conference.

After brief stopovers in Cheyenne and Boise, Wolfe arrived in Portland on June 8. He was invited to join an experiment in tourism by Edward Miller, Sunday editor of the *Portland Oregonian,* and Ray Conway, an executive in the Oregon State Motor Association. Miller and Conway asked Wolfe to join them as they toured eleven national parks by auto in a two-week period. The excursion was meant to prove that all of the Western national parks could be visited within an average two-week vacation. The trip was conceived as travel promotion and proved to be a grueling drive. Wolfe eagerly accepted the invitation, believing it an excellent opportunity to absorb the West. He kept a record of his impressions in a six-by-nine-inch ledger, doing most of his writing at night in lodges.[2] By the time the journey ended at Mount Rainier on July 2, he had traveled 4,632 miles in thirteen days.

Before ending his western journey, Wolfe mailed the following postcard to Mrs. Roberts from Bryce Canyon, Utah.

Postmarked June 26, 1938   *Postcard of Point Supreme, Cedar*
Breaks National Monument, Utah;
Harvard, bMS Am 1883.2 (294)

You can't take it with you – neither can you send it on a post card, but maybe this will give some idea.

T.W.

Wolfe during his tour of eleven national parks; pictured here at Zion National Park in Utah, June 25, 1938. By permission of the Thomas Wolfe Collection, Pack Memorial Public Library, Asheville, North Carolina

1. Posthumously published as *Thomas Wolfe's Purdue Speech: Writing and Living,* ed. William Braswell and Leslie A. Field (West Lafayette, Ind.: Purdue University Studies, 1964).

2. The journal of his excursion was published as *A Western Journal: A Daily Log of the Great Parks Trip, June 20–July 2, 1938* (Pittsburgh: University of Pittsburgh Press, 1951). For a more complete transcription of the journal, see Wolfe, *Notebooks of Thomas Wolfe,* 2:963–91.

77

ON JULY 4, 1938, from the New Washington Hotel in Seattle, Wolfe wrote his final letter to Mrs. Roberts (and one of the last letters he wrote). On July 5 he left on his ill-fated voyage to Victoria and Vancouver in British Columbia. He planned to be gone for a day or two and was eager to return and have his journal of the Great Parks trip typed. However, during his passage on the coastal steamer *Princess Kathleen,* he shared a pint of whiskey with a man he referred to afterward as a "poor shivering wretch."[1] Evidently the man was ill with pneumonia or influenza and passed it on to Wolfe. Wolfe contracted a respiratory infection that soon activated the dormant tuberculosis in his right lung, which eventually resulted in his death from brain tuberculosis.

July 4, 1938

ALS, 1 p., Harvard, bMS Am 1883.2 (294)
New Washington Hotel letterhead

Seattle

[Written in Wolfe's hand on upper left margin]
address is still c/o <u>Miss Nowell</u>

Dear Mrs Roberts: Your letter was forwarded on to me here. I think you are grand to go to so much trouble for me, and if I blow off clouds of volcanic steam, don't think I don't appreciate all you have done and are doing. I was ready to drop when I left N.Y. six weeks ago, but I've seen a whole new continent, the entire West, and now I'm writing thousands of words a day again. I'll be back in N. Y. some time this month: meanwhile I'm trying to rewrite and put the fifty thousand words or more I've written on this trip in a typed mss.[2] – When I arrived here last night, after traveling 5000 miles around the whole West in the past 14 days,[3] I found a telegram from my editor at Harper's telling me he had read the 2,000,000 word[4] rough draft I left with him of the new book, that it was "magnificent in scope and design" – and far and away the best thing I'd ever done.[5] With this wonderful assurance I'm going back and try to live up to it until it's finished as I want it. All your help is gratefully appreciated. Best wishes to you and Mr R – Tom Wolfe

[Written on top margin]
P.S. I heard from Fred this morning about Ralph. It is very sad, but now I hope things take a better turn. – T.W.

---

1. Nowell, *Thomas Wolfe,* 424.
2. Wolfe's western journal contained only about 11,400 words.
3. Actually 4,632 miles in thirteen days.
4. The manuscript Wolfe left with Edward Aswell totaled over 1,200,000 words.
5. Aswell's Western Union telegram of July 1, 1938, reads: "DEAR TOM, YOUR NEW BOOK IS MAGNIFICENT IN SCOPE AND DESIGN, WITH SOME OF THE BEST WRITING YOU HAVE EVER DONE. I AM STILL ABSORBING IT, CONFIDENT THAT WHEN YOU FINISH YOU WILL HAVE WRITTEN YOUR GREATEST NOVEL SO FAR. HOPE YOU COME BACK FULL OF HEALTH AND NEW VISIONS" (*Harvard*).

78

Postmarked July 21, 1938   *ALS, 2 pp., UNC*

My dear Tom,

It is a vast relief that we read that you are better.

I know that, even though better, you are too weak to be bothered by a letter. Only let me say here that your talk this summer, and your recent letters have convinced us that you are only on the threshold of your career, and there is nothing for you to do but to get well, and that quickly, so that you can go forward.

The sudden shock of seeing your name in the paper[1] as of one desperately sick took my mind – galloping back through the years, to your boyhood, and on to this hour, and, so far as I know, this is your first serious illness. Because of this, you have been free to perform the truly colossal work that you have. This should cheer you to pull out fast. How thankful we all are that the news changed so quickly from despair to hope.

If you are strong enough to smile, you may give a little grin to the remembrance of the great figure you cut in the Shakespeare pageant twenty-two years ago this spring. This is one of the things I recalled as I went back through the years.[2]

Tom, we think about you hourly, and long for continuing good news.

Much love,

Margaret R –

1. "THOMAS WOLF, NOTED NOVELIST, SERIOUSLY ILL AT SEATTLE, WASH," *Asheville Times,* July 15, 1938. The first two paragraphs below the headline continue: "Stricken last Wednesday with pneumonia, Thomas Wolfe, of Asheville, author of 'Look Homeward, Angel' and 'Of Time and the River,' is seriously ill in Firlawn sanitarium, Seattle, Wash. Mrs. Julia Wolfe, his mother, has been notified here. Mrs. Wolfe was notified yesterday of her son's condition. The attending physician, Dr. E. C. Ruge, told Mrs. Wolfe that her son was suffering a severe attack of pneumonia, but was 'past the crisis.'"

2. In her memoir of Thomas Wolfe, Mrs. Roberts recorded this:

In the Spring of 1916 it looked as if his love for drama was to have fulfillment. The private schools of the city united to give a pageant in celebration of Shakespeare's Tercentenary. Tom, who was to be Prince Hal was openly delighted.

The costumes, ordered from Philadelphia, were very late in arriving. I had to go on to the pageant grounds to round up the smaller boys, and so did not learn that Tom's costume was far too short. (If you want to get the picture, bear in mind that he was fifteen years old and six-feet, two).

J. M. and Margaret Roberts, 1940. Courtesy of Jerry Israel, Asheville,
North Carolina

To get him dressed and into the procession, one of the teachers pulled out for him relics of some former festivities—and imagine my horror when, peeping from behind a sheltering bush to watch our boys, I saw charming Prince Hal parading forth in a curious make-shift costume.

The tragi-comedy of this occasion he tells with considerable accuracy in "Look Homeward, Angel." We, carelessly (but not callously) failing to realize how the wearing of the queer costume had destroyed his pleasure, so eagerly anticipated, treated the incident as a minor casualty so incidental to amateur theatricals, and laughed heartily about it. It was a considerable time before he could respond with more than a rueful smile. (Roberts memoir, 12)

◦◦◦

In the summer of 1938, Wolfe, desperately ill, was admitted to a private sanatorium, Firlawns, twelve miles from Seattle at Kenmore. When he seemed unable to make a complete recovery, he was sent to Providence Hospital in Seattle the first week of August. The physicians believed he had an abscess or a tumor on his brain. They recommended that he be taken to Johns Hopkins Hospital in Baltimore, where the leading brain surgeon in the country, Dr. Walter E. Dandy, could examine him.

After arriving by train in Baltimore on September 10, Dr. Dandy examined Wolfe, and following a trephining procedure, he diagnosed tuberculosis. According to Dandy, Wolfe had contracted tuberculosis of the lung at some time during his youth. The lung healed, sealing the tubercles inside. When Wolfe contracted pneumonia in July, the lesion reopened and the tubercles suffused his bloodstream and infected his brain. Surgery was performed on September 12 (a cerebellar exploration), but to no avail. Wolfe died on September 15, at 5:30 A.M. His death certificate lists the immediate cause of death as "Tuberculous Meningitis" with contributing "Pulmonary Tuberculosis."

Mrs. Roberts learned of Wolfe's death from a radio announcement and went into a long period of deep grief.[1] During the funeral at First Presbyterian Church in Asheville, the minister, Dr. Robert F. Campbell, quoted from *Of Time and the River:* "And which of us shall find his father, know his face, and in what place, and in what time, and in what land?"[2] When Mrs. Roberts knew that Campbell was adding religious connotation by stressing "his" and "father" with special emphasis, she wanted to fire back with "Not capitals! No capitals there!"[3] "Father" and "His" were capitalized in the *Asheville Citizen's* reportage of the funeral.[4]

Margaret Roberts outlived Wolfe by more than eight years. Her husband recalled that, confined to her bed for almost two years with cancer, "she suffers a good deal though she makes so little to do over the discomfort that we

Margaret Roberts at the age of sixty-four, in 1940. Courtesy of Jerry Israel, Asheville, North Carolina

Grave of Margaret Roberts at Riverside Cemetery, Asheville. At the bottom of the stone is a quotation from Wolfe's *Look Homeward, Angel:* "She remained, who had first touched his blinded eyes with light." Photo by Ted Mitchell

hardly realize that she is going through it."[5] Her daughter, Margaret Rose Roberts, left a moving account of the last hours of the woman who had been such a vital force in Thomas Wolfe's life:

> Mother was confined to her bed from August 1945 to the day she died —almost two years. It seemed like an eternity to me because I was taking care of her. She couldn't stand the thought of having an outside nurse around her when she was so ill.
>
> A day or so before she died I was afraid I would not be able to handle it any longer. I was worried that Mother might go into convulsions. There was a trained nurse we knew, Annie Laurie Leech—but this was not the same Annie Laurie who nursed Tom just before he died.[6] Mother loved her and Annie took care of her at the end.
>
> Before Daddy and I went to bed that night we told Annie, "You have to call us while Mother's still breathing. We want to be with her before she dies."
>
> Very early in the morning, long before light, Annie called us. She said she thought the worst was over. Mother was breathing calmly. We went in and stayed with her. She died while Daddy held her hand on one side of the bed and I held her hand on the other side. I slipped off her wedding ring and have worn it ever since.[7]

Margaret Roberts died at 2 A.M. on May 9, 1947, in her home at 10 North Dogwood Road.[8] The funeral took place at four o'clock on May 11, a sunny and mild spring afternoon in the mountains. Former students of Mrs. Roberts served as active and honorary pallbearers. Because she was a professed atheist, her family had difficulty in finding a minister willing to change the traditional funeral service. Finally, a congregational minister, the Reverend A. C. Todd, was located, and the funeral was held not in a church but at the Morris-Gearing funeral home. All references to God were removed from the service. A few words were spoken by her husband of the long and happy life they had shared, and Mrs. Roberts's favorite sonnet—Shakespeare's "Shall I Compare Thee to a Summer's Day?"—was read. She was buried, in accordance with her request, at Riverside Cemetery, on a hillside and within view of Thomas Wolfe's grave.

1. Margaret Rose Roberts to Ted Mitchell, undated interview notes.
2. Wolfe, *Of Time and the River*, 2.
3. Turnbull, *Thomas Wolfe*, 321. Margaret Rose Roberts was Turnbull's source.
4. *Asheville Citizen*, September 16, 1938.
5. J. M. Roberts to Mabel Wolfe Wheaton, April 11, 1947 (ALS, 2 pp., *UNC*).

6. Annie Laurie Crawford was a young registered nurse who befriended Wolfe at Providence Hospital in Seattle and nursed him on the long train trip to Johns Hopkins Hospital. Crawford watched Wolfe's cerebellum operation, and of Wolfe's family and friends, she was the sole witness to his death.

7. Margaret Rose Roberts to Ted Mitchell, interview, February 8, 1995.

8. By 1947 Mrs. Roberts's cancer had metastasized. Her death certificate gives the immediate cause of death as cardiac failure resulting from hypertension caused by a previous exophthalmic goiter.

Background Readings

Donald, David Herbert. *Look Homeward: A Life of Thomas Wolfe.* Boston: Little, Brown, 1987.

Ensign, Robert Taylor. *Lean Down Your Ear upon the Earth, and Listen: Thomas Wolfe's Greener Modernism.* Columbia: University of South Carolina Press, 2003.

Mauldin, Joanne Marshall. *The People and Places of Thomas Wolfe's "Look Homeward, Angel": From the 1929 Scribners Edition.* Weaverville, N.C.: Privately printed, 2002.

Nowell, Elizabeth. *Thomas Wolfe: A Biography.* Garden City, N.Y.: Doubleday, 1960.

Turnbull, Andrew. *Thomas Wolfe.* New York: Charles Scribner's Sons, 1967.

Wisdom, William B. *My Impressions of the Wolfe Family and of Maxwell Perkins.* Edited by Aldo P. Magi and David J. Wyatt. N.p.: Thomas Wolfe Society, 1993.

Wolfe, Thomas. *The Autobiographical Outline for "Look Homeward, Angel."* Edited by Lucy Conniff and Richard S. Kennedy. N.p.: Thomas Wolfe Society, 1991.

———. *The Letters of Thomas Wolfe.* Edited by Elizabeth Nowell. New York: Charles Scribner's Sons, 1956.

———. *The Letters of Thomas Wolfe to His Mother.* Edited by C. Hugh Holman and Sue Fields Ross. Chapel Hill: University of North Carolina Press, 1968.

———. *Look Homeward, Angel: A Story of the Buried Life.* New York: Charles Scribner's Sons, 1929.

———. *The Notebooks of Thomas Wolfe.* Edited by Richard S. Kennedy and Paschal Reeves. 2 vols. Chapel Hill: University of North Carolina Press, 1970.

———. *O Lost: A Story of the Buried Life.* Edited by Arlyn and Matthew J. Bruccoli. Columbia: University of South Carolina Press, 2000.

———. *Of Time and the River.* New York: Charles Scribner's Sons, 1935.

———. *Thomas Wolfe's Composition Books: The North State Fitting School, 1912–1915.* Edited by Alice P. Cotten. Chapel Hill, N.C.: North Caroliniana Society and the Thomas Wolfe Society, 1990.

———. *The Web and the Rock.* New York and London: Harper and Brothers, 1939.

Wolfe, Thomas, and Aline Bernstein. *My Other Loneliness: Letters of Thomas Wolfe and Aline Bernstein.* Edited by Suzanne Stutman. Chapel Hill: University of North Carolina Press, 1983.

Wolfe, Thomas, and Maxwell E. Perkins. *To Loot My Life Clean: The Thomas Wolfe–Maxwell Perkins Correspondence.* Edited by Matthew J. Bruccoli and Park Bucker. Columbia: University of South Carolina Press, 2000.

Index

Page references in italics refer to illustrations.

Roberts, Margaret, (*continued*)
on Wolfe's composition books, 3–6; on
Wolfe's development, 93–94; on Wolfe's
illness, 182; Wolfe's letters to in *Atlantic
Monthly,* xxii–xxiii; Wolfe's letters to
purchased by Wisdom, xxiv–xxv; on
Wolfe's novels, 133–34; on Wolfe's oratory of "Gettysburg Address," 94, 99;
on Wolfe's success, 47, 90, 92. *See also*
Leonard, Margaret (Margaret Roberts)
Roberts, Margaret Rose, xxix, *xxxii,*
15n11, 71n3; on death of M. Roberts,
186; on death of Wolfe, 184; on
estrangement between Wolfe and her
parents, 133–34, 136, 145n7; on financial hardships of parents, 14n7, 67n7;
at Goucher, 94, 95n9, 97; on *Look
Homeward, Angel,* xliiin20, xliiin30;
at North State Fitting School, *xxxi;* on
parents, 122n4; on reunion between
Wolfe and her parents, 145n7, 149n3;
on M. Roberts as atheist, 8, 9n1; on
J. Roberts Jr., 53n2, 147n2; M. Roberts
on, 12, 22, 55, 57; on M. Roberts's
love for books, 67n7; and Wolfe's letters, xxiii–xxv
Roberts, Martha Elizabeth, *146,* 147n2
Roberts, Mary Frances, 66
Roberts, Mary Linn "Aunt Dolly," 21,
65–66, 67n6, 69–70
Roberts, Verna Britt, 39, 45, 51, 53n2,
146, 147n2
Roberts, William Marvin, Jr., 66
Roberts, William Orton, *37,* 41n2,
65–66, 67n6; in *Look Homeward, Angel,*
xxxviii–xxxix, 133; in *O Lost,* xiv–xv
Root, Edward Wales, 177, 178n3
Root, Elihu, 177, 178n4
Ruge, E. C., 182n1
Russell, Bertrand, 79, 79n6
Russell, Reid, *xxxii*

Saunders, A. P., 177, 178n5
Sayler, Oliver. See *Our American Theater*

Scribner, Charles, III, 108, 113n17
Scribner's. *See* Charles Scribner's Sons
Scribner's Magazine, 108, 114
Scudder, Lulu (character in *You Can't Go
Home Again,* based on Madeleine
Boyd), 112n3
Sell, Joseph, 154
Shakespeare, William: *Julius Caesar,* 40;
Macbeth, 98; "Shall I Compare Thee to
a Summer's Day?" 186; *The Tempest,*
167
Shakespearean pageant, xxxiii, 182, 182n2
"Shall I Compare Thee to a Summer's
Day?" (Shakespeare), 186
Shaw, George Bernard, 23, 24n1, 26
Sheba (Sister) (character in *Look Home-
ward, Angel,* based on Hortense Roberts
Pattison), xxxviii–xxxix, 133
Shelley, Percy Bysshe: "Adonais," 18,
19n5; "Alastor, or the Spirit of Soli-
tude," 18, 19n4; "Ode to the West
Wind" by quoted by Wolfe, 18, 19n8
Sheridan, Richard. See *Rivals, The*
Smith, Abe, 88n1
Smith, Al, 93
Steffins, Lincoln, 167n3
Stephens, Leslie, 25
Story of a Novel, The, xxxix, 133, *135*
Stott, Margaret, 94, 95n3
Strife (Galsworthy), 26, 28n7
Swift, Jonathan. *See* "Tale of a Tub, A"

"Tale of a Tub, A" (Swift), 25
"Tall Young Man," 62n1, 66
Tar Heel, The, 31, 32n6
Taxpayers' League of Asheville, 160, 162
Taylor, Joe, *xxxii*
Tempest, The (Shakespeare), 167
Theatre Guild, 33, 44, 110
Thomas, Fred, *xxxii*
"Thomas Bewick and His Tail Pieces," 14
*Thomas Wolfe's Composition Books: The
North State Fitting School, 1912–1915*
(Cotten), 4n1, 5n3